'Male' and 'Female' in Developing Southeast Asia

Cross-Cultural Perspectives on Women

General Editors: Shirley Ardener and Jackie Waldren,
for The Centre for Cross-Cultural Research on Women, University of
Oxford

ISSN: 1068-8536

Vol. 1: *Persons and Powers of Women in Diverse Cultures*
Edited by Shirley Ardener
Vol. 2: *Dress and Gender: Making and Meaning*
Edited by Ruth Barnes and Joanne B. Eicher
Vol. 3: *The Anthropology of Breast-Feeding: Natural Law or Social Construct*
Edited by Vanessa Maher
Vol. 4: *Defining Females: The Nature of Women in Society*
Edited by Shirley Ardener
Vol. 5: *Women and Space*: Ground Rules and Social Maps
Edited by Shirley Ardener
Vol. 6: *Servants and Gentlewomen to the Golden Land: The Emigration of Single Women to South Africa, 1820–1939*
Cecillie Swaisland
Vol. 7: *Migrant Women: Crossing Boundaries and Changing Identities*
Edited by Gina Buijs
Vol. 8: *Carved Flesh/Cast Selves: Gender Symbols and Sexual Practices*
Edited by Vigdis Broch-Due, Ingrid Rudie and Tone Bleie
Vol. 9: *Bilingual Women: Anthropological Approaches to Second Language Use*
Edited by Pauline Burton, Ketaki Dyson and Shirley Ardener
Vol. 10: *Gender, Drink and Drugs*
Edited by Maryon MacDonald
Vol. 11: *Women and Missions: Past and Present*
Edited by Fiona Bowie, Deborah Kirkwood and Shirley Ardener
Vol. 12: *Women in Muslim Communities: Religious Belief and Social Realities*
Edited by Camillia Fawzi El-Solh and Judy Mabro
Vol. 13: *Women and Property, Women as Property*
Edited by Renée Hirschon

'Male' and 'Female' in Developing Southeast Asia

Edited by
Wazir Jahan Karim

BERG PUBLISHERS
Oxford/Washington D.C., USA

First published in 1995 by
Berg Publishers
Editorial offices:
150 Cowley Road, Oxford, OX4 1JJ, UK
13590 Park Center Road, Herndon, VA 22071, USA

Library of Congress Cataloging-in-Publication Data

A catalogue record for this book is available from the Library of Congress.

British Library Cataloguing in Publication Data

A catalogue record for this book is available from the British Library.

ISBN 0 85496 905 5 (Cloth)
       1 85973 027 2 (Paper)

Printed in the United Kingdom by WBC Book Manufacturers, Bridgend,
Mid Glamorgan.

This book is dedicated to Sir Raymond and Lady Rosemary Firth whose pioneering research on anthropology in Malaysia introduced Southeast Asian ethnography to the future generation of anthropologists.

Contents

Notes on Contributors   ix

Foreword   xiii

PART I *Theoretical Overview*   1

Prologue: A Woman Looks Back on the Anthropology of
Women and Feminist Anthropology
    Rosemary Firth   3

1 Introduction: Genderising Anthropology in Southeast Asia
    Wazir Jahan Karim   11

2 Bilateralism and Gender in Southeast Asia
    Wazir Jahan Karim   35

3 Gender at the Margins of Southeast Asia
    Otome Klein-Hutheesing   75

PART II *Ethnography and Culture*   99

4 Modern Malay Women and the Message of the 'Veil'
    Judith Nagata   101

5 Engendering Disquiet: On Kinship and Gender in Bali
    Mark Hobart   121

6 Buddhism, Merit Making and Gender: The Competition
for Salvation in Laos
    Mayoury Ngaosyvathn   145

7 Vietnamese Women and Confucianism: Creating Spaces
from Patriarchy
    Stephen O'Harrow   161

8 Performance and Gender in Javanese Palace Tradition
    Felicia Hughes-Freeland   181

PART III *Methodological Issues*   207

9 Redefining the 'Maybahay' or Housewife: Reflections on
the Nature of Women's Work in the Philippines
    Jean Frances Illo   209

10 The Significance of 'Eating': Cooperation, Support, and
Reputation in Kelantan Malay Households
  Ingrid Rudie   227

11 Rewriting Gender and Development Anthropology in
Southeast Asia
  Penny Van Esterik   247

Index   261

Notes on Contributors

Rosemary Firth is currently retired. She completed two periods of fieldwork in Kelantan, Malaysia, in 1939–40 and 1963. She has taught at the Institute of Education, London University after the war. Her special interests have always been giving anthropological insights to lay audiences, especially in the fields of family life, women's affairs, nutrition and health. Her publications of main interest are, *Housekeeping Among Malay Peasants*, (Athlone, 1966), 'The Social Images of Man and Woman', Biosocial Aspect of Sex, *Journal of Biosocial Science*, 1970, Supplement No. 2 and 'From Wife to Anthropologist' in *Crossing Cultural Boundaries, The Anthropological Experience*, ed. Solon T. Kimball and James B. Watson (Chandler, 1972).

Jean Francis Illo is a research associate of the Institute of Philippines Culture, where she heads the Women's Studies programme. She is author of *Irrigation in the Philippines: Impact on Women and their Household; The Case of the Aslong Project, 1988* (Population Council, Bangkok), and co-author of *Women and Men in Rainfield Farming Systems: Case Studies of Households in the Bicol Region, 1988* (Institute of Philippines Culture) and *Fishers, Traders, Farmers, Wives: The Life Stories of Ten Women in a Fishing Village, 1990* (Institute of Philippines Culture). She has also written several articles on women and rural development.

Mark Hobart is currently Senior Lecturer at the Department of Anthropology, School of Oriental and African Studies, University of London. He has conducted extensive research in South Bali, and amongst his books are; *Ideas of Identity, the Interpretation of Kinship in Bali* (Universitas Udayana, 1980), *A Balinese Village Remembered* (University of Gadjah Mada Press, 1991) and *The Growth of Ignorance: A Critique of Development* (Routledge, In press). He has also contributed numerous chapters in books, including 'Is God Evil?', ed. Parkin (Blackwell, 1985) and 'Anthropos through the Looking-glass: Or How to Teach the Balinese to Bark' in *Reason and Morality*, ed. Overing (Tavistock, 1985).

Felicia Hughes-Freeland is a Lecturer in Social Anthropology at University College of Swansea, Wales. She has conducted extensive fieldwork in Java and Bali and has published articles on different aspects of Indonesian culture and social change with reference to Javanese performance. She is currently writing up her research, which has so far been expressed in an ethnographic film entitled *The Dancer and the Dance*, and is also working on a project about television and social change.

Wazir Jahan Karim is Professor in Anthropology at Universiti Sains Malaysia and currently Convenor of the Women and Human Resource Studies Unit. She is author of *Ma' Betisek Concepts of Living Things* (Athlone, 1981), editor and co-author of *Emotions of Culture: A Malay Perspective* (Oxford University Press, 1990) author of *Women and Culture: Between Malay Adat and Islam* (Westview, 1993) and co-editor and co-author of *Gendered Fields* (Routledge, 1992) . She has also published several articles on the Ma' Betise and the Malays, and is currently working on the anthropology of goods and consumption.

Otome Klein-Hutheesing, a former sociologist from the Netherlands, retrained herself as an anthropologist to do fieldwork amongst the Lisu of Thailand. She is author of *Emerging Sexual Inequality among the Lisu of Northern Thailand* (Brill, 1990) and has contributed a chapter to *Gendered Fields*, eds. D. Bell, P. Caplan and W. J. Karim (Routledge, 1991). She has also published several articles on women and rituals in Malaysia, and is currently researching on AIDS in Northern Thailand.

Judith Nagata is Professor of Anthropology at York University. Most of her research is concerned with various aspects of ethnicity and ethnic relations and religious change, both in North America and in Southeast Asia, particularly Malaysia, where she has spent many years conducting research on religion and ethnicity. Among the works resulting from these interests are *Pluralism in Malaysia: Myth or Reality?* (Brill, 1976), *Malaysian Mosaic: Perspective from a Poly-ethnic Society* (University of British Columbia Press, 1979), *The Reflowering of Malaysian Islam* (University of British Columbia Press, 1984), *Religion, Values and Development in Southeast Asia* (co-edited with Bruce Matthews; Singapore: Institute of Southeast Asian Studies, 1986). She is also the author of numerous articles on related topics of gender and class and of a volume on an American religious community, *Continuity and Change Among the Old Order Amish of Illinois* (AMS Press, 1989). More recently she has been involved in research on Asian and Southeast Asian migrants in Canada.

Mayoury Nagosyvathn is trained in legal studies and has been appointed Counsellor of the Royal Supreme Court of the Kingdom of Laos. She has lectured at the Royal Institute of Law and Administration, then the School of International Relations, and the High School of Law in Lao PDR. She was Deputy-Director for the Ministry of Justice from 1975 to 1978, and Deputy-Director for the Ministry of Foreign Affairs from 1979 to 1986. Since then, she has devoted her research to Southeast Asia history, ethno-sociology, as well as gender issues. She has received several fellowships and awards including a Fulbright, Senior Scholar based at Harvard University (U.S.A) and a fellowship at the University of Hawaii. She has written several articles, and co-authored books with Dr Pheuiphanh including *A Present of the Past Fifty Years (1778 to 1828) of Diplomacy and Warfare Among Mainland Southeast Asian Polities: Politics Nemesis in Modern Laos, Thailand and Vietnam* (New York: Cornell University's Southeast Asian Program), *The Lao in Australia: Perspective on Settlement Experiences*, 1993 (Australia: Griffith University), *Studies on Lao History and Historiography* (with Kennon Breazeale, co-editor) forthcoming.

Stephen O'Harrow has been teaching at the University of Hawaii in Honolulu since 1968, where he is Associate Professor of Vietnamese Studies, Chairperson of the Vietnam Studies Committee, and Coordinator of the Hawaii/Vietnam Exchange Program. Trained as a philologist, O'Harrow is currently working on computerised language teaching and reference materials in Vietnamese. Beyond his linguistic work, he is especially interested in the historical role of women and gender dynamics in Vietnamese society.

Ingrid Rudie is a senior lecturer at the Institute of Anthropology, University of Oslo. She began her research on the Malays in Kelantan in 1965, and has since returned in the mid 1980s to update her research on Malay family and economics. Amongst her publications are *Ceremonial, School and Market. On the Reproduction of Gender in East Coast Malay Culture* (NORAS, 1990) and *Carved Flesh/Cast Selves: Gender Symbols and Sexual Practices* (with co-editors Tone Bleie and Broch Due; Berg, 1993). She has also published several Chapters including 'A Hall of Mirrors: Autonomy Translated over Time in Malaysia', in D. Bell, P. Caplan and W. J. Karim (eds), *Gendered Fields* (Routledge, 1993).

Penny Van Esterik is an Associate Professor of Anthropology at York University, Toronto. Her principal areas of interest include nutritional anthropology, particularly infant feeding, cognitive and symbolic theory, and advocacy anthropology. In addition to past fieldwork on Thai symbolism, religion, and cultural history, she has recently worked with an interdisciplinary team studying the determinants of infant feeding in several developing countries. This work, *Beyond the Breast–Bottle Controversy* (also translated into Indonesian), has been published by Rutgers University Press. She co-directs the Thai Studies Project and directs a CIDA-funded linkage programme between York and Thai Universities in the area of women and development.

Foreword

This volume is a result of a Workshop organised by the Universiti Sains Malaysia-based KANITA Project (Women in Development) and UNESCO on 'Research Methodologies, Theoretical Perspectives and Directions for Policy in Gender Studies in Southeast Asia', held in December 1989, in Penang. It puts together a selection of the papers presented at the workshop and a few from invited contributors.

The chapters are organised into three parts, theoretical, ethnographic and methodological, and essentially express the viewpoints of Southeast Asianists concerned with the applicability of contemporary feminist theory in Southeast Asia. While a number of the writers attempt to form a critique of Western feminist theory, by demonstrating its inconsistency with cultural data, either ideologically or empirically, some appear sympathetic to the writings of feminist anthropology by elucidating the way in which Western knowledge through colonialism and modernisation has made men more 'public', and hence more important. Economic and development theory borrowed from the West emphasises male–female categories of work and production, according them a differential value that has engendered both economic renumeration and statistical and national accountability.

Many writers also show that religions which originated in patriarchal states outside Southeast Asia, such as Hinduism, Buddhism, Islam and Christianity, have contributed significantly to gender differentiation and the formal dominance of men in public and political life. However, underlying most of these papers is the association of women's power with popular ideologies derived from folk traditions. Rather than seeing male–female relations as separate, distinct and hierarchical, writers show how interfused male–female relationships are and how domestic and public boundaries overlap in social systems which are ego-centred and non-corporate. Women fare better under systems which de-emphasise corporate forms of grouping and membership. If any kind of feminist perspective has to emerge, it is to show that Southeast Asian categorical distinctions of the public and private, formal and informal are not as important as they are made out to be in social theory, and that differences in power between women and men suggest differences in domains of preference, perceived as complementary rather than hierarchical. In Southeast Asia, the history of inclusion of ideologies that formally preach patriarchy reflects a history of social tensions between popular bilaterality and religious orthodoxy. This introduces paradoxical statements and interpretations of gender relations within cultures.

Another point which is emphasised is the distinction between 'sameness' and 'equality', reflecting the Southeast Asian mode of thinking: that biology, physique and psychology are factors that make women different from men but in no way inferior to them. These factors have not reduced women's contributions to political, economic and social life, but, on the contrary, enable them to stabilise important institutions, which are being destabilised with economic development, modernisation and industrialisation. These pertain to the organisation of the family and household, the production and processing of food, the maintenance of health-care systems and the educational needs of children. The popular view that women are not the same as men and do different things does not generate a discourse that they are inferior or less important that men, at least not before they are told that they are by modernists, advocating Western models of change and development. Nevertheless, while tourism, prostitution, and production work in assembly lines, have placed a commercial value on women in ways more visible than before, there are signs and symptoms of resistance, a pull towards reducing hierarchies and differences through popular interpretations of gender relationships. In revivalist movements, for example, the external symbols of resistance seems to go contrary to notions of equality, yet the invisible message is anti-Western and anti-modern. Women became the ritual bearers of 'culture' emphasising a role more 'indigeneous' than 'commercial'. In modern economic activity, women are increasingly moving into the non-formal sector where they can continue with their entrepreneurial activities based in household production. This is a traditional way of recognising the household as 'public' and of linking the domestic with economic activity managed and controlled by women.

This volume will make an important contribution to the development of the theory and ethnography of Southeast Asia, particularly since publications on women and gender in this sub-region are still few to come by and, with the exception of one or two, continue to emulate predictions of Western theory that patterns of change and transformation are always hierarchical and irreversible, affecting women more adversely than men.

PART I

Theoretical Overview

Prologue: A Woman Looks Back on the Anthropology of Women and Feminist Anthropology

Rosemary Firth

It is good to find the Women's Studies Unit at Universiti Sains Malaysia, Penang presenting a collection of papers on gender relations from so wide an area and with such diverse viewpoints in this challenging new field.

Over half a century ago, my own Malayan fieldwork was probably one of the first published studies of women in Southeast Asia. But it was a study of women's roles, not a gender study in the modern theoretical idiom. The same is true of the work by other women anthropologists of that time. It is natural that each generation should approach old subjects in a style which differs from that of their elders. In this paper I shall take a backward look at anthropological work on women and by women in the last sixty years or so, which laid the foundation on which younger writers have built today.

The term Gender Studies is a recent innovation in anthropological discourse, while sex roles and relationships were a traditional subject of investigation even before Malinowski's study of kinship and sex in the Trobriands (1929). Ten years later, Phyllis Kaberry published her Australian *Aboriginal Woman, Sacred and Profane*. The introduction to that work makes it clear that she was concerned with the anthropology of women rather than with feminist anthropology. While women were the focus of her attention, her theme, she said, was 'one that involved a contrast and comparison of their activities with those of men, their cooperation and their shared beliefs'. In 1952 she published *Women of the Grasslands*, an original and witty study of the contradictions and complexities of attitudes and behaviour between the sexes in the Cameroons. Those women had no doubt about their importance in that society, in child-bearing, agricultural work and certain ritual practices, and they expressed it to her with some acerbity (1952: 150)

3

A woman is an important thing . . . she bears a child, then takes a hoe, goes to the field and is working there; she feeds the child there . . . What work can a man do? A man can only buy palm oil. Men only build houses . . . Important things are women. Men are little. What are the things of men? Men are nothing, have you not seen?

And they reminded her of the four days of mourning for a woman, in contrast to only three for a man.

In 1937 Camilla Wedgwood published her studies of *Women in Manam*, New Guinea. In 1959 Audrey Richards published *Chisungu*, her study of girl's initiation ceremonies in Northern Rhodesia (Zambia). In this she made clear that the rites were an initiation into womanhood and its responsibilities, since the girls were already sexually sophisticated. The rites were said to change the girls from 'an uncultivated weed', in the men's phrase, to 'women as we are', in their own terms. A study of the unusual familial and economic roles of women in Jamaica was Edith Clarke's book *My Mother Who Fathered Me* in 1957.

For these four women, all unmarried and collecting their material alone in the field, it must have seemed the most simple and natural thing to do, to study women: a man would have found it a more difficult task. Successful women in those days often did remain unmarried, but we cannot know if this was a deliberate choice or the unexpected result of the way their emotional energies were directed.

About 1958 the wind began to change a little. UNESCO convened a meeting in Calcutta in January of that year to discuss the contribution which the social sciences could make towards better mutual appreciation of Eastern and Western cultural values. Special emphasis was to be laid on the 'revolutionary changes in the status of women politically, legally, economically and educationally . . . in country after country in the last fifty years'. The preface boldly declared (1963: 13): 'In this book, UNESCO is daring to ask for trouble- to study the roles of the two sexes is to do just that. Probably no other topic excites more argument and less agreement and probably on no other topic is the argument more heated and the disagreement more profound.'

The book was edited by Barbara Ward, who contributed a clear introductory preface for lay readers. The articles covered Burma, Ceylon (as it then was), India, Indonesia, Laos, Malaya, East Pakistan, the Philippines, China, Singapore, Thailand and Vietnam. They were written by anthropologists, sociologists, educationists and political scientists of note, as well as by some 'ordinary housewives'; in some of these papers the sharp note of perceived injustice and inegality first began to appear.

In 1968 Edwin Ardener wrote a paper on 'Belief and the Problems of Women'. First delivered in Phyllis Kaberry's seminar in London, it was appropriately published in a *Festschrift* for Audrey Richards in 1972, edited in turn by Jean La Fontaine. Commenting on a later reprint, Ardener noted (1975: 20) that 'of that galaxy of female talent, none of the women were of a particularly feminist turn of mind'. It so happened, however, that when in 1964 I consulted Audrey Richards on how I might present the result of my second visit to Malaysia, she wrote to me: 'Women are News! as Rose Macaulay says; so you might write a selling book on the position of house-keepers the world over.' I did not do quite that in the 1966 edition of my book, except in so far as I outlined some of the technological developments which had altered the way of life of those peasant fisherman and their wives, and to which they had to learn to adapt.

In 1970 I was invited to give a paper on 'The Social Images of Men and Women' at a symposium on 'Biosocial Aspects of Sex'. Stressing the influence of upbringing and social expectations on the different behaviour of men and women in such matters as dress, hair style, bodily movement in sitting and carrying and using implements, I suggested that a world in which the sexes were not so differentiated, but regarded as similar and equal would lack the variety of much in art, myth and religious expressions. As Marilyn Strathern succinctly put it later, 'In many cultures notions about difference and similarities between the sexes are put to use . . . as a kind of language for talking about other things . . . as a source of symbolism' (1976: 49).

Issues such as these were not brought to the fore at the time Raymond and I first went into the field. A husband-and-wife team was indeed so unusual that there was a little precedent for any division of labour in field enquiry. If I had any model, it was that of Audrey Richards. I had met her in London at the London School of Economics and read her first book. It was a research study published before she was in the field among the Bemba. In the opening paragraph she boldly stated (1932: 1) 'Nutrition as a biological process is more fundamental than sex. In the life of the individual it is a primary and recurrent physical want, while in the wider sphere of society it determines the nature of social groupings and the form their activities take.'

In 1939–40 and again in 1963 I studied the position of women in Kelantan and their relation to men; since Raymond was recording fish catches on the beach every day it seemed logical that I should find out how fish are cooked and eaten within each household. From there on followed much else about the domestic life of women. Audrey's model, however, did perhaps deflect me from immediate concern with women's

6 | **Rosemary Firth**

roles and women's self-perception, although I was indirectly concerned with this.

In my own professional gender relations, my studies and those of Raymond were complementary. They were of equal value, and seen so by us, fitting in to each other both factually and theoretically, as my book has shown.

Our joint work might have been regarded as parallel to the gender relations among our Malay friends. In many ways we conformed to their gender patterns as time went on. But our aims and resources were very different, and in some spheres I occupied a special category, in which I was allowed to behave outside a Malay woman's normal gender role. At festivals of marriage or religious celebrations men did a great deal of the cooking. Notably, in the domestic finances of these peasants, it was the married woman who had charge of the family cash, and had a distinct voice in the family expenditure, including capital expenditures by the man, as for a boat or net. It is notable, too, that in Kelantan peasant women were much freer socially than their sisters in western Malaysia – particularly in that early period, except perhaps in Negeri Sembilan.

In 1972 I published a personal description of what it was like to do fieldwork overseas for the first time, and what sort of relations developed between the two of us as we worked. After the war, many married couples went into the field together, and divided their work in different ways, as must have seemed appropriate at the time. Sometimes this meant working in adjacent areas, sometimes on adjacent problems in one area: for example, the Freedmans in Singapore, the Berndts in Australia, the Stratherns in New Guinea, and the Ardeners in Nigeria. The intellectual climate in which they worked differed from that of the pre-war group, when the profession was still very small, and women were not expected to combine marriage and family life with a profession of their own. But when these couples returned home they often found that both partners could not easily get academic jobs. The earlier friend in feminist anthropology to see univerals of gender inequality in every culture studied was possibly a reflection of this Western experience of discrimination. I have been made aware of some personal strains myself, where there were tensions between private and public obligations or conflicts of loyalty in the family. On the whole I would hazard a guess that cooperation rather than conflict becomes the rule for anthropologists in marriage partnership. In some instances wives did better than husbands. Anthropologists learn flexibility and adaptability in the field, where they observe different codes of behaviour in all aspects of domestic life, so that it is easier for them, perhaps, than for some others to make personal adjustment within the culture of their own families.

Womens' liberation as an aggressive egalitarian movement began in the 1960s in America, whence it later spread to Britain. An early result in the United States was to stimulate a lecture course on women at Stanford in 1971. This produced in 1974 the classic collection *Woman, Culture and Society*, which was edited by Rosaldo and Lamphere. Not long after, an important conference on 'New Directions in Social Anthropology' was held in Oxford. Appropriately enough, it gave rise to a 'fringe meeting' of the Association of Social Anthropologists; this meeting was itself an innovation. It was a seminar *on* women *by* women in anthropology; it resulted in 1975 in the collection of essays edited by Shirley Ardener, with papers on female militancy in Africa, diplomats' wives, gypsy women and nuns. A whole new series followed under her editorship.

In retrospect 1970 seems to have been a turning-point, after which came a regular stream of writing – some would call it a flood – by women on women. Looking through the bibliographies only of some fifty books I had collected during my own teaching career between 1961 and 1978 I realise that no one person could easily be familiar with the whole of the literature on this subject. But in studying some of it again for this article, one thing has struck me which may be of some interest.

Thirty years ago the word gender was not found in the indexes of textbooks, encyclopedias or specific works on women, females or sex roles. Only very recently did it appear on the title-page of two collections I know, published in 1980 and 1989. Hence, its use in theoretical discussions on feminist anthropology is very recent. The first use which I can find is by the sociologist Ann Oakley (1972), and she takes the precaution of giving it a dictionary definition (from Webster's Third New International Dictionary): '**Sex**, the two divisions of . . . human beings respectively designated as male or female. GENDER . . . any of two or more subclasses . . . that are purely arbitrary but also partly based on distinguishable characteristics such as . . . sex (masculine, feminine . . .).'

Even in a paper written in 1973 Marilyn Strathern had found it useful to begin a definition of cultural stereotypes of males and females as *gender* as distinct from the physiological basis for discrimination as *sex*. However by the time her paper was published, in 1976, considerable literature had been published on women since then, which, she noted, had changed all that. In the collection she edited with Cormack in 1980, as in the collection of Jolly and MacIntyre in the Pacific area, in 1989, *gender* appeared boldly on the title-page.

I have not been able to keep in touch with recent indigenous scholarship in Southeast Asia and the concern of local scholars in the Third World not to be submerged by feminist approaches or Western paradigms of womanhood. But I can see the importance for social scientists, there and elsewhere beyond the West, in developing new theoretical viewpoints from local indigenous fieldwork.

In this prologue I have done little more than cast a rather hasty eye over the development of the early work of some anthropologists in the disputatious field of gender relations during my own working life. I was invited to give a personal view, and it must be clear that this is all I have done. It is a partial, as well perhaps as a one-sided view. In an attempt to bind together what I have said, I offer one final commentary on the problem at issue.

Structuralist analysis derives from the belief that binary thinking underlies all human mental functioning; from this basis 'gender studies' developed from the realisation that women had become a new analytical category. Lifted from the closed world of academic discourse, it is easy to see how such theories provided valuable ammunition in political and personal debate about the rights and duties of men and women in the real world. Early American writers on women's roles bore a strong political message. Questions are asked, Rosaldo and Lamphere affirmed (1974: 1; cf. H. Moore 1988) 'Not simply out of abstract intellectual curiosity, but because we are searching for ways in which to think about ourselves. Along with many women today, we are trying to understand our position and to change it.'

Fortunately, in my opinion, in the United Kingdom the tone of this kind of writing has recently become less strident – perhaps because of real changes in the position of women; while theoretical writing has developed a wider focus on positive images of identity, looking at complementarity and cooperation as well as conflict (Harris 1978). Change in perception of gender identity over the life-span is also described in Gaynor Cohen's collection, *Social Change and the Life Course* (1987), which has an exceptionally useful list of references.

An Islamic community cannot be the easiest place in which to develop feminist thinking or dispassionate gender studies; but from what I can read in these papers emerging on Southeast Asia, Southeast Asian women and men remain as innovative and flexible in thought and action as I noted in my first visit to a changing Malaysia in 1963. Some anthropologists believe that they should be more concerned with observing society than in trying to change it. It is clear to me in respect of sex roles and gender relations that, in doing the first, they have indirectly had an important influence on the second. And that is as it should be, I believe.

Notes

1. In the domestic field there was much more equality and cooperation than in the public and political. Men caught the fish, it is true and women took part in the salting and drying of fish for domestic use and for sale (see Rudie's comments on Kelantan women, as concerned with both food and money projects, in this volume).
2. Raymond and I wrote up our materials in consultation. But owing to publication difficulties and war obligations, my book was published first, his not appearing until three later than mine.

Bibliography

Ardener, E. (1972). Belief and the Problems of Women. In J. S. La Fontaine (ed.), *The Interpretation of Ritual: Essays in Honour of A. I. Richards*. London: Tavistock. (Also in S. Ardener (ed.) 1975.)

Ardener, S. (ed.) (1975). *Perceiving Women*. London: Malaby Press.

—— (1978). *Defining Females*. London: Croom Helm.

—— (1981). *Women and Space*. London: Croom Helm.

—— (1984). See Callan and Ardener.

Benedict, M. and Benedict B. (1982). *Men, Women and Money in Seychelles*. Berkeley: University of California Press.

Callan, H. and Ardener, S. (eds) (1984). *The Incorporated Wife*. London: Croom Helm.

Cohen, G. (1987). *Special Change and the Life Course*. London: Tavistock.

Cormack, C. and Strathern, M. (1980). *Nature, Culture and Gender*. Cambridge: Cambridge University Press.

Firth, R. M. (1943). *Housekeeping Among Malay Peasants*, London School of Economics, Monographs on Social Anthropology, No. 7. London: Lund Humphries. Second edn 1966, London: Athlone Press.

—— (1970). The Social Images of Man and Woman. *Journal of Biosocial Science*, Supplement No. 2.

—— (1972). 'From Wife to Anthropology'. In S. T. Kimball and J. A. Watson (eds), *Crossing Cultural Boundaries*. San Francisco: Chandler.

—— (1973). Anthropology in All Directions (Report on ASA Conference). *Contemporary Review*, Vol. 221, No. 1293.

Firth, R. W. (1946). *Malay Fishermen: Their Peasant Economy*. London: Kegan Paul. Second edn 1966, London: Routledge and Kegan Paul.

Fortes, M. and Meyer, D. (1969). 'Psychosis and Social Change among the Tallens'. In M. Fortes (ed.), *Psychiatry in a Changing Society*. London: Tavistock.

Harris, O. (1978). 'Complementarity and Conflict: An Andean View of Women and Men'. In J. S. La Fontaine (ed.), *Sex and Age as Principles of Social*

Differentiation, ASA Monograph 17. London: Academic Press.

Jolly, M. and MacIntyre, M. (1989). *Family and Gender in the Pacific*. Cambridge: Cambridge University Press.

Kaberry, P. M. (1939). *Aboriginal Women Sacred and Profane*. London: Routledge.

—— (1952). *Women of the Grasslands: A Study of the Economic Position of Women in Bamenda, British Cameroons*, Colonial Research Publications 14. London: HMSO.

Moore, H. L. (1988). *Feminist Anthropology*. Cambridge: Polity Press.

Oakley, A. (1972). *Sex, Gender and Society*. London: Temple Smith.

Richards, A. I. (1932). *Hunger and Work in a Savage Tribe*. London: Routledge.

—— (1956). *Chisungu: A Girl's Initiation Ceremony among the Bemba of Northern Rhodesia*. Faber and Faber: London.

Rosaldo, M. and Lamphere, L. (eds) (1974). *Woman, Culture and Society*. Stanford: Stanford University Press.

Strathern, M. (1976). 'An Anthropological Perspective'. In B. Lloyd and J. Archer (eds), *Exploring Sex Differences*. London: Academic Press.

Ward, B. E. (ed.) (1963). *Women in The New Asia*. Paris: UNESCO.

Wedgwood, C. H. (1937). 'Women in Manam', *Oceania*, Vols. 7 and 8.

1

Introduction: Genderising Anthropology in Southeast Asia

Wazir Jahan Karim

The Gender Debate in Western Theory

Reviewing some of the earlier perspectives on gender in history, social scientists usually begin by making some objective observation on the position of women in the past. The Morgan view (1871; 1962; 1963) that societies originally maintained structures that were matriarchally defined was rejected by social and cultural anthropologists mainly because empirical evidence did not support his notion of matriarchies as preceding other kinds of social systems. More importantly, his underlying assumption, that women in matriarchally ordered structures assumed more power and control than men, contained serious limitations. Further evidence of the power of the mother's brother over land and other forms of property threw light on women's symbolic rather than real power, provoking the thought that matriarchy was merely a conceptual formula for anthropologists looking for convenient labels to classify societies.

However, his ideas, rephrased in Engels's (1884), *The Origin of the Family, Private Property and the State* and Marx's theory of the social division of labour, encouraged social scientists to renew their faith in the idea that patriarchal trends in social organisation, ordered by Western modes of capitalism and industrialisation, have indeed emerged and encouraged trends towards women's 'devaluation' in society. What is seldom discussed is the way and extent to which systems might be 'equal' or bilateral in form. Conversely, patriarchal trends may exist in tension with folk traditions which define women's position in ways similar to that of men. In this context, to what extent are the newly emerging patriarchal trends 'structural'? What newly emerging systems of values are apparent that can assure the social scientist that these trends actually transform gender relationships in ways which are long-lasting and permanent? How have gender relationships been denuded in ways which have adversely affected women, and what is the evidence to show that social change has affected women more than men? These are some of the issues which will be raised in this volume on gender.

The perspective that macro developments from outside produce effective change in relationships between men and women has contributed to much binary thinking in the social sciences, where so-called 'egalitarian societies', said to contain gender relationships of symmetry, have been compared and contrasted to 'class-structured societies' containing relationships of gender asymmetry or inequality. To illustrate, E. B. Leacock (1978, 1981a,b,c), writing on the Montagnais-Naskapi, a foraging community, highlighted its egalitarian features in relation to the sexual division of labour. She maintained that the autonomous nature of relationships between men and women was gradually eroded when the society was brought under the control of French missionaries like Le Jeune, who imposed male and female differences in behaviour and organisation according to the European values and norms of the time. Consequently, a patriarchal trend was manifested and maintained through male domination. These structural transformations over time are explained by researchers' providing an external view of women's power in society, usually defined in terms of formal and public venues of decision-making where autonomy and personal freedom is safely guarded. But power can be invisible, informal, non-bureaucratised and alienated from the system of privileges and rights sanctioned by the State. These are the ways women and less privileged classes have articulated their 'power' in Southeast Asia. With women, added strategies of power are 'silence' (in contrast to public protests) and withdrawal (in contrast to affirmative action). These 'intangibles' are always interpreted as sources of women's strength in communal relations. Non-cooperation in political and religious activity is also feared by men, since most of them realise that they cannot assume important formal offices without the support of wives and important members of the female community. Though it is important to objectify folk experience of power through externally prescribed definitions, it is equally important to know if these interpretations coincide with cultural constructs of the same thing. In discussing 'change' in gender relations, are we as social scientists able to understand how societies alter or modify their own gender constructs in the long term ? Can one confidently state that the resulting changes reflect permanent hierarchies between men and women?   With urbanisation and industrialisation, to what extent do pre-existing perceptions of gender guide current folk notions of women and their relationships with men?

The view that colonisation or industrialisation radically brings about male domination cannot provide adequate answers simply because it maintains the underlying assumptions that social rules invariably lead to an inequality that becomes a permanent rule for future social discourses between women and men. One way in which anthropologists have attempted to overcome this patronage of Western wisdom is to accept social inequality as a fundamental social construct in all cultures (Gough 1965, 1975; Rosaldo and Lamphere 1974; Reiter 1975; Raphael 1975). Since basic biological and sexual differences already exist, cultural systems merely serve to interpret and elaborate upon rules of relationships between men and women. Thus cultures only differ in the extent to which gender is used as a rule, formal or symbolic, to sort out hierarchical forms of relationships between men and women.

With this basic assumption safely formulated, some researchers set about explaining it in terms of institutions which have long been embedded in the complex history and social systems of different populations. Reiter (1975: 11) introduces her volume of cross-cultural studies on women by stating that the 'subjugation of women is a fact of our daily existence, yet it neither began with modern capitalism nor automatically disappears in socialist societies'. Gough (1975) asserts that differences between the status of men and women exist even in foraging cultures and are equally prominent in so-called matriarchal or matrilineal societies like the Hopi of Arizona, the Nayar of Kerala and the Minangkabau of Sumatra. She states that, in such cultures, women and children invariably fall under the greater or lesser authority of male kinsmen from the matrilineage (eldest brother, mother's brother, eldest son). She concludes that 'there is in fact no true "matriarchal" as distinct from "matrilineal" society in existence or known from literature, and the chances are that there never has been' (1975: 54).

This theme is further developed by Rosaldo and Lamphere, who agree that 'all contemporary societies are to some extent male-dominated' and that 'sexual asymmetry is presently a universal fact of human social life' (1974: 3). The notion of persisting forms of male domination and patriarchy throughout history is often demonstrated through detailed ethnography using structural or symbolic analysis.

This line of thinking again runs contrary to the rigorous inquiry into gender symbolism, which has been a stronghold of social anthropologists concerned with linking empirical data with perspectives of gender. Such insiders' writers show that variations in folk constructs on ideas of 'male' and 'female' and the likely relationships between women and men do not necessarily live up to Western universalisms of sex and gender based on notions of hierarchies and oppositions between culture and nature, public and private. Through symbolic analysis, MacCormack and Strathern in a collection of articles argued against the 'putative universality of the nature–culture categories' applied to male–female relationships (1980: vii). MacCormack in her critique of this feminist approach in anthropology argued that the 'genderizing' of anthropology should be done in the context of the relativity of ideas and morals on which anthropology was built. She asked, 'Might we then conclude that both men and women are nature and culture, and there is no logic compelling us to believe that at an unconscious level women, because of their naturalness, are opposed and subordinate to men?' (1980: 17).

The symbolic analysis of gender in anthropology, however, did not transcend the structuralist framework, since relativisms established in cultural analysis assumed that change was less important than cultural consistency (Harris 1978; Strathern 1980). Influence on gender analysis produced a period of disenchantment with cultural relativity and an attempt to renew universalistic notions of women's subordination in Western theory (see Caplan 1989).

The volume by Ortner and Whitehead (1981) rejected the structuralist line and stated that a new symbolic mode of analysis should be developed – one which allowed gender to be observed in the context of prestige systems. Reviewing a variety of prestige-systems in different cultures, these authors argue that kinship, motherhood and the mother–son bond enhance the prestige of men rather than women, and that this heightens with advancing religious orthodoxy (1981: 1–128). I would argue to the contrary that this does not clearly happen in Southeast Asia and that the flexibility of interpretation over prestige gives women and men sufficient leverage to operate power to the advantage of the 'self'. While it is evident that the indigenous milieu of gender relations rests uneasily on Indic–Buddhist and Islamic traditions in cultural history, male dominance in these areas of orthodoxy has not necessarily removed women from other public religious activity – in particular folk spiritualism, which expresses the heart and soul of the Southeast Asian. How important is State politics and formal religion to women? Are women in Southeast Asia like Western feminists, making an argument for equality in all spheres of male dominance; or do they see these spheres as alternative paradigms of power and prestige, complementing those they already have?

In this book, authors have avoided the stereotypical definition of 'power' as a social derivative of the 'State' and 'powerlessness' as a social derivative of 'people' at the grass roots. In Southeast Asia we know this is not true, since power at the grass roots is as public and important as the power of men allied to the State. As long as biology and sex are not used as a criterion for 'power', women can continue to generate activity which will bring them visibility and prestige. Moore argues that an investigation into the constructs of 'women' and 'men' is essential, and that these categories should not be assumed. She states that 'biological difference between the sexes tell us nothing about the general social significance of that difference' (1988: 7). The construction of ethnocentrism and racism might tell us something more about women and men, since these two forces have historical and cultural origins. In racism, biology might be used as an issue of differentiation; but the fact that it is utilised, manipulated and applied makes it cultural, rather than natural. In her volume, she concludes that anthropology is in a position to reformulate feminist theory, because (compared with other disciplines in the Social Sciences) it can more successfully remove social data from Western bias and Eurocentrism. The future of feminist anthropology, she states, is in a movement away from 'sameness' to 'difference', and in this women anthropologists have to realise a lack of academic cohesion when discussing issues of women's oppression.

Strathern (1988), reflecting again on theories of male dominance, cautions anthropologists against applying universalisms in gender relations and gender theory, since these universalisms are based in the researcher's familiarity with Western modes of social relations, where a threat to individuality and personal autonomy is construed in terms of hegemony and domination. She argues that Melanesian men and women do not represent themselves as separate autonomous beings. Melanesian women obey men, and are often beaten by them; but one must examine the system of providing this kind of advantage to men. Is it 'natural' and 'universal' that men dominate women, or are acts of domination 'tantamount to no more than taking advantage of this advantage' (1988: 327). It is easier for men in some cultures to take advantage of brute strength and rules which endorse the use of brute force over women; but this is by no means a standard formula for intersexual domination.

With the post-modernist disenchantment with Marxism, many writers began to have recourse to European philosophies concerned with the development of the history of knowledge and the history of ideas. Approaches linked to the constitutive nature of the process of knowledge production (Bourdieu 1980; Fabian 1983) have repopularised most of the major works of Foucault, which highlight history as processes of knowledge construction within culture. Foucault, in *The History of Sexuality* saw historical processes as linked to the relations of power amongst unequals from which emerged hierarchies of gender. He argued that European eighteenth-century culture focused on 'specific mechanisms of knowledge and power centring on sex' (1978: 103). The power specialists of succeeding epochs continued with more effective strategies of concretising gender, articulated in the final exploitation of women in capitalist technology.

Here, we have an example of European social history generating processes which encouraged rules of domination in terms of gender; but *The History of Sexuality* deals specifically with an interpretation of power from a Western paradigm which argues that gender inequality is an expression of inequality generated from the traditions within. Scholars researching on women in non-Western cultures may have to examine critically the relevance of *The History of Sexuality* to local data. The questioning of the relevance of 'grand theories' to anthropological data is meaningless if the conclusion is to look at yet another alternative within Western discourse. This alternative is also 'Eurocentric', and one concerned with establishing yet other universals through the European experience of modernity. The assumption that one should begin with the premise of unequal power generating gender hierarchies is not necessarily relevant in non-Western civilisations in Southeast Asia, which derive a theory of knowledge from concepts and values of bilateralism: the need to maintain social relationships through rules of complementarity and similarity rather than hierarchy and opposition, and the need to reduce imbalances in power through mutual responsibility and cooperation rather than oppression and force. This is the perspective adopted by the author in the chapter on gender and bilateralism: that the bilateralism of social relationships in many parts of Southeast Asia diffuses distinctions of hierarchy and difference in relationships of rank, class and gender, rendering clear structural dissimilarities between the Southeast Asian and the South Asian models.

Hutheesing in this volume attempts to answer this fundamental question in interpretation through observing minority–majority relations in Southeast Asia, and their impact on the dynamics of the lives of minority men and women. In Southeast Asia, deforestation and the dwindling subsistence economy have created serious economic hardships among men and women of highland and lowland minorities. Both men and women are forced to reexamine their relationships to one another. 'Men without honour and women without repute' is the indigenous view of contemporary gender relations amongst the hunters and gatherers of the hills, albeit one expressed differently through contrasting sexual metaphors. For example an uprooted Lisu tribesman is still a paying customer in Chiengmai, downing bottles of Mekong beer as he prepares to sleep with his prostitute; but the uprooted Lisu female in Chiengmai will always *be* the prostitute. Hutheesing suggests that it is not so much patriarchy or male domination which surfaces, but the degradation of the moral worth of a person, which may have differential consequences on the sexes. Is the destruction of the tribesman through alcoholism any worse or better than that of the tribeswoman through venereal disease? This is a difficult question to answer. If, as a result, women become more depressed and suicidal, does this show that they see the changes as affecting them in a worse way; or is this a typical 'female' reaction to crisis situations in the past and present? Male–female reactions and responses to critical changes in life situations may be a meaningful reflection of gender and the meanings it provides to systems of power and prestige.

An Appeal for an Anthropology of Informality in Southeast Asia

Subaltern social analysis, popularised through and enriched through social critics like Fanon (1968) and Freire (1970, 1972; Freire and Foundez 1989), may best capture the semiotics of gender relations in Southeast Asia. It attempts to centralise the informal and private, providing better insights into daily activities which concern the actors of culture. Scott's study, *The Weapon of the Weak* (1985), based on research in rural Malaysia, is a fine example of the importance of informal codes of behaviour which are spontaneously practised by rural Malays dealing with impossible hierarchies of rank in formal public bureaucracies; but it does not include observations of women's pervasive image in this culture of informality. Errington sees this to be possibly *the* dominant sphere of decision-making of women in island Southeast Asia, and indeed of Southeast Asians in general. She writes:

> We also tend to identify 'power' with activity, forcefulness, getting things done, instrumentality, and effectiveness brought about through calculation of means to achieve goals. The prevalent view in many parts of island Southeast Asia, however, is that to exert force, to make explicit commands, or to engage in direct activity – in other words, to exert 'power' in a Western sense – reveals a lack of spiritual power and effective potency, and consequently diminishes prestige (1990: 5).

Errington then goes to describe how this Western Eurocentric bias has been responsible for perpetuating the image of Southeast Asian women as conniving and calculating, constantly manipulating public structures through their sexuality and money to achieve power and prestige.From my observation, in reality, to do things through informal structures *is* the proper way, and one which is fully acceptable within the confines of custom (*adat*). This is powerfully reflected in the tensions between *adat* and Islam in Malaysia and Indonesia, which is the informal structure of gender relations 'struggling to be free' to achieve recognition and autonomy within the confines of a heavily bureaucratised, male-dominated Islam (see Karim 1992). Among other things it explains the preference for witchcraft and sorcery instead of direct confrontation (Karim 1990). Seldom are formal complaints made, and seldom is the target aware who are actually the people conducting the campaign. Anonymity and invisibility are carefully preserved, and the targetted person is unable to 'clear the air' or resolve the problem directly. 'What is the point of being an invisible enemy?' a Western observer may ask. 'One never gets the satisfaction of telling the person one is in disagreement with him or her; nor does one get the credit of being an opponent.' To a Southeast Asian, satisfaction and accomplishment is best linked to anonymity. Knowing is enough.

What Errington does not also discuss is the way in which codes of 'proper' behaviour through island Southeast Asian rules of *adat* are most actively used in conflict situations. When public hierarchies of class and gender are imposed upon people, then in class situations, rather than oppose these hierarchies, women and men resort to non-cooperation — polite non-committal statements at meetings, leaving in a group by the back door, circulating poison-pen letters about officers who have been unduly 'difficult' in exerting authority and forming or joining alternative groups competing with those developed by the bureaucracy. Conflicts in gender hierarchies usually centre around situations of harsh authoritarian styles of decision-making from husbands and fathers. Many alternatives are resorted to, including staying silent about personal earnings and expenditure, declaring that a visit to a sister or aunt is overdue and then taking off without waiting for an answer, serving food without eating and observing complete silence for days. The idea is to discourage open confrontation and to develop instead a form of hostile 'harmony' which will be uncomfortable for the person who is the source of irritation. The absence of an emotional reaction forces the authoritarian male to change his approach to decision-making. Men usually break under the strain of this friendly animosity, and mill around helping to carry a plate or two, in the hope that it can be met with a responsive smile. After a week they behave like whipped dogs. Many Western-trained bureaucrats administering a clerical pool of women socialised through these idioms of *adat* fail to achieve higher productivity when a formal style of administration is used – minutely following job descriptions; questioning medical leave; and denouncing the sale of cloth and crockery during office hours and cheating on the punch-card machine. (A popular mode is to punch on and, after the lunch hour, between 1.00 pm to 2.00 pm, to relax in the office, and then to disappear for the real lunch between 2.00 and 3.30 pm. To reject the imposition of formality in the workplace is not unusual. The bureaucrat who points this out as irresponsible is marked down, and work productivity drops dramatically. The clerical pool starts asking to be transferred out to other departments, and this looks bad on the bureaucrat's record. Many of them overcome this by teasing the girls excessively, complimenting or scolding them in the local dialect with a lot of gusto and charm, and agreeing to buy some of the items being sold in the office. They then become popular, and work productivity increases. Many men who do this boast that they can get girls to type any hour of the day or night without complaint.[1]

Women in Southeast Asia are publicly visible; but they are not visible in formal politics or the great religions endorsed by the State. Their inputs into politics and religion exist in the informal sphere; but this informal sphere is so visible and important that it is hard for social scientists to come up with one general statement to the effect that women are less important in politics and religion. Indeed most political and religious activities are enacted within this informal sphere. What value differences in terms of power and prestige do men and women hold between themselves, and what kinds of shifts in systems of power and prestige have women worked out to diffuse male centres of political and religious control? A Western feminist perspective for example may allocate the activity of local female devotees in Buddhism to the 'periphery', but is this 'periphery' one which is based in feminist thinking or in the people's ideology? What is the local popular view of women's informal labour inputs in religious ceremonies, food preparation and feasting in formal state religions? Do men and women view this kind of work in terms of concepts of the 'periphery' or 'centrality', or are these merely discourses of feminist anthropologists based on Western values of work – where the reward has to be immediately gratifying, it has to be based on a practical notion of utility, should be easily converted into monetary measurements, should give one access to other sources of power and lastly should provide a sense of autonomy and personal freedom. Deferment, patience, spirituality, invisibility, transference and other social intangibles are intrinsic features of a Southeast Asian social system, and become sources of resistance and strength. Do we then argue that those who practise these social intangibles are powerless, dependent and weak, that these values make them conniving and manipulative, since they have to overcome their lack of access to more formal sources of power; or do we say that, given a social system which allows these social intangibles to become valuable human resources, and strategic bases for establishing core human relations, those who use them are in fact operationalising their culture in a constructive and productive form?

Southeast Asian men who depend on the formal and public are indeed the true 'modernists'. They need a formal office and public credentials to demonstrate their 'power'. From the few men who are able to do so, the feminist comes to view all men as 'powerful'. Yet class and cultural variables separate men from one another as much as women are separated from them. A review of past and current works on women and gender in Southeast Asia may be helpful in putting some of these points across. They also provide vital sources of contemporary ethnography intersecting in time and place with the research undertaken by the authors of this volume.

Gender in Southeast Asian Ethnography: Ironing Out Differences Between Sexism in Research and Sexism in Culture

Social Scientists who have been concerned with correcting feminist approaches in Southeast Asian ethnography have directly and indirectly elucidated the complexities of Southeast Asian social systems in relation to village and political life. Thailand in particular has been the focus of much of this academic discussion. The 'loose structure' controversy of the 1950s and 1960s affected the kinds of questions researchers asked of the Thai social system regarding woman, family life and village organisation. The notion that Thai society lacked well-defined social roles (Embree 1950) was contradicted by later researchers who, focusing on women and gender relations, found the society to be more 'structured' than was earlier assumed (Eberhardt 1988).

Most of this research was conducted in North Thailand (Turton 1972; Potter 1977; Wijeyewardene 1977; Eberhardt 1988; Hanks 1988; Kammerer 1988), and accounts of matrilateral bias in the kinship system, preference for matrilocal residence, and the organisation of ancestral spirit cults around women not only elucidated the important role of women in North Thai society, but also introduced significant ethnographic variations that did not support the notion of Thai society being devoid of 'structures' and 'social roles'. Changes in perception of Thai society developed through research on kinship, gender and the family, which in turn became important areas of investigation for other scholars seeking to understand the complexity of Thai political and social life.

In other words, researchers concerned themselves with gender in order to draw meaningful conclusions about social relationships in general and village political life in particular. This was extended to peasant-based Thai communities in the North and South.

In Thailand, research in villages and towns indicated the need to study politics and religion through variable gender roles, which were asymmetrical ideologically, but less so in practice. Formal and informal definitions of Theravada Buddhism had to be considered together, for each respectively served to mystify and demystify gender relationships at different levels of activity. In Buddhism in practical activity women became the 'gate keepers' of the faith; Buddhism was almost completely dependent on women to uphold central ritual and merit-making 'activities'. Hence the gender perspective demystified the role of Theravada Buddhism in Thai society as strengthening the religious and political lives of men (Van Esterik 1982a,b,c; Kirsch 1982). These writers concluded that articulations of gender relationships must include informal and interpersonal definitions; the demystification of roles usually occurs on this level of interaction, away from public view. In this book, Mayoury Ngaosyvathn puts forward a similar argument for the Lao. Buddhism as 'State-sponsored' gives men a greater avenue for formal power. Spiritualism, as 'village-sponsored', gives women a wider avenue for informal power. Monkhood, the monastery and merit-giving form the bastions of the Lao male order; but women, through hard work and enterprise, are the merit-receivers. The wheel of fortune turns! Monkhood is a strategy for women's, receiving merit, from men, who make it.

More recently the problematic Southeast Asian social structure has been redebated through the notion of the 'village community', which writers like Kemp (1988a, 1989) and Breman (1988) argue exists only in sociological and administrative theory. Kemp goes so far as to say that the 'village' is not a feature of traditional Southeast Asian State systems, with the possible exception of North Vietnam (1988: 10). The State uses the 'village' as a primary unit of local administration; but 'this is not the continuation of tradition; it is the invention of it' (1989: 10). By inventing the 'village', the State manages to introduce the notion of a 'community', which becomes an important feature of social life. Significantly Thai social scientists appear to disagree with this view, arguing that the word *ban* or 'village' is not a recent political invention, but a pre-capitalist institution dating back to the thirteenth century (Nartsupha 1989: 3). The *Sakdina* concept meaning 'authority over the rice-field' does not imply *a State* dominating the peasantry but the claim of a local political entity over food-producing units, which were autonomously managed. The Thai farm family lived in small household units, but maintained a cooperative labour unit with others; and this corporate structure diffused attempts by other political entities to extend political control over land and labour resources.

In a similar vein, the theme of the Southeast Asian State controlling the 'state of the arts' appears in Hughes-Freeland's analysis below of court dances in Java, except that she uses it to show the weakness of male-centred power centres over history, and how their attempts to create new visual arts in dance, by highlighting the male as a symbol of active culture, breaks down as the peasant tradition takes over. The folk tradition of favouring both sexes in dance and drama provides more fluid and flexible sexual images. Finally, it is the dance rather than the dancer which triumphs, showing the transcendental state of gender and sexuality in the performing arts.

The force of Southeast Asian informality strikes wrong cords with male-centred debates in the ethnography of Southeast Asia. European and local scholars again highlight the 'public' and 'formal', caught up in paradigms they have created for themselves to help understand the Southeast Asian peasant tradition better. The 'village community' does not exist in Southeast Asia, except in Vietnam, stated some European observers. What one observes are creations of the State over history, designed to control peasant activity and movements. Yet the concept of the 'village community' is questionable; Southeast Asians have not presupposed similar structures in village life to those found in European feudal and contemporary villages, so why the fuss and bother to see through it? Rosaldo (1989) in *Culture and Truth* questioned the ethnographic lens which is made in Europe (168–245). I may add that spare parts cannot be found in Southeast Asia. European and local Southeast Asian actors met at a conference at Lund (1989).[2] Breman's 'Shattered Image' of the village in Colonial Asia (1988) and Kemp's 'Seductive Mirage' of the Southeast Asian village (1988a) stood out in startling contrast to local Thai interpretations of the 'village community' within the State (Nartsupha 1989; Pantasen 1989). The village in Thailand is like a 'Paradise Lost and Found', argued the Thai scholars. The government had 'found' it to be a viable unit of economic production, and is rebuilding a new morality based on the old. Breman and Kemp were not amused. They argued rather persuasively against the use of a 'made in Thailand' brand of anthropology, which was not only unpatented but lacked the quality control of the European version. Why was Breman shattered and Kemp unseduced; and why were the Thais keen to convince them to use a Thai lens?

In the next exciting episode, I became an interested observer of this debate, which occurred at an early stage of this conference. Facts became fantasy as the scene before me transformed to a Ramayana epic. The Thais, as Rama and Sita, were the actors of this epic, fighting off their enemies, the race of Europeans. The spectators were also Europeans, who somehow stood out as a mega force against the bespectacled minority Southeast Asians present. Drained of their cosmic powers after being transplanted to EKSA, the powerful European Kingdom of Social Anthropology, Rama and Sita accused the Europeans of stealing their 'village community' from its sacred site in Thailand. It was now hidden in this European Kingdom; and only these Europeans had the magical key. Rama and Sita were at their mercy. The two Europeans announced loudly, 'Only we know where your village community is. Only we know the secret place where it is hidden.' 'Give us back the village' begged Rama. Cried Sita, 'What am I without my community?' Rama roared, 'I rule the village Kingdom, I have been king for years, what is a kingdom without a King?' 'This is all your fault' grumbled the Europeans. 'We followed you around for years. We spoke your language and tried to understand you. You did not give us a proper location of your whereabouts. We had to find it by ourselves. We had to make up our own concepts and definitions. We were clear when you were not, were active while you remained passive, constructive when you were elusive. You kept on disappearing each time, showing off your powers of invisibility and invulnerability in Oriental fashion. We are tired of this mirage. We have taken control of the village and the community. It will be returned if you promise to master the magic book of anthropology.'

The European spectators murmered nervously. Sweat broke out amongst them. 'Would this mean that the Southeast Asians could transform into Southeast Asianists, like us?', one asked. 'Won't they use this newly found magic against us and drain us of our powers?, shouted another. 'We have been learning their language for years, now they must learn ours, as long as they are on the soil of our European Kingdom.' Another exhorted, 'Unite, peace upon the kingdom, conflict will drain us of our powers and the Gods will punish us. We will be sent back to the land of Southeast Asia and will have to look for something again, dammit.'

Returning back to the scene of the conference I thought Rama and Sita would have done better and would have refound their 'village community' faster if they had said, 'Thank God you did not find the "village community". We do not have a problem with it, because we do not need to revisit our country each time to understand the nature of our social life. The Thai village is invisible and incoherent because we are an evasive lot; and even more so when it comes to Western theory and social analysis. No wonder the men did not gather around you and the women continued to eat rice when you dropped into our villages. No wonder no harvest dance was performed and no death materialised before your eyes. If there were no indications of a social life it is because obscurity is our theme and avoidance our method. It merely means that we do not have to worry if we have a village or a community or both or neither. We do not need a coffee shop to unravel a political discourse or neighbourhood for the women to discuss a coming feast. Anthropologists who come here have to understand that we choose to construct ourselves in this way, which is the Thai way; and if our evasiveness and loose sense of identity causes a problem, remember that we are Buddhists, and as Buddhists we are also visitors. The only difference is we "stayed".'

We should also ask ourselves if the 'Shattered Image' and 'Seductive Mirage' are a proper reflection of village life in Southeast Asia. An anthropologist, Janet Carsten, researching in Teriang, a Malay fishing village in Langkawi Island, described (personal communication) how she had to gracefully decline eager invitations from Malay women to follow the path of Islam. 'They were disappointed she did not convert; but her fostermother was consoled in the fantasy that she had had an English husband, and Janet was her child. Many mats and baskets were woven for Janet to take home to her "village" in England, a village spiritually connected with Teriang, invisible to the Malay naked eye but visible in their dreams. The nightmare of dealing with a "stranger visitor" became dreamy contentment as they used their "made in Malaysia" ethnographic lens to ease the unfamiliar and dangerous into the boundaries of the "community". Normal social relations could then be resumed.' 'Be one of us' is a good demonstration of a 'community', the collective need to remove 'stranger' categories, to absorb the unknown and fearful and transform it to a familiar whole. Her research further demonstrated how women uphold the network of social and community relations neglected by men through their preoccupation with fishing (1989). Marie Andree Coullard, another women anthropologist researching on the Malays, had a similar experience in Kedah, of women wanting to transform her into a good Malay and Muslim (personal communication). Again they did not succeed, and no one gained any spiritual merit (*pahala*) for this effort.

They did, however, succeed in making a confident connection with the unfamiliar, and the triumph of having widened the cosmogenic boundaries of the village. Is the independent variable here gender, as argued by Carsten, where men divide and women unite, that women reprocess impersonal transactions through kinship and make them into viable community resources? Is the responsibility of the *village* 'male' and the *community* 'female'? Do women fill in the empty cells of the village and domesticate it with their own skilful techniques of human resource management, exchanging food with one another, organising rotating credit pools and persuading elders to stay with them to take care of their children? Or is this a new kind of sexism in anthropology, where everything women do seems to be going right for others, since it is directed towards the achievement of the Collective?

Hobart's discussion on the gender of kinship in Bali directly and indirectly refutes the argument that the Southeast Asian village does not have a 'community'. In dispelling conventional anthropological classifications of kinship, Hobart states that a much better approach to kinship is to study the patterns of social formation of groups centring around important spheres of economic, social and ritual activity, since it is in these spheres that consanguinity, affinity and temporality converge to form cohesive action groups. Temple congregations (*pamaksaan*, *daduya* or *soroh*, followed by the name of the worship group) is one such example, where the criterion of membership is a loose flexible arrangement based on agnatic descent (*sakeng purusa*) and 'coming from the same mother's womb' (*semeton*). This expresses a structure of complementarity, linked to the perceived function of males and females. Localities are also defined in terms of sites of worships or shrines (*sanggah*), which usually originate from female deities. Women pray at both marital and natal shrines. Hence, despite the formal classification of kinship based on agnatic descent or *purusa*, community relations takes on a flexible genderless arrangement of people linked together by descent or parentage (*saturunan*), marriage and territoriality.

Discussing this book with Rosemary and Raymond Firth (1990) the latter said that he had to confess that gender analysis did not seem right anthropologically. 'Gender' is neuter, you have to talk about 'women' or 'men' or 'women' and 'men', but you cannot talk about them in terms of abstract concepts of human relations, as what appears in the English language as 'gender'. Rosemary was much more supportive, hence her agreement to contribute the 'Prologue' to this book, which sets off the background story of the 'gendering of anthropology'. I defended my stand in this book by stating that English grammar aside, and other regions apart, anthropologists should be concerned with gender as an abstraction of social relations merely because biology or sex is not always such a clear principle of differentiation of power or prestige. Western themes of feminism cannot envisage a situation where male and female relations are managed in a way as flexible and fluid as they are in Southeast Asia. These relationships appear hierarchical on the formal level and as contrasting as the village is to the State; but in day-to-day activity, through the family and social life, men and women go about doing things which are important to them without asserting who are or which sets of activities are more valuable or indispensable. The 'State' is metaphorised in men and the 'village' in women, and the former seems more visible than the latter, and hence more powerful and dominant. But a State without people to respond and react to it does not exist. From where could it derive its sources of power, wealth, and prestige, and who would back it to say that it is there, vibrant and alive, ready to establish forms of social control over the other? Ngaosyvathn, discussing men and women in spiritual worship and Buddhism, puts up this defence. Male–female relations, she argues, are similar to social symbiosis. In religion men and women attempt to derive their legitimacy in different ways; but it is clear that notions of power and dominance exist in both spheres. Buddhism is more explicit in form, since it is State-sponsored, and spiritualism more implicit, since it communally shared.

Ngaosyvathn's discussion links up very closely to O'Harrow's on Vietnamese women and their relationship to Confucianism, except that O'Harrow probes more deeply into the psychic relationship of women to men and to other women who gain dominance through patriarchy (mother-in law; sister-in law). O'Harrow argues that dominant ideologies like Confucianism create different levels of male dominance in the family and society. Women adopt positions which ignore these levels by creating a psychic withdrawal from 'real' men into 'dream men' and then waiting for the right spaces to re-enter the system when they can dominate the family again. Finally, male–female relationships permeate economic and social life in disparate forms, contradicting the ideology of Confucianism which is prevalent.

Comparing Confucianism in Vietnam to Islam in Malaysia, Nagata's analysis of veiling amongst Malay women is yet another example of how a Eurocentric perspective of gender contradicts the new Islamic consciousness emerging amongst the educated and politicised. She explains how a symbol of dressing which in the West conveys a gendered derogatory image of women, takes on a local and global metaphor of anti-modernism amongst the educated classes. Conformity to symbols of resistance in economic, political and ritual life does not denote 'powerlessness' or 'domestication' but rather an active reconstruction of the image of the person amidst a world where modernity is equated with progress and virtue. This conformity also challenges the Malaysian Government's emphasis on modernity, providing an alternative interpretation of 'change' – a movement away from State control towards a participatory grass-roots mode.[3]

Adopting State ideologies, men in personhood may use the rhetorics of Confucianism, Buddhism or Islam to say they are more 'powerful'; but how is this operated when they face their mothers or wives? Part of the problem of studying gender in Southeast Asia is that social scientists tend to see male dominance in religious and political life as 'traditional' and 'customary', whereas what really happens is that men tend to articulate this dominance as 'traditional' and 'customary', and women and male scholars begin to perceive gender relationships through the interpretations of men. What researchers have to do is to provide evidence that, in Southeast Asia in particular, women allow men to dominate religious and political life in formal and public activity but continue to uphold important areas of decision-making in the informal sphere. Like the finer black print on an insurance form, they determine some important rules of decision-making, and hence should be 'read' properly. Debates on the 'village' and 'village community' and State–village relations by numerous social scientists tend to adopt the common male view of the 'formal', bureaucratised and 'ritualised' being more important to the people than the 'informal', 'personal' and 'non-ritualised'. On this second level of social interaction, relationships of gender, rank or class do not necessarily imply hierarchies of power or dominance, and even if they do, they exist in favour of women rather than men.

Methodological Issues

The analysis of traditional roles of women as mother, housewife, farmer or artisan in feminist anthropology has usually been made within the ambit of the sub-discipline of the 'anthropology of work'. Researchers mostly begin with the paradigm that the traditional roles of women as mothers or housewives have not changed significantly since the family system evolved, despite the fact that women are now employed formally in corporations and agencies outside the home. The issue of 'double-day work' has become a popular pursuit of feminist researchers, concerned with the additional workload of working women in the domestic sphere.[4]

In Southeast Asia, this problem has been discussed widely, with many researchers showing that industrialisation and modernisation have not reduced women's domestic chores, since men have not taken over some or a fair share of the domestic responsibilities of women (Heyzer 1986; Ng 1987; Hing Ai Yun *et al.* 1984). While these studies can be easily verified through time-allocation surveys of women's activities in the domestic and non-domestic sphere, other studies are emerging in the region to suggest that the problem should be analysed through local constructs and definitions of 'work' as understood by the men and women themselves. Many activities that researchers have often viewed as 'domestic', such as cooking and the fetching of water and firewood, are in Southeast Asia integrated into home-based production work, which has an economic and commercial value beyond the normal consumptive needs of the family and household. So-called 'domestic' activities are often part of a continuous chain of productive enterprises linked to a woman's need to obtain independent sources of income. Significantly, a common situation develops in Southeast Asia whereby women utilise household resources, including children's labour, to obtain money to spend and invest without their husband's knowledge. Conversely, men who work outside the family and household bring home a pay-packet which is taken over by their wives. That women handle money in modern and rural Southeast Asia has been widely attributed to their skills at budgeting and accounting, derived from house-keeping and independent economic enterprises (Firth, R.M. 1943; Papanek and Schwede 1988). What these studies note is that in Southeast Asia the distinction between the domestic and non-domestic is not so easily discerned. Furthermore, the value placed on work at home is high, because women can operate a flexible range of productive activities from a varied range of capital, labour and environmental resources that come under their control. This Southeast Asian characteristic is well brought out by Rudie's study of constructions of the Malay household unit in Kelantan. She demonstrates how Malays nucleate or disperse capital and human resources depending on the needs and requirements of the moment. Women of different natural units, 'the nuclear family or extended family', would link up for food, labour or shelter, establishing a repertoire of social units, linked to the 'house', household and environmental resources. Conversely, they may unlink themselves when situations change, so that persons and children may belong to a number of multifocal social units with varying connotations of 'space'. An open-ended system of social relations is created, with undifferentiated boundaries of private and public, personal and communal. From these linkages, it is possible to identify the core who control resources, for these units constantly centre around them. That they are not differentiated by gender but economic productivity is significant. An understanding of gender relations in rural Southeast Asia needs to take this into consideration, for access to resources and working capacity are important determining variables of power, overriding other considerations of biology and gender.

Illo's approach is an interesting contrast, in that she focuses on personhood rather than 'action units'. She argues that the concept of *Maybahay* or housewife does not convey women's domesticity *vis-à-vis* the family and household, but a diffused status of home-making and economic responsibilities connected to the regeneration of the household unit. They define their roles as important and essential, but tend to elevate the roles of men in economic production, mainly because men engage in activities which are more 'central', that is falling into State definitions of work and productivity. Hence they tend to see male contributions to agriculture and household economics as more important because of formal and public perceptions of work perpetuated by government agencies. This reflects an earlier-stated argument that women acquire differentiated values of work in terms of gender through development programmes which focus on male activities.

This brings us to the study by Van Esterik on anthropology, gender and development in Southeast Asia. She argues similarly that the productive and reproductive labour of women in Southeast Asia are so closely interlinked in a network of economic activities which are home-based that the analytical constructs of work, production and reproduction perpetuated by Western analysts cannot be applied. Hence development models using these constructs will not be able to capture women's real contributions to the economy. To introduce supplementary training programmes for women in agriculture amounts to a degradation of women's contributions to economics. They have to enjoy the same 'centrality' as men, if not more. Supplementary training programmes for men in home-based economics should be introduced instead, considering their inferior skills in budgeting, accounting and housekeeping. This would also enable women to participate in economic decision-making on a more public level. The convergence of the formal with the informal may give a truer picture of the pre-modernist Southeast Asian woman in work and development, since she is already working, producing and reproducing.

The perspective employed by many social scientists suggests that development agencies have the effect of restructuring gender rules, in a direction detrimental to women (Boserup 1970; Rogers 1979; Jain 1980).

Since planners and decision-makers in agriculture and industry are male, male-dominated or male-oriented, sexual or biological rules continue to be utilised and enhanced to ensure the success of such policies. In some cases, however, pre-existing egalitarian rules of gender may be ignored to ensure the greater participation of men. However, many of these earlier writers did not touch on the psychological impact of development on women: that policies which are male-focused may change local perceptions of gender, in particular women's perceptions of the work done by men and women. What development planners have to do now is to rectify the damage done by local and international development agencies by incorporating more egalitarian rules of decision-making. In the case of Southeast Asia, these rules do not have to be newly created; merely revived.

Notes

1. I suspect that this is a general Southeast Asian code of 'proper' behaviour, and not one restricted to island Southeast Asia alone. I have observed many similar situations in Thailand, for example, when informality is the preferred rule of conduct. It is extremely rude to draw public attention to a person's conduct, particularly if the comment is negative, even for those Thais who have been trained abroad. One of my Thai colleagues actually left a high-level ILO meeting permanently when an ILO official asked her if she could kindly attend all the sessions instead of using up some of the time to make social calls. Southeast Asian observers of this scene were shocked that this official confronted her. He was supposed to pretend he did not notice it, and make a mental note not to invite her again.

2. The Sixth Annual Conference of the Nordic Association for Southeast Asian Studies (NASEAS), September 28 – October 1, 1989, Lund, Sweden.

3. The Malaysian example of fundamentalism is one which spontaneously opposes modernism. In contrast, Singapore's example, of fundamentalism in reviving Confucianism, is one which exists in forced marriage with modernity.

4. Refer to Chapter 2 of this book and Heyzer 1986 on women's work in Southeast Asia in general. Lewenhak gives an overview of women's work history in *Women and Work* (1980). See also Bruce and Dwyer's *A Home Divided* (1988), which deals with the unequal distribution of work within household-based production units.

Bibliography

Boserup, E. (1970). *Women's Role in Economic Development*. New York: St Martin's Press.

Bourdieu, P. (1980). *Le Sens Practique*. Paris: Editions Minuit.

Breman, J. (1988). *The Shattered Image: Construction and Deconstruction of the Village in Colonial Asia*, CAS 2. Dordrecht: Foris Publications.

Bruce, J. and Dwyer, D. (1988). 'Introduction'. In J. Bruce and D. Dwyer (eds), *A Home Divided: Women and Income in the Third World*. Stanford: Stanford University Press, pp. 1–19.

Caplan, P. (1989). *The Social Construction of Sexuality*. London: Routledge.

Carsten, J. F. (1987). Women, Kinship and Community in a Malay Fishing Village on Pulau Langkawi, Kedah, Malaysia. Unpublished Doctorate Thesis, London School of Economics and Political Science.

—— (1989). 'Cooking Money: Gender and the Symbolic Transformation of Means of Exchange in a Malay Fishing Community'. In J. Parry and M. Bloch (eds), *Money and the Morality of Exchange*. Cambridge: Cambridge University Press, pp. 117–41.

Eberhardt, N. (ed.) (1988). *Gender, Power and the Construction of the Moral Order: Studies from the Thai Periphery*, Monograph No. 4. Madison: Center for Southeast Asian Studies, University of Wisconsin.

Embree, J. (1980). 'Thailand – A Loosely Structured Social System'. *American Anthropologist*, 52: 181–93.

Engels, F. (1884). *Origin of the Family, Private Property and the State*. Chicago: Charles H. Kerr.

Errington, S. (1990). 'Recasting Sex, Gender and Power: A Theoretical and Regional Overview', in J. M. Atkinson and S. Errington (eds), *Power and Difference: Gender in Island Southeast Asia*. Stanford: Stanford University Press, pp. 1–58.

Fabian, J. (1983). *Time and the Other*. New York: Columbia University Press.

Fanon, F. (1968). '*The Wretched of the Earth*', trans. C. Ferrington. New York: Grove. (First published 1961.)

Foucault, M. (1978). *The History of Sexuality*, Vol. 1. New York: Pantheon Books.

Freire, P.(1970). *Pedagogy of the Oppressed*. New York: Penguin.

—— (1972). *Cultural Action for Freedom*. New York: Penguin.

Freire, P. and Foundez,A. (1989). *Learning to Question*. New York: Continuum.

Gough, K. (1975). 'The Origin of the Family'. In R. R. Reiter (ed.), *Towards an Anthropology of Women*. New York: Monthly Review Press.

Hanks, J. R. (1988). 'The Power of Akha Women'. In N. Eberhardt (ed.), *Gender, Power and the Contruction of the Moral Order: Studies from the Thai Periphery*, Monograph No. 4. Madison: Center for Southeast Asian Studies, University of Wisconsin.

Harris, O. (1978). 'Complementary and Conflict: An Andean View of Women and Men'. In J. S. La Fontaine (ed.), *Sex and Age as Principles of Social*

Differentiation. London: Academic Press.

Heyzer, N. (1986). *Working Women in Southeast Asia: Development Subordination and Emancipation*. Stratford: Open University Press.

Hing Ai Yun, Rokiah Talib and Nik Safiah Karim (1984). *Women in Malaysia*. Petaling Jaya: Pelanduk Publications.

Jain, D. (1980). *Women's Quest for Power*. New Delhi: Institute of Social Studies.

Kammerer, C. A. (1988). 'Shifting Gender Asymmetries Among Akha of Northern Thailand'. In N. Eberhardt (ed.), *Gender, Power and the Construction of the Moral Order: Studies from the Thai Periphery*, Monograph No. 4. Madison: Center for Southeast Asian Studies, University of Wisconsin.

Karim, W. J. (1990). 'Prelude to Madness: The Language of Emotion in Courtship and Early Marriage', in W. J. Karim (ed.) *Emotions of Culture: A Malay Perspective*. Singapore: Oxford University Press.

—— (1992). *Women and Culture: Between Malay Adat and Islam*. Boulder: Westview.

Kemp, J. H. (1988a). *Seductive Mirage: The Search for the Village Community in Southeast Asia*, As 3. Dordrecht: Foris Publications.

—— (1988b). *Community and State in Modern Thailand*, Bielefeld Working Papers No 100. Bielefeld: Sociology of Development Research Centre, Bielefeld University.

Kirsch, A. T. (1982). 'Buddhism, Sex-Roles and Thai Society'. In P. Van Esterik (ed.), *Women of Southeast Asia*. DeKalb: Northern Illinois University, pp. 16–41.

Leacock, E. (1981a). 'Introduction: Engels and the History of Women's Oppression'. In E. Leacock, *Myths of Male Dominance: Collected Articles on Women Cross-Culturally*. New York: Monthly Review Press, pp. 13–32.

—— (1981b). 'Status among the Montagnais-Naskapi of Labrador'. In E. Leacock, *Myths of Male Dominance: Collected Articles on Women Cross-Culturally*. New York: Monthly Review Press, pp. 39–62.

—— (1981c). 'Women's Status in Egalitarian Society: Implications for Social Evaluation'. In E. Leacock, *Myths of Male Dominance: Collected Articles on Women Cross-culturally*. New York: Monthly Review Press, pp. 138–87.

Lewenhak, S (1980). *Women and Work*. Glasgow: Fontana Books.

MacCormack, C. P. and Strathern, M. (eds) (1980). *Nature, Culture and Gender*. Cambridge: Cambridge University Press.

Marx, K. (1952). *Capital*, F. Engels (ed.), Chicago: Encyclopaedia Brittanica, Inc. (First Published 1886).

Marx, K. (1972). *Manifesto*. In *Marx–Engels Reader*, R. C. Tucker (ed.). New York: Norton, pp. 331–62.

Moore, H. (1988). *Feminism and Anthropology*. Cambridge: Polity Press.

Morgan, L. H. (1871). *Systems of Consanguinity and Affinity of the Human Family*. Washington: Smithsonian Contributions to Knowledge, Vol. 17.

—— (1962). *League of the Iroquois*. New York: Corinth Books.

—— (1963). *Ancient Society,* E. Leacock (ed.). Cleveland: World Publishing Co.

Nartsupha, C. (1989). 'The Village Economy in Pre-Capitalist Thailand', 6th Annual Conference of the Nordic Association for Southeast Asian Studies (NASEAS), Lund (Sweden).

Ng, C. (1987). 'Agricultural Modernization and Gender Differentiation in a Rural Malay Community 1983–87'. In C. Ng (ed.), *Technology and Gender: Women's Work in Asia.* Serdang: Women's Studies Unit, Universiti Pertanian Malaysia.

Ortner, S. B. and Whitehead, H. (eds) (1981). *Sexual Meanings: The Cultural Construction of Gender and Sexuality.* Cambridge: Cambridge University Press.

Pantasen, A. (1989). 'Agro-Industry and Self-Reliance Strategies in Thailand'. 6th Annual Conference of the Nordic Association for Southeast Asian Studies (NASEAS), Lund (Sweden).

Papanek, H. and Schwede, L. (1988). 'Women are Good with Money: Earning and Managing in an Indonesian City'. In J. Bruce and D. Dwyer (eds), *A Home Divided: Women and Income in the Third World.* Stanford: Stanford University Press.

Potter, S. (1977). *Family Life in a Northern Thai Village: A Study in the Structural Significance of Women.* Berkeley: University of California Press.

Raphael, D. (1975). 'Women and Power: Introductory Notes'. In D. Raphael, (ed.), *Being Female.* The Hague: Mouton Publishers, pp. 111–16.

Reiter, R. (1975). *Towards an Anthropology of Women.* New York: Monthly Review Press.

Rogers, B. (1979). *The Domestication of Women: Discrimination in Developing Societies.* New York: St Martins Press.

Rosaldo, M. Z. and Lamphere, L. (1974). 'Introduction'. In M. Z. Rosaldo and L. Lamphere (eds), *Women, Cultural and Society.* Stanford: Stanford University Press, pp. 1–6.

—— (1974). 'Women Culture and Society: A Theoretical Overview'. In M. Z. Rosaldo and L. Lamphere (eds), *Women, Culture and Society.* Stanford: Stanford University Press, pp. 17–42.

Rosaldo, R. (1989). *Culture and Truth: The Remaking of Social Analysis.* Boston: Beacon Press.

Scott, J. (1985). *Weapons of the Weak: Everyday Forms of Peasant Resistance.* New Haven: Yale University Press with Kuala Lumpur: University of Malaya Press.

Spiro, M. E. (1967). *Burmese Supernaturalism,* New Jersey: Prentice Hall.

Strathern, M. (1980). 'No Nature, No Culture: The Hagen Case'. In C. MacCormack and M. Strathern (eds), *Nature, Culture and Gender.* Cambridge: Cambridge University Press, pp. 174–222.

—— (1987). *Dealing with Inequality: Analyzing Gender Relations in Melanesia and Beyond.* Cambridge: Cambridge University Press.

—— (1988). *The Gender of the Gift: Problems with Women and Problems with*

Society in Melanesia. Berkeley: University of California Press.

Turton, A. (1972). 'Matrilineal Descent Groups and Spirit-Cults of the Thai-Yuan in Northern Thailand'. *Journal of the Siam Society*, 60: 217–56.

UNU/KANITA (1986). Workshop and Meeting on 'Women's Work and Family Strategies in South and Southeast Asia'. Proceedings. Penang: KANITA.

Van Esterik, P. (1982a). *Women of Southeast Asia*, Center for Southeast Asian Studies, Occasional Paper No. 9. DeKalb: Northern Illinois University.

—— (1982b). 'Women Meditation Teachers in Thailand'. In P. Van Esterik (ed.), *Women of Southeast Asia*. Center for Southeast Asian Studies, Occasional Paper No. 9. DeKalb: Northern Illinois University.

—— (1982c). 'Lay Women in Theravada Buddhism'. In P. Van Esterik (ed.), *Women of Southeast Asia*. Center for Southeast Asian Studies, Occasional Paper No. 9. DeKalb: Northern Illinois University.

Wijeyewardene, G. (1977). 'Matriclan or Female Cults: A Problem in Northern Thai Ethnography'. *Mankind*, 11: 19–25.

2

Bilateralism and Gender in Southeast Asia[1]

Wazir Jahan Karim

Bilateralism as a System of Social Relations

The classification of kinship systems according to specific types, based on rules of incest, descent, inheritance, marriage and residence has given preference to formalistic explanations and descriptions of relationships of biology and affinity. Social and cultural anthropology, through the rigorous comparative analysis of structure, defined an extensive variety of kinship types in Africa. The patrilineal descent system of the Nuer (Evans Pritchard 1950) and Tallensi (Fortes 1949) contrasted with the matrilineal Ashanti (Fortes 1950) and Bantu (Richards 1950), and both with the double-descent system of the Yako (Forde 1950) and the dual descent of the Nuba (Nadel 1950). In Southeast Asia and the Pacific, the emphasis on the residential rule produced the cognatic descent kinship types, with variations along a continuum of preferential rules from patrilaterality to bilaterality and matrilaterality. The emphasis on the rule of residence as a determinant of a basic kinship unit suggests that numerous variations of local groupings can occur, forming a composite index of people united by consanguinity, marriage, friendship and adoptive or fictitious kin relations. Local social groupings of this kind have had prominence in anthropological literature, from Firth's 'ramage' (1951: xx) to Lévi-Strauss's 'undifferentiated' descent systems (1969: xxviii).

Island Southeast Asia, in particular from Southern Sumatra to the Malay Peninsula, Indonesia West of the Torres Straits, and the Southern Philippines, seems to replicate this pattern of social grouping. Kinship rules of bilaterality characterised by fluid loose interlocking social networks of a depth of three to four generations merge comfortably with the egocentricity of social behaviour, where hierarchies of rank, gender and class are formally given significant recognition, but undergo a metamorphosis of meaning, moving from heterogeneity to homogeneity on the level of interaction in daily life. Many of the earlier researchers on kinship bilaterality have pointed this out before (Murdock 1960; Djamour 1959; Winzeler 1974, 1976), and a consensual opinion is that rules of kinship bilaterality are incorporated into other organisational structures of society, in particular into class and gender. While a ranking system based on inherited titles (Kings, chiefs, subjects) may emphasise descent, this only comes to mean something when it can be demonstrated by a display of power – for example by command over the labour and resources of a local grouping (Gullick 1965; Siegel 1969; Karim 1992; Razha 1993). Otherwise, a King and his chiefs may find themselves hopelessly defunct. To command this kind of attention, they have to demonstrate honour and generosity by cultivating benevolence, charity and a fair system of reward.[2] The relationship has to demonstrate social reciprocity before the role of 'protector' or 'loyal subject' can be assumed. Similarly, sex and sexuality are important factors in gender relations, with women actively cultivating sexual experience independently from family censorship. Numerous Southeast Asian cultures allow both men and women to explore their sexual differences freely, without inhibition and without shifting the natural attributes which both sexes have to offer one another – women as 'feminine' and sexually accommodating, as mothers, home-makers, food processors and keepers of communal and ritual relations; men as 'masculine' and sexually aggressive, as fathers, hunters, economic providers and guardians of political and religious institutions.[3] The complementarity of sex roles and priorities are undifferentiated by social status. Both sexes are valued for their ability to cultivate the roles of man and woman, husband and wife, and power is defined in the way so-called natural differences are cultivated to the optimum, to bring out the best in the person in relation to the other. If the traditional complementary system is stretched further, and men want to assume the roles of women as dancers, wedding specialists and ceremonial cooks, and women the roles of men as politicians, business managers and shamans, both can do the same without much discussion and dialogue, so long as the result conforms to the intersexual third dimension of 'behaviour' provided for men and women who cross boundaries.

Indeed many authors have remarked on the unique acceptability of unisexuality in Indonesia, particularly in Bali (Geertz 1973; see also Hobart, this volume); and this has to do with the fluidity of sexual boundaries and the choices open to both sexes to overplay or downplay feminine or masculine roles, depending on the context of reference.

Errington suggests that in island Southeast Asia, male and female power is not something that has to be publicly demonstrated, in the Western, European sense. The forceful demonstration of power is a sign of weakness and 'diminishes prestige' (1989: 5). This is something difficult for Europeans to understand, and exceedingly so for feminists, who see femininity, domestication and bedroom decision-making as ploys of the oppressed female.

This brief description of bilaterality has been mainly intended to introduce the concept of 'bilateralism' – the composite meanings of ideas of complementarity unaccompanied by statements of differential value, and the egocentricity of behaviour allowing status differences to be reduced within and without local groupings. Bilateralism in Southeast Asia is mainly featured in the island complex of Malaysia, Western Indonesia and the Philippines, and in *societies* in East Indonesia, *Kalimantan* and *Sumatra*. In Malaysia and Indonesia a manifestation of this is the metaphorical naming (through terms of address) of people beyond the local grouping by kinship terms, as if to recreate the intimacy and familarity of consanguinal and affinal ties in local groupings in other spheres of life. Everywhere patron–client and employer–employee relations in economic and political affairs are neutralised by terms like *pa'cik* (uncle) and *ma'cik* (aunty) in Malaysia and *bapak* (father) and *ibu* (mother) in Indonesia. In Malaysia, the usage of classificatory kinship term, of eldership and siblingship is gendered across three generations: *dotok* (grandfather) and *nenek* (grandmother) for the grandparental generation, *pa'cik* and *ma'cik* for the parents' generation and *kakak* (elder sister), *abang* (elder brother) and *adik* (younger brother and sister) for ego's generation kinship terms above grandparent's and below ego's generation are neutered eg *anak* (child), *cucu* (grand-child), *cicit* (great-grand child) and *piut* (great-great-grand child). Great grandparents are referred to as *tok*, *nenek* or *moyang* (yang) without reference to sex. In Indonesia, it has been argued that classificatory kinship terms like *bapak*, *ibu* and *saudara* (literally a 'male relative', but meaning in practice a combination of 'male friend' and 'kinsman') and *saudari* (a combination of 'female friend' and 'kinswoman') were popularised by Bapak Soekarno, the first President of the Republic of Indonesia, who, as an opponent of Dutch rule, strove to develop sentiments of nationalism and patriotism through an egalitarian naming system, reducing the hierarchical status system of Javanese, Batak, Bugis and Balinese societies. Obviously the reason why it was adopted so successfully and became an integral part of Indonesia's discourse is the preference for a 'culture of informality', as seen in the way in which customary and modern measurements of social refinement (*kehalusan*) are measured against a 'superior's' ability to assume a personal conduct of modesty and humility. Similarly other terms, like *bong* (brother) and *mas* (friend), express the same egalitarian mode of communication, giving similar emphasis to a culture of informality. In Malaysia and Singapore terms like *ma'cik* and *pa'cik* have become translatable in the English language into 'uncle' and 'auntie', and every child is trained to address elders of the parental generation in this way, regardless of whether they are kin, affines, friends or the European tourist offering a friendly handshake. A significant development of this culture of informality is the way in which Malaysian and Indonesian Chinese and Indians adopt these terms of address naturally in everyday life.

By 'bilateralism', then, I also imply the simulation of kinship structure and sentiment in the wider spheres of personal and public life and the conflation of hierarchy against egocentricity.[4] The 'self' is pitted against the 'other' by a multiplicity of role behaviours which give the individual the chance to adjust situationally and contextually to the preferred pattern of relationship required at any time. While this may be true of many cultures outside Southeast Asia, particularly with the introduction of new social and economic influences from industralisation and modernisation, historical evidence points to Southeast Asia as a classic 'entrepôt' of Brahmanic and Confucianist traditions, which successfully permeated local cultures by absorbing rather than dismissing what was already there. It has been suggested by Winzeler (1976) that the late and incomplete processes of state-formation in Southeast Asia were due to the prevalence of 'bilaterality' (here conceptualised as bilateralism). 'Processes of state formation' refers to the development of more centralised modes of political control that challenge localised systems of power relations within the indigenous population. These generalities hold true for both mainland and insular Southeast Asia, where kingships could not produce highly centralised forms of organisation comparable to South Asian and European states. For example, in Malaysia's pre-colonial history Malay kings (*raja*, *sultan*) were created by the establishment of patrilineages with fictitious genealogies produced from Indic royal descent systems outside the peninsula. The absence of patrilineages or patrilineal systems of descent amongst the indigenous Malay population of the time suggests that the formal constructions of the Malay state were superimposed upon a local history which interpreted political leadership rather differently (see Bowen 1983; Karim 1992). Bilateralism was a popular local construct of social relations and a mode of conceptualising relations of politics, amongst others. Also the values of balance, flexibility, interchangeability and fluidity, transcending higher levels of interaction based on religion, economics and politics, made it difficult for patriarchally ordered kingship systems to domesticate the masses. Whether the context of reference is Malaysia, Indonesia or Thailand, the creation of flexible boundaries of action seems to be valued for most relationships of gender, class, religion and politics.

This argument appears to be supported by Geertz's description of Southeast Asian religion, in particular Islam: 'the patriarchy of the Great Tradition could not so easily subdue the bilaterality of the masses, since each religion was adopted eclectically, achieving only ritualistic and symbolic legitimacy amidst the more individualistic egocentric animism' (1968: 13). The continuing role of animism, shamanism and spirit mediumship in Southeast Asia further supports this argument. Amidst the élitism of Hinduism, Buddhism and Islam in Southeast Asia, animism encourages the democratisation of power between the masses and the élites and between men and women, providing a sense of personal autonomy in daily life.

An important feature of Southeast Asian bilateralism is the status of women *vis-à-vis* men. Studies of Southeast Asian kinship systems directly and indirectly suggest that the fluid interlocking social networks developing from consanguinal and affinal relationships encourage a diffusion of status concepts relating to gender. McKinley (1983) makes a case for the importance of siblingship, which reduces sexual differences among those of the same generation and in turn highlights seniority and eldership. Winzeler (1974, 1976) describes gender relations in Southeast Asia as complementary but non-hierarchical. Penny Van Esterik (in the present volume) lists several factors as indicative of women's high value in Southeast Asian society – pioneering land development; extensive labour inputs in agriculture and farming; wet rice production and domination over farm-management systems; distance between the patriarchal state and local culture; bilateral kinship and substantial matrilocal residence; land inheritance by women and control over money and household finances. Papanek and Schwede (1988) emphasised control over finances as an important source of autonomy, rendering women free to invest in business and other enterprises. Errington in her theoretical overview of sex, gender and power in Southeast Asia reaffirms the complementarity of men's and women's work 'and the relative lack of ritual and economic differentiation' in both mainland and island Southeast Asia (1989: 1). She is however careful to exclude patrilineal societies in Sumatra, in particular the Batak, and Eastern Indonesia from these generalisations. Errington suggests that one reason why Southeast Asian women have attracted so little attention in feminist studies is precisely because they seem to be already valued and enjoy high status, in particular when comparisons are made with women in South and West Asia and the Horn of Africa. Ward (1963) very clearly noted the differences between the Southeast Asian region and South Asia, where women never seemed to enjoy the geographical mobility, visibility and economic power so characteristic of women in island Southeast Asia.

In mainland Southeast Asia, where Confucianist ideology served to impose more gender hierarchies upon local cultures, women were still capable of managing farms and trade entirely on their own (see O' Harrow in this volume). A point which is seldom mentioned in anthropological research is the rubbing effect of Southeast Asian gender bilateralism within the Nanyang Chinese and Tamil populations which rose to economic prominence during English and Dutch colonial rule in the nineteenth century. While the skeletal structures of patrilineal descent continue to be maintained amongst Southeast Asian Chinese and Indians, significant changes are now taking place in towns and cities, suggesting the increasing value placed on women. My own observation as a Malaysian and Southeast Asian has revealed interesting changes – Chinese women taking over family businesses as the men dabble in the new high-status professions of electronics and computer science; gender impartiality over the formal education of daughters, particularly at the tertiary level; a growing preference for neolocal residence and the nuclear family, which reduces the dominance of the husband's parents over the wife; reversal of traditional rituals like the sitting of the family dinner on Chinese New Year, now held in the residence of the girl's parents where there is an overall dominance of daughters; and the transmission of property to daughters in the form of gifts to prevent a monopoly of ownership by the firstborn son. In Tamil families, similar changes are taking place in economics and education; but an important additional feature of assimilation to a Southeast Asian ideology of bilateralism is the avoidance of dowry amongst the lower and middle classes, and the increasing stigma attached to keeping mistresses or secondary wives.[5] Nevertheless, laws in Malaysia and Singapore have made polygyny illegal for non-Muslims; legal reform seems to proceed in accordance with the emerging public consciousness of the high worth of women in society.

Living in a pluralistic society like Malaysia, it is apparent that a pan-ethnic consciousness of women's rights is emerging in the concern and commitment Malaysian women seem to show for the negative consequences of religious revivalism (among Muslim, Christian, Buddhist and Hindu communities) on the status of women. Tension and resistance over the dominance of male representations of the 'self' against the female 'other' in revivalist movements are significant in Thailand, Malaysia, Singapore, Indonesia and the Philippines, and one has only to look at the weekly forums, seminars and workshops on women's issues held by public institutions and non-governmental commissions to realise this. The increasing interest in universities and institutions of higher learning in Women's and Gender Studies and the selection of assignments and thesis topics on Women's and Gender-related issues also confirms this. At the grassroots, political parties and farmers' associations are also more concerned with presenting 'the women's point of view', not only to solicit public support from women but also to demonstrate that women at home have always had a public space which has not been denied by men. Indeed, in my many conversations with leaders in Arqam, a Malaysian Muslim sectarian movement that has a prescribed code of veiling for women that consists in covering the total face and body and exposing no more than the eyes, I am often told that I am prejudicial to the cause, since I place an overall emphasis on the dressing code as a metaphor of women's oppression in Muslim society (see Nagata, this book). Denying my prejudice, I in turn argue that Malay women through *adat* have always had a proper Muslim dress code, in the shape of the *selendang* (long veil) and *baju kurung* (a long loose blouse worn over a sarong), and all Arqam is doing in fact is imitating 'Arab' dress styles alien to Malay culture. They in turn remark that, dressing aside, Arqam women have complete control over business enterprises developed by Arqam. When questioned on the rampant practice of polygyny in Arqam, many say that it is a practice followed only among the leaders, and that not all Arqam men are for it. A decade ago, this kind of dialogue over the rights of women in Arqam would never have taken place, and the Arqam response would have been aggressive rather than defensive. The numerous political statements made in the press in late 1994 on the censorship of Arqam did not directly touch on the public image of Arqam women in full *purdah* (see Karim 1992), but the general rift is that Arqam's activities are extremely deviant (*songsang*) and upset the middle road of Islamisation advocated by the State. Conceptually and metaphorically, this middle road oscillates between the practical working arrangement of Malay customs (*adat*) in everyday family and social life and the political need to encapsulate Muslims in a global and local *ummah* — a consciousness of cohesion and unity through religion, a siblinghood which is gender-free, unlike the concept of 'brotherhood' or 'sisterhood', which divides other congregations by sex. The middle road is again expressive of the bilateralism in Muslim Southeast Asia, which means doing things the

Malay, Indonesian or Filipino way, rather than the Arab or Western way. In its absolute form, emulation of West Asian or European/American life-styles is not only unidentifiable in everyday life, but would be socially demeaning. I would now like to focus on bilateralism as seen through the text of academic research and popular writings and observations in order to elucidate some important features of gender complementarity without differential status. The discussion will focus on island Southeast Asia west of the Torres Straits; but a comparison will be made with mainland Buddhist communities, particularly that of Thailand, to study the extent to which bilateralism applies.

Perspectives on Malay and Minority Women in Malaysia: Cultural Reconstitution in Social Change

Anthropologists researching in Malaysia have devoted most of their attention to the Malays (Firth, Raymond 1966; Firth, Rosemary 1966; Swift 1963, 1965; Wilder 1970, 1982; Banks 1983) or minority Orang Asli[6] (aboriginal) groups living in or at the periphery of the tropical and mangrove rain forests of the peninsula (Carey 1976; Benjamin 1976, 1980; Dentan 1968; Endicott 1979; Karim 1981a,b; Howell 1984). In the 'Malay Studies' component, the emphasis on economic organisation, family and kinship systems and local political institutions have bypassed theoretical conceptualisations of gender in the way it is discussed today. What is not clearly formulated is the way in which female autonomy in family, community and economic relations reflects a specific kind of male–female relationship in Islam and a political bureaucracy dominated by men. Women's control over household finances and personal income, management of land, and extensive entrepreneurial activities have not been properly analysed in culture or history, since anthropologists have made their observations in terms of formal kinship or feminist theory, which are both theoretically restrictive to the kind of social observations made in this study.

Studies on the 'Orang Asli' have devoted less attention to gender and more to religion, ecology and cosmology; yet implicit in all major observations of the 'Orang Asli' is the principle of equality, mutual sharing, communal cooperation and reciprocity, on all levels of interaction within the family, household and wider descent group. Cultural studies in Sabah and Sarawak (Freeman 1970, 1971; Appell 1976; Dahlan 1983; Nicholaisen 1989) have mostly adopted 'structural–functionalist' or ecological models with little emphasis on women and gender, except for the volume on *Female and Male in Borneo* (Sutlive 1991), which offers an interesting range of chapters on the variations of gender relations in relation to sexuality. In anthropology, studies of Chinese and Indian women in Malaysia have been insignificant, and the few which have emerged recently have been collections on the sociology of women (Oorijitham 1984; Chia 1984; Lebra and Paulson 1980). Where anthropological research has been conducted on these ethnic minorities, the thrust has been Marxist or neo-Marxist, within the context of economic history, class and ethnic pluralism.

The seventies and eighties seem to be the decades for sociological studies of women. Widespread industrialisation, rapid modernisation and ill-conceived development policies generated interest in and concern for women in traditional and modern sectors of work and employment (Hing 1984; Hing, Safiah and Rokiah 1984; Ackerman 1984; Jamilah 1984; Mazidah and Safiah 1986; Maznah 1987; Ng 1987a,b). The use of terminologies of 'exploitation', 'marginalisation', 'invisibility', 'missing', 'devalued', 'powerless' and 'statusless' not only expressed the feministic mood of scholars, but also more serious and deep-rooted misconceptions of women by administrators, planners, politicians and agents of development. Migrant Malay women were subject to work discrimination in factories, while women of all ethnic communities were given job descriptions which defined women's work as inferior to men's and meriting lower wages and social benefits. Writers also argued that agricultural modernisation and rural development appeared to enhance gender differentiation (Sundaram and Tan 1985; Ng 1987b). Anthro-pologists, working on ethno-medicine, midwifery (Laderman 1982, 1983, 1991; Karim 1984) and political culture (Manderson 1980, 1983; Karim 1982, 1983, 1987) echoed the concern of sociologists that women could not effectively compete with men within the formal medical and political bureaucracy.

The feminist–Marxist perspective in gender studies developed from a wider theoretical conceptualisation of Malaysia's economic history as moving, without a pause, from feudalism and colonisation to global capitalism. Increasing disparities in class were given priority over ethnicity or culture; and these studies attempted to elucidate women's marginality within economic forces of transformation. More recently, the observation of differential responses to work and employment amongst women provoked much more rigorous cultural analysis on gender. Ong's (1987) study of spirit-possession as symbolic resistance to capitalistic modes of production within the parameters of factory work showed Malay women's ability to reconsolidate their inferior position within the production line and to challenge male authority. She argued that 'in the absence of a union, covert revolts sometimes developed into acts of retaliation against factory men, the intimate supervisors as well as tormentors of operators in daily life' (1987: 211). Malay women, more than the Chinese or Indians, were inclined to express themselves through spirit-possession, and this she explains in terms of the cultural constitution of Malay women, which evokes a particular psychological response to work stress and gender hierarchy. Peletz's (1988) study of *adat pepateh* (matrilineal kinship) in Negeri Sembilan is another attempt to demonstrate cultural continuity in the context of Islamic revivalism. Islamisation processes have led to a great assertion of Shariah laws in the distribution of property and inheritance. Yet, despite these trends, *adat pepateh* is reconstituted through perceptions of gender relations where the social valuation of women is reproduced through laws of property ownership and inheritance.

Another critique of applying universalisms in feminist theory has been my own study of the unity and tensions between *adat* (culture) and Islam in Malay social history. The cultural milieu of *adat* has provided Malay women with a keen sense of independence, mobility, entrepreneurship and (with seniority and age) prestige. Islam has been subject to different interpretations over history; but it is only when its formulation has been more patriarchal or fundamentalistic that Malay women have been subject to increasing domination by men. I attempted to show how Malay constructions of gender have been produced by a social and political history unique to the region in which Malay identity was crystallised (Karim 1992). This identity through a synthesis of *adat* and Islam at times generated equitable relations of gender (as when *adat* was crystallised in pre-colonial history) and at other phases less equitable relations (the development of Western democracy through the political party system and Islamic fundamentalism). I argued that the strength of Malay women lies in *adat*, and that of Malay men in Islam, because women are able to develop a better sense of autonomy and self-identity through *adat*, and men through Islam. Shifting constructions of gender (in the direction of 'the *adat*isation of Islam' when male–female participation in Islam evokes the bilateral features of family and social organisation) and the 'Islamisation of *adat*' (when male–female participation in *adat* becomes hierarchical in a way closer to West Asian structures of family and social organisation) explains the essence of gender relations in Malay society. *Adat* and Islam generate a dialectical thinking mode over history, with *adat* as the constant 'equaliser' or 'moderator' for women.

The diversity of Malay women's social roles and the multiplicity of choices available in performing them makes the Malay social system rather different from those found in other Muslim societies in Asia. Where Malay women's sphere of influence is limited, in Islam, *adat* attempts to diffuse rules of separation, hierarchy and prestige by giving women dominant roles in *rites de passage* concerning *sunna* Islamic customs of sacrifice (*korban, akikah*) at childbirth, circumcisions, weddings and feasts of rejoicing and blessings (*do'a selamat, Murhaban, Tah'lil*). Indeed, in urban areas where Malay women have opportunities to organise themselves independently from men through membership in women's organisations like the Women's Institute, women's branches of the national party like Wanita Umno, or smaller neighbourhood groupings organised through systems of *usrah*, Malay women conduct these religious feasts and ceremonies independently of men (Karim 1992). Numerous ritual ceremonies have been observed where prayers are led by women in an all-female congregation. The few husbands who attend do not have any ritual function, and only come to partake in the feasting.

In Malay society, as in other Island Southeast Asian systems, tradition safeguards the autonomy of Malay women in the way in which they can compete with men and other women to establish a niche for themselves in politics and government. Here, Malays differ significantly from their Muslim counterparts in West and South Asia. Despite the prevailing forces of fundamentalism and in spite of the more rapid acquisition of modern Western values by the Chinese and Indians, Malay women more than any other ethnic group in Malaysia have been successful in defending their rights to political representation. Doubtless they have also been used by their male counterparts in party politics, and have become the 'hands and feet' of the government (Barisan Nasional, or 'National Front'), campaigning obsessively for votes in towns and villages. This has curbed their ability to compete equally with men in the national arena of politics; but it has created a group of highly politically conscious rural and urban women, who are actively involved in political decision-making at the grass-roots, state and national levels. In this sense, in Malaysia, Islam has not seriously curbed existing venues for political participation and communication.

Indonesian Themes of Bilateralism: The Complexity of Social Realities

The first-ever significant observations of gender in Indonesian can be located in the letters of Kartini, published in 'Letters of a Javanese

Princess' and interpreted by Sitisoemandari Soeroto (1984 [1977]) in the form of a biography. Concerned with the role of domesticity of upper-class Javanese women of the Raden class, she wrote passionate commentaries on the need for formal education rather than protected tutelage, for women, and the need for women to question institutions of feudalism and polygamy which diminished the status and dignity of Javanese women. Though Kartini is, in her own terms, a female heroine (Sri Kandi) of early twentieth-century Java, and is usually politically linked to Javanese–Indonesian nationalism, many have argued that she is more catalytic to the women's movement in Indonesia than the nationalist movement (Vreede-de Stuers 1965; Sitisoemandari Soeroto 1984; Solichin Salam 1981). The structural rigidities of gender relations in upper-class Javanese Society appear to be inconsistent with the all-encompassing social construct of bilaterality and the public value of 'motherhood' (*Keibuan*), which transcends class boundaries. In Javanese society, motherhood generally offers women infinite possibilities of social and communal activity beyond the domain of the family and household. Kartini exclaimed in a letter to a friend, Stella, 'Yet the mother is a shrine . . . Do we ever call out the name of "Father!" in illness or suffering? Do we ever call out father for assistance?' (Sitisoemandari Soeroto 1984: 113).

The theme of gender underlies many Indonesian classical works produced by Minang, Javanese and Batak writers. Indonesian writers of the 1920s echoed some of the internal contradictions between patriarchy and the autonomy of women in romantic fiction, notably Merari Siregar in *Azab dan Sengsara*, Marah Rusli in *Siti Nurbaya*, Hamka in *Tenggelamnya Kapal v.d. Wijck* and Sutan Takdir Alisyahbana in *Layar Terkembang*. Of these Hamka was most concerned with the intracultural complexities of relationships in Indonesian society. His famous *Tenggelamnya Kapal v.d. Wijck* (1975) bore the argument that men without sisters in Minangkabau society lacked the strong links of membership they needed to feel 'Minangkabau'. Yet, to *merantau* (roam) in search of group identity and membership was a fruitless task, since other communities instinctively shut them out. Hence Minangkabau men would always experience social alienation and a sense of powerlessness, despite arguments assuring their inclusion.

The recurring themes of these novels were constraints in love and personal expression imposed by institutions of class, eldership, debt-bondage and colonialism. From the thirties onwards, novels began to depict women in more positive terms, most notably in the work of Pramoedya Ananta Toer *Bumi Manusia* and Sri Subakir's *Seribu Burung*

Layang-Layang di Tangerang. Jakop Sumardjo (1981) suggests that the end of colonialism symbolically shifted the mood of novels to optimism and positivism – perceptions of personal and human relationships become more realistic, since the need to convey political messages become less acute. To take the argument further, the more oppressive patriarchal structures of upper-class Javanese society, which sought an alliance with Dutch colonial rule, simultaneously lost their hold over the family and the household as Indonesia won its freedom against colonialism. Javanese women, in particular, began to pay more attention to personal identity, achievement and professionalism, exploring their potential in directions other than the family. Though this argument seems to apply mostly to Javanese upper-class families, Indonesian nationalism, Westernisation and modernisation affected the lives of Indonesian women in all strata of society, providing them with an impetus to achieve success and achievement in individual terms.

The 1970s and 1980s produced works from women who were concerned with female emancipation in intellectual and class terms. Julia I. Suryakusuma (1981) perceived Indonesian women's emancipation as parallel to Western liberalism and feminism. This she argued, affected the professional middle and upper classes more than anyone else. Women's control over the family and household was still apparent; but she saw this and their new professionalism as sources of women's strength, rendering their role in society as more global, integrated and comprehensive. However, she argued that modernisation and Westernisation affected social constructions of gender in a direction of hierarchy. As women competed with men, they became less secure emotionally and sexually. Men eventually displayed more autonomy and women more dependence. The liberation of Indonesian women, argued another writer (Hersri 1981), was only possible when both sexes removed biological images of gender from day-to-day activity. Biology had been moulded into cultural constructs which were detrimental to women.

Although outstanding works in Indonesian anthropology has been produced in the fields of culture and religion (Geertz 1960, 1973, 1980; Palmier 1960; Siegel 1969), politics, class and the peasantry (Geertz 1960; Kartodirdjo 1975; Dewey 1962), the subject of women only became indirectly visible through studies of the family and kinship systems (De Josselin de Jong 1951, 1960, 1977a,b, 1980a,b, 1984; Geertz, H. 1961; Geertz, H. and C. 1975). Spearheading this fascination with matriarchy and matriliny in Sumatra and the state of Negeri Sembilan in peninsular Malaysia, De Josselin de Jong made significant observations about Minangkabau matrilineal society. The high position accorded to women was mainly symbolic and ritualistic, with the sister's brother (*mamak kepala waris*) controlling public decision-making relating to land and politics. Yet the principle of transmitting rights of membership, inheritance and communal property through women rather than men was to the Minangkabau the most salient component of their culture and history. It was Minangkabau women, rather than the men, who controlled the links to cultural continuity and identity.

Increasing Western literature on the power of men in matriarchal society, in tradition, modernisation and change (Gough 1975; Webster 1975; Sack 1974; Kahn 1976; Stivens 1981) provided a pessimistic vision of the future of women living under matriliny in Southeast Asia. These Marxist approaches suggested that matriliny could not assure Minangkabau women personal autonomy in decision-making because colonial history and modern economic developments acted contrary to women's interests. Recent studies of legal sociology and anthropology in Indonesia (Benda-Beckmann, F. von 1979; Benda-Beckmann, K. von 1984, 1988a,b; Benda-Beckmann, F. and K. von 1984) have argued that increasing lack of consensus between women and men on the implementation of *adat perpateh* under colonial and modern law (the registering of communal land or *harato pusako* under the name of the *mamak kepala waris*; conversion of communal land to individual titles; recognition of the head of household as the husband) demonstrates women's dissatisfaction with state legal processes. This articulation of dissatisfaction and reluctance on the part of male representatives to take over management of *harato pusako* is a critical point of debate. It appears that, today, the most important organisational unit in Minangkabau society is the nuclear family, rather than the lineage or *suku*. If so, and if decision-making in the family and household is ego-centred, as it is in many parts of Southeast Asia, does participation in this minimal unit of organisation affect Minangkabau women any differently from those of other societies? Since Southeast Asian social systems centred around residential groupings, and the nuclear family and household is usually the foundation for women's public value and communal achievement, Minangkabau women should not be excluded from this observation. Anthropologists should be looking to see how the nuclear family in matrilineal or patrilineal systems eventually diffuses formal constructions of kinship.

In Java, Hilda Geertz conducted a study of the social organisation of the family and kinship system. She found it to be essentially ego-centred and non-corporate, giving significant importance to the freedom of the individual (1961: 4). She argued that since the family and household is the most important organisational unit in Java, women tend to monopolise a significant amount of decision-making relating to finance and household management – a point later reaffirmed by Papanek and Schwede (1988). While differentiation of economic activity exists, women have successfully competed with men in entrepreneurial activities and many run large enterprises alone or with other men (1961: 122). Again, the emphasis on traditional structures of kinship provides us with information on gender in certain spheres of activity but excludes more general observations of male–female relations outside the context of the family or household. The bilaterality of kinship extends into the bilateralism of gender, but on this level of observation other factors like class, politics and religion come into play, necessitating a different kind of analysis. Feminist anthropology provides an example of analysis of this kind, except that it has failed adequately to relate gender to the specificities of Southeast Asian ethnography.

The Balinese family study (Geertz, H. and C. 1975) also suggests similar symmetries in gender relationships within the family and household. Despite the transmission of hereditary temple houses and land through the principle of patrifiliation, men and women have equal rights and responsibilities in domestic and economic matters. Relationships between spouses are more equal than hierarchical. The Geertzs state, 'The women of these family groups, even when born elsewhere and marrying in, are not second-class members but have full rights and responsibilities' (1975: 56). Here, we have a similar gender theme to that among the Minangkabau, when a formal rule of descent, in this case, patrifiliation, does not prevent men and women from achieving personal autonomy in different spheres of life. Furthermore, since the management of temple activities is an obsession with Balinese women, one could conclude that what they lack in formal rank, they gain in public ritual life (see Hobart, this volume).

More recently, research on rural women focused on issues of female autonomy and power over labour, land and capital resources. Pudjiwati Sajogyo (1983) in her research on gender relations in Western Java saw class and affordability as important variables determining female autonomy. Women with land or capital had gender autonomy in household decision-making, farm management or entrepreneurial activities; but women without any of these resources became more dependent on their spouses. Invariably this dependency was reflected in gender relationships within the political bureaucracy and market economy. It was usual for the poor and landless to exploit whatever limited resources they had for cash earnings. Many poor women sought jobs as domestic servants. This brought them into a new form of domesticity, where relationships were hierarchical in class rather than gender terms. Sukanti's research (1986) on domestic servants in Jakarta reinforces this view but stresses the need to view servitude in economic and cultural terms. Stoler (1977) also employs an economic–cultural perspective in her analysis of labour relations, for she explains how capitalism and class formation affect women differently. Women retain control over labour and capital resources as successfully as men, as long as they are in an economic position to do so. Women of the poorer classes suffer the dual role of waged labourers and mothers; but since they have more alternatives to 'sell' their labour than their poorer male counterparts, they tend to be economically more productive. What these studies say for gender relations among the rich and poor is that generalisations do not hold even in class terms. Poor women are generally more resourceful than poor men and rich women as resourceful as rich men. That rich women are more successful materially than poor women is an obvious universal which needs little intellectual thinking. The Southeast Asian model generally indicates productivity and resourcefulness as general characteristics of women across class strata.

In Bugis society, the topic of gender has been recently studied in 'emic' (insider) terms according to cultural constructs of 'value', 'position' and 'importance'. Millar's (1983) interpretation of gender amongst the Bugis is particularly important, for it notes that observations made by anthropologists in 'structural' or 'class' terms do not necessarily reflect indigenous modes of interpreting gender. That women serve men their meals did not, to the Bugis, constitute an act of gender stratification or hierarchy. The women argue that 'food-serving' is not an indicator of subservience, and that sexual stratification is generally unimportant in Bugis society. What is more important is that women can do some things better than men and men other things better than women. They conclude that both men and women are important.[7] The research has important bearings on the relationship between gender, autonomy and domesticity. The 'folk view' of bilateralism does not exclude the important role of women in the family and household; but it is through domesticity that women gain an important public value. Through it, women gain an official status as respectworthy elders. This position is further exploited for commercial venture and financial gain. Hence again, motherhood diffuses boundaries between the public and domestic and gives women the legitimacy to explore other forms of personal or social activity outside the family.

Philippines as an Ideological Confluence between Bilateralism and Feminist Theory

As in Indonesia, anthropological research in the Philippines has brought out the rich cultural diversities which exist within the country. The early studies of the Ifugao (Barton 1969), the Tausug (Kiefer 1972), and the Kalinga (Dozier 1967) were presented in structural–functional terms expressing the self-containment of each culture coexisting with others within a pluralistic social system. Women and gender were not topics which generated interest in anthropological research. Instead, religion and society were topics which gained prominence (Fox 1970; Gibson 1986), often with an emphasis on the symbolic associations between ideology and economic life. M. Rosaldo's study of *Ilongot Notions of Self and Social Life* (1980b) expresses the impact of symbolic analysis on Philippines ethnography. Indeed, studies of sex and gender were developed through symbolic theory during the earlier phases of feminist influence, when the binary notion of women as nature and men as culture gained some attention in anthropology.

In other areas in the social sciences, feminist research in the early 1930s was undertaken by local sociologists and political scientists inspired by the controversy surrounding the Western suffrage movement and women's political status in society. The Philippines' close links with the United States generated keen interest in the American media and in American literature on women. Feliciano (1982: 2) wrote that, by the 1950s, the number of articles on Filipino women, published and unpublished, had 'increased by leaps and bounds', by then amounting to more than two hundred. From the 1960s academic and applied institutions of research attracted feminist scholarship in social science in areas relating to abuses of women in the mass media, exploitation of women migrant workers, problems of detribalisation amongst upland women, the need for legal reform in labour laws, parental custody, divorce and the increasing participation of women in the political life of Filipino society.

The interdisciplinary mode of research in women's and gender studies was preserved in the important area of rural development, where a number of 'impact studies' were conducted in relation to wet-rice cultivation and mixed crop farming (Miralao 1980; Illo 1987; Illo and Veneracion 1988; Borlagdan 1987). These studies forcefully drew attention to women's vital contribution to farming and farm management; however, there was little gender equity in access to development resources. Families and household operated a complex system of labour relations, where men and women undertook independent as well as joint activities in the production of food and the generation of income. Hence, since farming societies operated within a 'gender-neutral paradigm', it was difficult to understand why development projects were for the most part male-specific and did not project a clear understanding of the crucial role of women in agriculture.

An interesting academic observation which emerged from these studies was the way in which men and women viewed 'work' and 'productivity'. In highly diversified farming and production systems, women's activities were more complex *vis-à-vis* men's and involved the balancing of time and labour between home and farm production. Although most activities in home production were linked to farm production, women tend to view a major portion of work (life-sustaining activities) as 'non-work', and hence felt less productive than men. Illo suggests that this was provoked by a confusion in work definitions within the village. Since female work was more diffused and complex, existing in many different domains in contrast to the more specialized, visible variety of farm work conducted by men, women were less able to account for their own productivity *vis-à-vis* men (see also Illo, this volume).

This diffusion in and confusion over 'work' and 'productivity' is not a Philippine problem specifically, but draws attention to the problem of employing 'emic' perspectives in research without a more objective evaluation of gender roles. Obviously, women's role in farming becomes more diffused and confused as the alternatives for work expand in different directions and some come to be regarded as more 'productive' (i.e. useful, economically remunerative) than others. I would like to add that another reason why women and men categorise 'life-sustaining activities' as non-work (i.e. non-productive) is because economic remuneration for these activities does not exist and labour is viewed as 'free'. Women who do food-catering at home or outside it and feed their whole family on catered food or unsold food packets see cooking as 'work' and 'highly productive'. Hence women give different importance to different kinds of work, and the further the work is from purely life-sustaining activities the more important or productive it is made out to be. Finally, to spice the argument further, women's perception of the value of 'work' again differs from their perceptions of the value of a 'woman'. A woman's work may be conceived as 'non-productive' in the domestic domain; but the women may construct her own self-image as 'important', as the Akha, Balinese and Bugis studies have shown. She views herself as important for her many social contributions, which are founded in domesticity but extend beyond it into wider public economic and spiritual life; and this point is usually endorsed by men.

As was indicated in the introduction, a fair share of Western feminist theory in cultural anthropology has been generated from research conducted in the Philippines. Rosaldo (1974) based her ideas on the universality of female subordination in culture on her analysis of nature–culture, public–private oppositions in Ilongot society. In 1975, in a paper with Atkinson entitled 'Man the Hunter and Women: Metaphors for the Sexes in Ilongot Magical Spells', these views were further expanded in their analysis of the cultural constructions of men as 'autonomous' and women as 'relational'. In 1980, this view was further modified in an article by Rosaldo in *Signs* on the importance of articulating Western feminist theory in cross-cultural terms. Like Thailand, the Philippines has also experienced a phase of self-criticism through relying on feminist perspectives on the universality of male dominance. The 'central–peripheral' theme is not clearly elucidated as in Thailand; but the theoretical assumption of male dominance as a universal has been highlighted and refracted through local ethnography.

Is Bilateralism Operational in Mainland Southeast Asia? Focus on Thailand, Vietnam and Laos

Research on women and gender in Thailand has had to resolve the seeming contradictions between the 'unusually high public profile of women' and the peripheral position Thai women occupy in relation to Buddhism (Eberhardt 1988a: 3, 78). However, early structuralist approaches focused only on specific institutions of religion, politics or ecology and thus did not address this contradiction directly or indirectly (Embree 1950; Tambiah 1970; Walker 1975).

The earlier perspective of Embree (1950) of a loosely-structured Thai society with ill-defined social rules of behaviour provoked much research on the Thai family and village organisation, leading some writers to conclude that the family and village were indeed more stable and structured than had been assumed (Kingshill 1960; Wijeyewardene 1967; Turton 1972; Potter 1977). Northern Thai society in particular provided evidence on the centrality of women in village life, although most of these arguments were located in kinship analysis and religion. The preoccupation of women with concepts of fertility, procreation and motherhood provided them with a cosmogonic force both feared and respected by men.

Current academic concerns for the Thai and Southeast Asia 'village community' (Kemp 1988a,b; 1989a,b; Breman 1980, 1988), exclude most of the earlier discussion on the 'centrality' of women in the context of family, neighbourhood and friendship relations. In Thailand, interfamilial relationships activated by women, through food production, ritual festivity, market strategies and peer-group socialisation generate important areas of networking, sharing and exchange. Focus on the interpersonal, informal and non-bureaucratic spheres of action elsewhere elucidates women's vital contributions to community relations in different Southeast Asian cultures (Carsten 1989; Karim 1992). The structuralist approach of the 'village community' theory has once again removed women to the periphery, imposing a confusion between the 'peripheralisation' of women by anthropologists and the peripheralisation of women in actual life.

Research on Thai women in lowland urban centres developed radical feminist perspectives, mainly because of the peripheral roles women assume once they migrate to or reside in the city. Pasuk Phongpaichit (1980), in her research on female migrants in Bangkok, discussed how initiation into urbanisation and city life also implied initiation into prostitution: there were no other venues of work opened to unskilled young women from the villages. Khin Thitsa's studies of women in prostitution, spirit-mediumship and the monastery again expressed the marginalisation of Thai women in the city (1980, 1983).

Arguments on the 'centrality' and 'peripheralisation' of Thai women in particular and mainland Southeast Asian women in general now begin to develop a theoretical theme of their own. Rather than gender, geographical or demographic displacement and the resulting cultural decontextualisation of women (and men) are contributory factors to marginalisation. Pre-existing structures of 'maleness' and 'femaleness' may be complementary without being hierarchical; but once new meanings of gender are acquired from the towns and cities the bilateralism of gender is transformed into hierarchy. Minority Thai women from the North are transformed to the periphery when they encounter the nation's centre in the South. Hence a general theme to be learned from Thai ethnography is that while peripheral cultures uphold the centrality of women in society, central cultures appear to encourage their peripheralisation. However, it is also significant that these studies have focused on women in occupations which are 'marginal' in the eyes of the anthropologist and of Thai middle-class society – prostitutes, vendors, nuns and spirit-mediums. Value connotations attached to particular occupations by Eurocentric or local middle-class definitions have to be discarded before conclusive evidence of women's peripheralisation can be obtained. Furthermore, other areas of research, such as market women and women entrepreneurs, might draw attention to the 'centrality' of Thai women in urban society. The anthropologist who has chosen a feminist perspective on gender can easily select a sector to demonstrate the contents of this paradigm. Hence it is important to include self-perceptions and self-definitions of work and value in order to remove preconceived definitions of social change in urban society.

In 1975, Kirsch contributed a significant discussion to the interpretation of of gender in Thai society by arguing that Thai women engaged extensively in self-entrepreneurial activity and less so in public decision-making because of Buddhism. This gave them a centrality which religious orthodoxy denied. Buddhism, with its emphasis on monkhood and monastic activities, encouraged men to occupy a central position in religious activity, both ritualistically and symbolically. That Buddha was a male with the highest Karma ever achieved in humankind implied that men rather than women were best able to achieve this. However, inequality through Karma did not imply male–female dichotomies of inequality. Indeed, Keyes (1984) argues that, textually, Buddhism orders a separate but equal 'view of men and women'. Inequality was the resulting practice, reinforcing a view that Buddhism was more concerned with male hegemony.

Others have argued that both in thought and ritual Buddhism was linked in a complex hierarchical way to gender, age, seniority and style of life. As has been explained by Eberhardt (1988a: 79) the asymmetry between the sexes in the Theravada Buddhist ideology, then, is but one of a whole series of hierarchical relations thought to exist between all beings. However, that Buddhist ideology influences images of gender and gender relations is an important academic and practical concern. Eberhardt (1988b) in her study of Mya Tsing, a Shan women who mastered the *Kwaam tai* traditional style of singing, discussed the apparent ambivalence and confusion expressed by Shan men and women towards this singer. On the one hand, she did not demonstrate the attributes of decorum, propriety and domesticity prescribed for women through Buddhism and Shan concepts of gender. On the other, both sexes were fascinated by her brilliance, vitality and sexuality. She also seemed to have produced daughters with the same kind of physical and sexual attributes. Eberhardt argues that contradictions exist between ideological and real images of women. The 'problem' of Mya Tsing, she suggest, 'is not clearly traceable to Shan gender images, Buddhist beliefs, or attitudes towards singers *per se*. Rather, it is the convergence of all of these general cultural notions with the particular and idiosyncratic features of Mya Tsing's life that make her an anomalous figure to the people of Baan Nok' (1988b: 77).

In the light of this analysis, researchers are able to review the more positive linkages which women can establish with Theravada Buddhism. Van Esterik (1982c) shows how a variety of roles and identities have been created for women through Theravada Buddhism. Women were more motivated to indulge in activities relating to ritual merit because it gave them more 'prestige' and 'public recognition' (Eberhardt 1988b: 80). Shan culture, with its emphasis on female domesticity, did not provide the opportunities for public life that women were seeking; but they found these in Buddhism, even if the avenues so provided were limited.

Generally here, an example is provided of patriarchy within the cultural milieu of gender relations. Buddhism may or may not reinforce patriarchy. To compensate for their formal exclusion from decision-making, women deliberately penetrate the public ritual sphere of Buddhism by partaking in merit-making activities. Affordability also allows women to assume the position of patron or sponsor, extending their entrepreneurship in ritual. Generally, such studies demystify the role of men in Buddhism, while demonstrating the crucial role of women in maintaining the Buddhist folk tradition. In religion and ritual, they are both entrepreneurial and competitive. In a sense, the visibility of women in the informal economic sector had been extended further in the direction of Buddhism. Other studies have shown that this has been achieved without loss of their earlier spirituality in folk religion. Significantly, Spiro's study of Burmese supernaturalism (1966) further reinforces this argument for the women of Northern Burma.

Post-modernist research in Northern Thailand appears to be concerned with the dialectics of interpretation of gender, giving emphasis to 'popular' or 'folk' perceptions and integrating these perceptions with other levels of constructs derived from class, age or seniority. As research proceeds to the macro-structures of peripheral and mainline cultures, the need for a multi-level analysis becomes apparent. Thus Kammerer (1988), in her study of gender relations among the Akha of Northern Thailand, discusses the bilateral balance of relationships between men and women. Akha bilateralism embodies a basic organisational principle of separation, in which however separation does not necessarily imply hierarchy or inequality. Asymmetrical gender relations are significant in the absolute powers women have in the religious–cosmological sphere, where they control the linkages between history and the present world through their direct relationship to ancestors and descendants of the Akha. Significantly, that women serve food to men did not denote domesticity. Like the Minahasa, the Akha argue that women and men are equally important. These statements confirm Hanks's earlier observations of Akha women, in their capacity to generate cosmological powers and to drain the powers of others (1962; Hanks and Hanks 1963; Hanks 1988).

Kammerer suggests that the crucial cosmological linkage between the marital couple, rice ritual and ancestor offerings underlies shifting gender asymmetries in Akha culture. With increasing deforestation and land shortage, women as a group lose their control over ricelands and cease to participate in fertility and ancestor rituals (1988: 45). Hence they lose their powers to immortalise Akha culture. Here lies the dialectic between bilateralism and ecological change, where gender relations undergo asymmetry in a direction detrimental to women.

Conversion to Christianity is yet another factor which reinforces these contradictions. However, Kammerer does not discuss how declining hunting activities amongst men now place them in a disadvantageous position *vis-à-vis* women, the family and the household. On the basis of general observations of the desertification of natural habitats of minorities in mainland Southeast Asia, I would argue that Akha culture as a whole is being visibly threatened, affecting not only relationships of gender but the crucial balance of economic and political relations between minorities of the North and majority groups of the South.

Understanding Gender through Buddhism in Vietnam, Kampuchea and Laos

The interplay between Buddhism, socialism and gender in mainland Southeast Asia outside Thailand has not been clearly understood, since writers have in one way or another been influenced by different time perspectives, drawing attention to different systems of gender against specific events in local history. A paper by Chantou (1984) discusses the demographic and cultural displacement of women and men during the Pol Pot regime in the 1970s and the inability of women to cope with their lives without men at the end of the regime in 1979. The surplus of women (between 60 and 70 per cent in towns and villages) enabled women to take over many jobs previously reserved for men, including high-level public and managerial appointments; but the need for male companionship, sex and marriage placed men in a more advantageous position in relation to women, prompting them to explore adultery and polygamy openly or in secret. Hence the war was both advantageous and disadvantageous to Kampuchean women. Socialism in war and peace is a difficult problem to handle sociologically without bringing in issues of the family and gender; but the concern with war has not provided readers with much insight into the system of gender relations under more stable political conditions. Perhaps, since these conditions do not exist, it might be necessary to see how political instability as a permanent way of life reinforces particular kinds of gender and sexual activity, which become 'cultural' in the long term.

In Laos, writers tend to use 1975, the year of the formation of the Socialist Republic, as a convenient baseline date for comparing events. Earlier Buddhist and later socialist time constructs have been adopted to suggest overt gender hierarchies in the former and greater equality in the latter (Ngaosyvathn 1989). Yet the attempt on the part of the State to integrate Buddhism with socialism suggests that Buddhism continues to be a vital force within Laotian society; but how this affects women in family relations, law and politics is again unclear. To what extent has the Laotian state developed a religious interpretation which upholds the equality of the sexes in Buddhist ideology and ritual activity? How is pre-socialist Buddhism different from post-socialist Buddhism? If the differences are significant, and Buddhism continues to be gender-structured, other questions arise, as to whether a socialist ideology has increased inconsistences in the people's view about women in general and about women in association with Buddhism.

Generally researchers concerned with the interplay between Buddhism and gender tend to agree that Buddhism overtly discriminates against women both ideologically and in practical activity. A powerful factor which backs this is people's view that parents obtain merit from sons who become monks. Since women are forbidden to become monks, they cannot transfer this vital form of merit-making to their parents, and so suffer adversely as daughters (Van Esterik 1982a; Ngaosyvathn 1989; Keyes 1984). However, the relationship between merit-making activities directed towards the self and parents stemming from the various roles of monks, nuns and women devotees is again unclear. All writers invariably make two contradictory statements, that women are the most conspicuous merit-makers in Buddhism in Southeast Asia, and that the ritual importance of women in Buddhism is diminished by the overall public dominance of men in Buddhism. It seems that this inconsistency reveals two notions of 'public value', one, the important public position of men as monks and formal bearers of Buddhism; and the other the important social value of women as devotees, recognised publicly but seldom stated, except recently through anthropologists. The difference in the position of women and men in Buddhism, then, is that women's importance remains unstated, though undenied, whereas men's importance is stated and frequently acclaimed. Sacred texts and quotations from Buddha are constantly used to reaffirm the latter; and, since the bearers of these statements are men, contrary statements suggesting the importance of equality amongst devotees of Buddhism are not brought to the fore. Obviously, women devotees have not begun interpreting the texts to their advantage in the way that men have. This poses an important critique of hermeneutic theory, which does not allow for the possibility of interested interpretations of the texts by participants in the culture. Local interpretations may associate or dissociate textual meanings from social reality, depending on the political and social motives of the interpreters. The role of hermeneutics in anthropology has been limited to the wisdom of humanist and orientalist students of the texts; but folk interpretations of the text need to be studied further in anthropology, since this is where semiotics provides the best answers to power in gender.

Studies of gender in Vietnam have to a certain extent moved into this complex sphere of semiotics. O'Harrow's research (1989) on gender in Vietnam elucidates significant contradictions between men's public statements of themselves and their informal observations on women. Many of these statements reflect their powerlessness in dealing with women. They mystify their importance, yet do not really believe in it themselves; and the strategies employed by women in language, in confronting the problem of matriarchy (the husband's mother) and patriarchy (husband; father) through metaphorical language and dreaming expresses the social tensions amongst women across generations and between women and men, within and across generations (see also Harrow, this volume). In language and daily activity, women create privacy and autonomy in interpersonal relationships and economic activities, dispelling the power of the older generation and the husband over them. An elusive woman is hard to control, since she gives the illusion of subservience, yet remains stubbornly evasive in character. Some of these psychological dimensions of communication in gender relations need to be explored to obtain a proper view of personal and social conduct on the interpersonal level. If social structures are not compatible with social relationships, the discrepancy between ideology and action should be examined more critically to obtain a better understanding of gender in practical life.

White (1989) has attempted to adopt a non-Western feminist discourse by applying a 'deconstructionist approach to a study of Vietnamese popular consciousness' – dialogues in plays, movies, lonely hearts columns and newspapers. She demonstrates the continuity of Vietnamese ideas of the power of women within the household ('the general of the interior') and market-place, and the way in which State socialism splits men and women through the Peasant Union and the Women's Union, thereby encouraging a popular public view that women are not farmers (although most of them are) and need not be directly involved in economic change. Again the psychological dimensions of male–female relationships within the family and community are unrepresented and unidentified in the State bureaucracy, and new contradictions begin to emerge between the power of women in family and culture and their empowerment by the State. This seems to be a repeat of a typical Southeast Asian model of change and development: that women continue to experience contradictory statements of their usefulness and power, and that the public view usually contradicts the popular.

Conclusion

In this chapter I have attempted to argue that Southeast Asia provides a field area for the application of bilateralism as a conceptual model of social organisation. In island Southeast Asia in particular, and in parts of mainland Southeast Asia, bilateralism is the operational principle of activating relationships of kinship, gender and class, where complementarity of roles and statuses is not clearly associated with formal hierarchical distinctions of power or authority. The sources from which individuals obtain ascribed and achieved forms of power, from birthrights or descent to competitive ranking systems, or through gender or control over capital and other forms of economic resources, are usually understated and even concealed, so as to provide the 'other' with possibilities of introducing levelling mechanisms, both metaphorically and in a real sense. One of the most powerful pervasive mechanisms for neutralising social differences is the spontaneous adoption of bilateral kinship terms, where status differentiation is only expressed intergenerationally. Society becomes a metaphorical replica of the family and kinship unit, and every individual is linked to another through a system of fictitious kinship, highlighting rules of eldership and siblingship. In gender, what has been previously expressed as the 'high status of Southeast Asian women' is in reality effective and productive use of biology and sex where boundaries are left open and fluid to enable either sex to develop experiential knowledge of the activities of the 'other'.

The study of the anthropology of informality: the development of social retreats in everyday life away from formal structures of organisation has not been given much attention in recent anthropology. Southeast Asia however provides an interesting arena for studies of this kind, which in the field of gender also serves to question earlier assumptions of 'relational' behaviour between men and women.

Notes

1. This discussion on bilateralism was first conceived in a 1988 pre-conference session of the twelfth IUAES (International Union of Anthropological and Ethnological Sciences) Congress in Zagreb. The title of this meeting was 'Anthropological Perspectives on Research and Teaching Concerning Women'. This chapter is substantially different from the earlier piece, which focused mainly on kinship bilaterality. I am grateful to Khoo Khay Jin and Razha Rashid for their comments on bilateralism. While the chapter is mainly a theoretical rethinking of Southeast Asian social organisation and gender, it includes many personal observations of everyday life in Malaysia and Indonesia, two 'field' areas extremely familiar to the author.

2. In my research for *Women and Culture: Between Malay Adat and Islam* (1992) I gave much attention to the informal structure of Malay politics, which I had described as the 'moral polity' of the masses. A Eurocentric observation of Malay forms of leadership might view the system as formalistic and hierarchical, yet, when an examination is made of the attitudes of followers towards Chiefs and Kings, it is quite obvious that the formal structures of leadership are not allowed to develop to ensure the complete privilege of the powerful. The withdrawal of loyalty and support is also an important source of power among followers, and this has been and continues to be a sensitive observation among formal leaders.

3. Notions of 'feminine' and 'masculine' are here used in a general sense to describe female and male values of desirable conduct, except that one should note the Southeast Asian association of 'femininity' with 'sexuality', through openly expressive body language, speech and dressing. The idea is not to conceal sexuality in the West and South Asian way, but to show it; but rather than showing it through visible glimpses of the naked flesh, the body is covered in closely fitted blouses and sarongs for women and dashing head scarves and loose shirts for men. Hand gestures, facial expressions and conversational styles then emulate the dressing preference; non-Southeast Asianists might find this provocative and openly flirtatious; but to Southeast Asianists, the message is usually one of innocent friendliness. Muslims strongly influenced by West Asian images of the 'concealed women' tend to see the Southeast Asian style of dressing and conversation as unIslamic, and

hasten to impose Islamic concepts of *aurat* (modesty) upon local women.

4. 'Egocentricity' has often been alleged as a reason behind the failure of development projects requiring cooperation and collective responsibility in Malaysia. Gullick (1984) has argued that Malays in particular work best when labour is redeemed for cash (*upah*), and least when institutions of *kerah* (forced labour) or *gotong-royong* (voluntary group labour) are applied.

5. Indian custom has made it virtually impossible for women to leave their husbands when a marriage fails; but an increasing number of Indian women are now seeking divorce. Currently many continue to work after marriage to obtain an independent source of income.

6. The term *Orang Asli* literally means the 'original people'. They form part of a under-referential group of *bumiputeras* (son of the soil) that comprises the indigeneous populations of the peninsula. This term excludes only the Chinese and Indian populations of Malaysia.

7. A common factor about food preparation in Southeast Asia is the importance given to women in control over food resources in the household. Indeed in Malay and many other Indonesian communities, the person who distributes the food is as important as the person who brings it in. See Carsten (1989) for her analysis of food resources in relation to cash.

Bibliography

Abraham, R. G. (1978). 'Aspects of the Distinction between the Sexes in the Nyamwezi and some other African Systems of Kinship and Marriage'. In J. S. La Fontaine (ed.), *Sex and Age as Principles of Social Differentiation*, ASA Monograph 17. London: Academic Press.

Ackerman, S.E. (1984). 'Impact of Industrialisation on the Social Role of Rural Malay Women'. In Hing Ai Yun, Nik Safiah Karim and Rokiah Talib (eds), *Women in Malaysia*. Kuala Lumpur: Pelanduk Publication.

Almagor, U. (1978). 'Gerontocracy, Polygyny and Scarce Resources'. In J. S. La Fontaine (ed.), *Sex and Age as Principles of Social Differentiation*, ASA Monograph 17. London: Academic Press.

Appell, G. N. (ed.) (1976). *Studies in Borneo Societies: Social Process and Anthropological Explanation*, Center for Southeast Asian Studies, University of Northern Illinois, Special Report No. 12. DeKalb: Northern Illinois University.

Bamberger, J. (1974). 'The Myth of Matriarchy: Why Men Rule in Primitive Society'. In M. Z. Rosaldo and L. Lamphere (eds), *Women, Culture and Society*. Stanford: Stanford University Press.

Banks, D. J. (1983). *Malay Kinship*. Philadelphia: Institute for the Study of Human Issues.

Barton, R. F. (1969). *Ifugao Law*. Berkeley: University of California Press. (First published 1919, University of California, Publications in American Archaeology and Ethnology.)

de Beauvoir, S. (1953). *The Second Sex*, transl. and ed. by H. M. Parshley. New York: Knopf.

Benda-Beckmann, F. von (1979). *Property in Social Continuity: Continuity and Change in the Maintenance of Property Relationships through Time in Minangkabau*, Verhandelingen van het Koninklijk Instituut voor Taal-, Land- en Volkenkunde 86. The Hague: Martinus Nijhoff.

Benda-Beckmann, K. von (1984). *The Broken Stairways to Consensus: Village Justice and State Courts in Minangkabau*, Verhandelingen van het Koninklijk Instituut voor Taal-, Land- en Volkenkunde 106. Dordrecht–Cinnaminson: Foris Publications.

—— (1988a). 'Social Security and Small-Scale Enterprises in Islamic Ambon'. In F. von Benda-Beckmann, K. von Benda-Beckmann, *et al.* (eds), *Between Kinship and the State: Social Security and Law in Developing Countries*. Dordrecht–Holland/Providence USA: Foris Publications.

—— (1988b). 'Development, Law and Gender-Skewing: An Examination of the Impact of Development on the Socio-Legal Position of Indonesian Women, with Special Reference to Minangkabau', Paper presented at the Seminar on 'The Socio-Legal Position of Women in Changing Society', IUAES Commission on 'Folk Law and Legal Pluralism', Zagreb.

Benda-Beckmann, F. von and Benda-Beckmann, K. von (1984). 'Transformation and Change in Minangkabau'. In K. von Benda-Beckmann, *The Broken Stairways to Consensus: Village Justice and State Courts in Minangkabau*, Verhandelingen van let Koninklijk Instituut voor Taal-, Land- en Volkenkunde 106. Dordrecht–Cinnaminson: Foris Publications.

Benjamin, G. (1976). 'Austroasiatic Subgroupings and Prehistory in the Malay Peninsula'. In P. N. Jenner (ed.), *Austroasiatic Studies*. Hawaii: University of Hawaii Press.

—— (1980). 'Semang, Senoi, Malay: Cultural, History, Kinship and Consciousness in the Malay Peninsula'. Canberra: Department of Prehistory and Anthropology, Australian National University.

Bhar, S. (1984). 'The Status of Simunul Bajau Women in Sabah'. In Hing Ai Yun, Nik Safiah Karim and Rokiah Talib (eds), *Women in Malaysia*. Kuala Lumpur: Pelanduk Publications.

Borlagdan, S. B. (1987). *Working With People in the Uplands: The Bulolakaw Social Forestry Experience*. Quezon City: Institute of Philippines Culture, Ateneo de Manila University.

Boserup, E. (1970). *Women's Role in Economic Development*. New York: St Martin's Press.

Bowen, J. R. (1983). 'Cultural Models for Historical Genealogies: The Case of the Melaka Sultanate'. In K. S. Sandhu and P. Wheatley (eds), *Melaka*, Singapore: Institute of Southeast Asian Studies and Kuala Lumpur: Oxford University Press, 1, 162–79.

Breman, J. (1980). *The Village in Java and the Early-Colonial State*, CASP 1. Erasmus University: Rotterdam.

—— (1988). *The Shattered Image: Construction and Deconstruction of the Village in Colonial Asia*, CAS 2. Dordrecht: Foris Publications.

Burling, R. (1965). *Hill Farms and Paddy Fields: Life in Mainland Southeast Asia*. Englewood Cliffs, NJ: Prentice-Hall.

Carey, I. (1976). *Orang Asli 'The Aboriginal Tribes of Peninsular Malaysia'*. Kuala Lumpur: Oxford University Press.

Carsten, J. (1989). 'Cooking Money: Gender and Symbolic Transformation of Means of Exchange in a Malay Fishing Community'. In J. Parry and M. Bloch (eds), *Money and the Morality of Exchange*. Cambridge: Cambridge University Press.

Chan, H. C. (1975). *Notes on the Mobilization of Women into the Economy and Politics of Singapore*, Occasional Paper No. 23. Singapore: Department of Political Science.

Chang, Chen-Tung (1975). 'A Sociological Study of Neighbourlines'. In S. Yeh (ed.), *Public Housing in Singapore*. Singapore: Singapore University Press.

—— (1976). 'The Changing Socio-Demographic Profile'. In R. Hassan (ed.), *Singapore: Society in Transition*. Kuala Lumpur: Oxford University Press.

Chantou, Boua (1984). 'Draft Report on the Situation of Women and Girls in Kampuchea', Country Paper circulated at the Workshop on 'Research Methodologies, Perspectives and Directions for Policy in Women/Gender Studies in Southeast Asia', KANITA/UNESCO, Penang.

Cheng, S. (1977). 'Singapore Women: Legal Status, Educational Attainment and Employment Patterns'. *Asian Survey*, 17:4, 368–73.

Chia, Oai Peng (1984). 'The Legal Status of Women in a Multi-Racial Malaysian Society'. In Hing Ai Yun, Nik Safiah Karim and Rokiah Talib (eds), *Women in Malaysia*. Kuala Lumpur: Pelanduk Publications.

Conklin, H. C. (1957). *Hanun'oo Agriculture: A Report on an Integral System of Shifting Cultivation in the Philippines*. Rome: Food and Agricultural Organisation of the United Nations.

Cucchiari, S. (1981). 'The Gender Revolution and the Transition from Bisexual Horde to Patrilocal Band: The Origins of Gender Hierarchy'. In Ortner and Whitehead (eds), *Sexual Meanings: The Cultural Construction of Gender and Sexuality*. Cambridge: Cambridge University Press.

Dahlan, H. M. (1983). 'Urbanisation and the Destruction of Subsistence Reproduction: The Case of Maludam Peasantry', Paper presented at the Seminar on 'Third World Urbanisation and the Household Economy', 27–29 June. Penang: Universiti Sains Malaysia.

De Josselin de Jong, P. E. (1951). *Minangkabau and Negeri Sembilan: Socio-Political Structure in Indonesia*. Leiden: E. Ydo. (Third impression: 1980.)

—— (1960). 'Islam Versus *Adat* in Negeri Sembilan (Malaya)'. *Bijdragen*, 116:1, 158–203.

—— (1977a). 'The Participants' View of their Culture'. In idem (ed.), *Structural Anthropology in the Netherlands: A Reader*, KITLV, Translation Series 17. The Hague: Martinus Nijhoff. (Originally published in Dutch in 1956.) pp. 231–52

—— (ed.) (1977b). *Structural Anthropology in the Netherlands: A Reader*, KITLV, Translation Series 17. The Hague: Martinus Nijhoff.

—— (1980a). 'The Concept of the Field of Ethnological Study'. In James J. Fox (ed.), *The Flow of Life: Essays on Eastern Indonesia*, Cambridge, Mass. and London: Harvard University Press, pp. 317–26.

—— (1980b). *Minangkabau and Negeri Sembilan: Socio-Political structure in Indonesia*. The Hague: Martinus Nijhoff. (Third impression; first impression 1951.)

—— (ed.) (1984). *Unity in Diversity: Indonesia as a Field of Anthropological Study*, Instiuut Voor Taal-, Land- en Volkenkunde. Dordrecht: Foris Publications.

Dentan, R. (1968). *The Semai: A Non-Violent People of Malaya*. New York: Holt, Rinehart and Winston.

Dewey, A. (1962). *Peasant Marketing in Java*. New York: Free Press.

Djamour, J. (1959). *Malay Kinship and Marriage in Singapore*. London: Athlone Press.

Dozier, E. P. (1967). *The Kalinga of Northern Luzon, Philippines*. New York: Holt, Rinehart and Winston.

Dube. L., Leacock, E. and Ardener, S. (eds) (1986). *Visibility and Power: Essays on Women in Society and Development*. Delhi: Oxford University Press.

Dunham, A. (1983). Women's Work in Village Industries on Java. Unpublished Ph.D. Thesis, University of Cornell.

Eberhardt, N. (ed.) (1988a). *Gender, Power and the Construction of the Moral Order: Studies from the Thai Periphery*, Center for Southeast Asian Studies, Monograph No. 4. Madison: University of Wisconsin.

—— (1988b). 'Siren Song: Negotiating Gender Images in a Rural Shan Village'. In N. Eberhardt (ed.), *Gender, Power and the Construction of the Moral Order: Studies from the Thai Periphery*, Center for Southeast Asian Studies, Monograph No. 4. Madison: University of Wisconsin.

Ebihara, M. (1974). 'Khmer Village Women in Cambodia: A Happy Balance', Matthiasson (ed.), *Many Sisters: Women in Cross-Cultural Perspective*. New York: Free Press.

Embree, J. (1950). 'Thailand – A Loosely Structured Social System'. *American Anthropology*, 52: 181–93.

Endicott, K. (1979). *Batek Negrito Religion: The World-View and Rituals of a Hunting and Gathering People of Peninsular Malaysia*. Oxford: Clarendon Press.

Errington, S. (1989). 'Recasting Sex, Gender and Power: A Theoretical and Regional Overview'. In J. Atkinson and S. Errington (eds), *Power and Difference: Gender in Island Southeast Asia*. Stanford: Stanford University Press.

Evans-Pritchard, E. E. (1950). 'Kinship and the Local Community Among the Nuer'. In A. R. Radcliffe-Brown and D. Forde (eds), *African Systems of Kinship and Marriage*, pp. 360–92. London: Oxford University Press.

Firth, Raymond (1951). *We the Tikopia: Kinship in Primitive Polynesia*. Boston: Beacon Press.

—— (1957). 'A Note on Descent Groups in Polynesia'. *Man*, No. 2, 4–8.

Firth, Raymond (1966). *Malay Fishermen: Their Peasant Economy*. London: Routledge and Kegan Paul.

Firth, Rosemary (1966). *Housekeeping Among Malay Peasants*, 2nd edn. London: Athlone Press.

Fortes, M. (1949). *The Web of Kinship among the Tallensi*. London: Oxford University Press (for the International African Institute).

—— (1950). 'Kinship and Marriage among the Ashanti'. In A. R. Radcliffe-Brown and D. Forde (eds), *African Systems of Kinship and Marriage*, pp. 252–84. London: Oxford University Press.

Foucault, M. (1978). *The History of Sexuality*, Vol. 1. New York: Pantheon Books.

Fox, R. B. (1970). *Religion and Society among the Tagboriua of Palawan Island, Philippines*. Manila: National Museum.

Freedman, M. (1957). *Chinese Family and Marriage in Singapore*. London: HMSO.

—— (1966). *Chinese Lineage and Society*. London: Athlone Press.

Freeman, D. (1970). *Report on the Iban*, LSE Monograph on Social Anthropology, No. 41. New York: Athlone Press.

—— (1971). 'The Family System of the Iban of Borneo'. In J. Goody (ed.), *The Developmental Cycle in Domestic Groups*, pp. 15–52. Cambridge: Cambridge University Press; Chicago: Chicago University Press.

Geertz, C. (1960). *The Religion of Java*. Glencoe: The Free Press of Glencoe.

—— (1968). *Islam Observed: Religious Development in Morocco and Indonesia*.

—— (1973). *The Interpretation of Cultures*. New York: Basic Books.

—— (1980). *Negara: The Theatre State in Nineteenth Century Bali*. Princeton: Princeton University Press.

Geertz, H. (1961). *The Javanese Family: A Study of Kinship and Socialisation*. Glencoe: The Free Press of Glencoe.

Geertz, H. and Geertz C. (1975). *Kinship in Bali*. Chicago: University of Chicago Press.

Gibson, T. (1986). *Sacrifice and Sharing in the Philippine Highlands: Religion and Society among the Buid of Mindoro*. London: Athlone Press.

Gough, K. (1975). 'The Origin of the Family'. In R. Reiter (ed.), *Towards an Anthropology of Women*. New York: Monthly Review Press.

Grinjns, M. (1987). 'Tea-pickers in West Java as Mothers and Workers'. In E. Locher-Scholten and A. Niehof (eds), *Indonesian Women in Focus*, Verhandelingen van het Koninklijk Instituut Voor Taal-, Land- en Volkekunde 127. Dordrecht: Foris Publications.

Gullick, J. M. (1965). *Indigenous Political Systems of Western Malaya*. London: Athlone Press. (First Published 1958.)

—— (1984). 'The Entrepreneur in Late Nineteenth Century Malay Society', the Third James C. Jackson Memorial Lecture, 1984, Asian Studies Association of Australia; republished in *Journal of the Malayan Branch of the Royal Asiatic Society*, 58(1), 1985.

Hamka (1975). *Tenggelamnya Kapal Van der Wijck* (Microfilm). Penang: Universiti Sains Malaysia.

Hanks, J. R. (1988). 'The Power of Akha Women'. In N. Eberhardt (ed.), *Gender Power and the Construction of the Moral Order: Studies from the Thai Periphery*, Center for Southeast Asian Studies, Monograph No. 4. Madison: University of Wisconsin.

Hanks, L. (1962). 'Merit and Power in the Thai Social Order'. *American Anthropologist*, 64:6, 1247–61.

Hanks, L. M. and Hanks, J. R. (1963). 'Thailand: Equality Between the Sexes'. In R. Ward (ed.), *Women in the New Asia*. Paris: UNESCO.

Harris, O. (1978). 'Complementarity and Conflict: An Andean View of Women and Men'. In J. S. La Fontaine (ed.), *Sex and Age as Principles of Social Differentiation*, ASA Monograph 17. London: Academic Press.

Hassan, R. (ed.) (1976). *Singapore: Society in Transition*. Kuala Lumpur: Oxford University Press.

Hassan, R. (1977). *Families in Flats: A Study of Low Income Families in Public Housing*. Singapore: Singapore University Press.

Hersri, S. (1981). 'Wanita: Alas-Kaki di Siang Hari, Alas-Tidur di Waktu Malam'. *Prisma*, 7, July, 15–30.

Hing Ai Yun (1984). 'Women and Work in West Malaysia'. In Hing Ai Yun, Nik Safiah Karim and Rokiah Talib (eds), *Women in Malaysia*. Kuala Lumpur: Pelanduk Publications.

Hing Ai Yun, Nik Safiah Karim and Rokiah Talib (eds) (1984). *Women In Malaysia*. Kuala Lumpur: Pelanduk Publications.

Howell, S. (1984). *Society and Cosmos: Che Wong of Peninsular Malaysia*. Singapore: Oxford University Press. (Republished: University of Chicago Press 1989.)

Hutheesing, O. (1989). *Emerging Sexual Inequality Among the Lisu of Northern Thailand*. Leiden: Brill.

Illo, J. F. I. (1987). *Impact of Irrigation Development on Women and their Households: The Case of the Aslong Project*. Quezon City: Institute of Philippine Culture, Ateneo de Manila University.

——(1988). *Gender Issues in Rural Development: A Workshop Report*. Quezon City: Institute of Philippine Culture, Ateneo de Manila University.

Illo, J. F. I. and Veneracion, C. C. (1988). *Women and Men in Rained Farming Systems*. Quezon City: Institute of Philippine Culture, Ateneo de Manila University.

Jamilah, Ariffin (1984). 'Migration of Women Workers in Peninsular Malaysia: Impact and Implications'. In Fawcett, Khoo and Smith (eds), *Women in the Cities of Asia: Migration Urban Development*. Boulder: Westview Press.

Jay, R. R. (1969). *Javanese Villagers*. Cambridge, Mass.: MIT Press.

Jayawardena, C. (1977). 'Women and Kinship in Acheh Besar, Northern

68 | **Wazir Jahan Karim**

Sumatra'. *Ethnology*, 14:1, 21–38.

Kahn, J. (1976). 'Tradition, Matriliny and Change Among the Minangkabau of Indonesia'. *Bidjragen*, 32:1, 64–95.

Kammerer, C. A. (1988). 'Shifting Gender Asymmetries Among Akha of Northern Thailand'. In N. Eberhardt (ed.), *Gender, Power and the Construction of the Moral Order: Studies from the Thai Periphery*, Center for Southeast Asian Studies, Monograph No. 4. Madison: University of Wisconsin.

Karim, W. (1980a). 'Children of the Garden: Concepts of Size, Space and Time in Child Socialisation Among The Ma'Betise' and the Malays'. *Federation Museum Journal*, NS, 25, 151–8.

—— (1980b). 'The Affinal Bond: A review of Ma' Betise' Marriages on Carey Island'. *Federation Museum Journal*, NS, 25, 137–50.

—— (1980c). 'The Nature of Kinship in Ma' Betise' villages'. *Federation Museum Journal*, NS, 25, 119–36.

—— (1981a). *Ma' Betise' Concepts of Living Things*. London: Athlone Press.

—— (1981b). 'Ma' Betise' Concepts of Humans, Plants and Animals', *Bidjragen Tot De Taal-, Land- en Volkenkunde*, 137, 35–60.

—— (1982). 'An Evaluation of Participatory Research, as a Method in Developing Community Skills and Decision-Making'. *Convergence*, 15:4, 54–60.

—— (1983). 'Malay Women's Movements, Leadership and Processes of Change'. *International Social Sciences Journal*, 35:4, 719–31.

—— (1984). 'Malay Midwives and Witches'. *Social Science and Medicine*, 18:22, 159–66.

—— (1987). 'The Status of Malay Women in Malaysia: From Culture to Islam and Industrialisation'. *International Journal of Sociology of the Family*, 17:1, 41–55.

—— (1992). *Women and Culture: Between Malay Adat and Islam*. Westview: Boulder.

Kartini, R. A. (1976). *Letters of a Javanese Princess*. Transl. from the Dutch by Agnes Louise Symmers; ed. with an introduction by Hildred Geertz. Hong Kong: Heinemann Educational Books (Asia).

Kartodirdjo, S. (1975). *Protest Movements in Rural Java: A Study of Agrarian Unrest in the 19th and early 20th centuries*. Singapore: Oxford University Press.

Kaye, B. (1960). *Upper Nankin Street Singapore: A Sociological Study of Chinese Households Living in a Density Populated Area*. Singapore: University of Malaya Press.

Kemp, J. H. (1988a). *Seductive Mirage: The Search for the Village community in Southeast Asia*, CAS No. 3. Dordrecht: Foris Publications.

—— (1988b). *Community and State in Modern Thailand*, Bielefeld Working Papers No. 100. Bielefeld: Sociology of Development Research Centre, Bielefeld University.

—— (1989a). *Peasants and Cities: The Cultural and Social Image of Thai*

Peasant Village Community. Sojourn, 4: 6–19.

—— (1989b). 'Development and Invention of The Peasant Village: Some Southeast Asian Examples', Paper presented at the Nordic Association of Southeast Asian Studies Conference, Lund, 28 Sept. – 1st October.

Keyes, C. (1984). 'Mother or Mistress but Never a Monk: Buddhist Notions of Female Gender in Rural Thailand'. *American Ethnologist*, 11:2, 223–41.

Khin, Thitsa (1980). *Providence and Prostitution: Image and Reality for Women in Buddhist Thailand*. London: Change International Reports, Women and Society.

Kiefer, T. M. (1972). *The Tausug: Violence and Law in a Philippine Society*. New York: Holt, Rinehart and Winston.

Kingshill, K. (1960). *Bang Khuad: A Community Study in Thailand*, Association for Asian Studies Monograph, No. 10. New York: J. J. Augustin.

Kirsch, A. (1975). *Economy, Polity and Religion in Thailand*. In G. W. Skinner and A. T. Kirsch (eds), pp. 172–96. *Change and Persistence in Thai Society*. Ithaca: Cornell University Press.

Laderman, C. (1982). 'Putting Malay Women in their Place'. In P. van Esterik (ed.), *Women of Southeast Asia*, Center for South and Southeast Asian Studies, Occasional Paper No. 9. DeKalb: Northern Illinois University.

—— (1983). *Wives and Midwives: Childbirth and Nutrition in Rural Malaysia*. Berkeley: University of California Press.

—— (1991). *Taming the Wind of Desire: Psychology, Medicine, and Aesthetics in Malay Shamanistic Performance*. Berkeley: University of California Press.

La Fontaine, J. S. (ed.) (1978). *Sex and Age as Principles of Social Differentiation*, ASA Monograph 17. London: Academic Press.

Lebra, J. and Paulson, J. (1980). *Chinese Women in Southeast Asia*. Singapore: Times Book International.

Lévi-Strauss, C. (1969). *The Elementary Structures of Kinship (Les Structures élémentaires de la Parenté)*. Boston: Beacon Press. (First Published, 1949.)

Locher-Scholten, E. and Niehof, A. (1987). *Indonesian Women in Focus*, Verhandelingen van het Koninklijk Instituut Voor Taal-, Land- en Volkenkunde 127. Dordrecht: Foris Publications.

MacCormack, C. P. (1980). 'Nature, Culture and Gender: a Critique'. In C. P. MacCormack and M. Strathern (eds), *Nature, Culture and Gender*, Cambridge: Cambridge University Press, pp. 1–24.

MacCormack, C. P. and Strathern, M. (eds) (1980). *Nature, Culture and Gender*. Cambridge: Cambridge University Press.

Manderson, L. (1980). *Women, Politics and Change: The Evolution of the Kaum Ibu (Women's Section) of UMNO, 1945–72*. Kuala Lumpur: Oxford University Press.

—— (1983). *Women's Work and Women's Roles: Economic and Everyday Life in Indonesia, Malaysia and Singapore*, Development Studies Center, Monograph 32. Canberra: Australian National University.

Marah, Rusli (1963). *Siti Nurbaya: Kasih Tak Sampai*. Kuala Lumpur: Pustaka

Melayu Baru.

Mazidah, Zakariah and Nik Safiah Karim (1986). 'Women in Development: The Care of on All-Women Youth Land Development Scheme in Malaysia'. In L. Dube, E. Leacock, and S. Ardener (eds), *Visibility and Power: Essay on Women in Society and Development.* Delhi: Oxford University Press.

Maznah, Mohammad (1987). 'Production Relations and Technology in the Malay Handloom Wearing Industry'. In C. Ng (ed.), *Technology and Gender: Women's Work in Asia.* Serdang: Women's Studies Unit, Universiti Sains Malaysia.

Marx, K. *et al.* (1970). *The Woman Question: Selection from the Writings of Karl Marx, Frederick Engels, V.I. Lenin and Joseph Stalin.* New York: International Publishers. (First Published 1951.)

McKinley, R. (1983). 'Cain and Abel on the Malay Peninsula', Siblingship in Oceania: Studies in the Meaning of Kin Relations, ASAO Monograph No. 8. Lanham: University Press of America. (Originally published 1979, Ann Arbor: University of Michigan Press.)

Merari, Siregar (1965). *Azab dan Sengsara.* Djakarta: P.N. Balai Pustaka.

Millar, S. B. (1983). 'On Interpreting Gender in Bugis Society'. *American Ethnologist,* 10: 477–93.

Miralao, V. A. (1980). *Women and Men in Development: Findings from a Pilot Study.* Quezon City: Institute of Philippines Culture, Ateneo de Manila University.

Moore. H. (1988). *Feminism and Anthropology.* Cambridge: Polity Press.

Moyer, D. S. (1984). 'South Sumatra in the Indonesian Field of Anthropological Study'. In P. E. De Josselin de Jong (ed.), *Unity in Diversity: Indonesia as a Field of Anthropological Study.* Dordrecht: Foris Publications.

Murdock, G. P. (1960). 'Cognatic Forms of Social Organisation'. In G. P. Murdock (ed.), *Social Structure in Southeast Asia,* Viking Fund Publications in Anthropology, No. 29.

Nadel, S. F. (1950). 'Dual Descent in the Nuba Itills'. In A. R. Radcliffe-Brown and D. Forde (eds), *African Systems of Kinship and Marriage,* London: Oxford University Press, pp. 333–59.

Narli, N. (1986). Malay Women in Tertiary Education: Trends of Change in Female Role Ideology, Unpublished Ph.D. Thesis, Department of Anthropology/Sociology, Universiti Sains Malaysia.

Nicholaisen, I. (1989). 'Timber, Culture and Politics in Rural Sarawak'. Paper presented at the Nordic Association of Southeast Asian Studies Conference, Lund, 28 Sept. to 1 Oct.

Niessen, S. (1984). 'Textiles are Female . . . but what is Femaleness? Toba Batak Textiles in the Indonesian Field of Ethnological Study'. In P. E. De Josselin de Jong (ed.), *Unity in Divenity: Indonesian as a Field of Anthropological Study.* Dordrecht: Foris Publications.

Ng, C. (ed.) (1987a). *Technology and Gender: Women's Work in Asia.* Serdang: Women's Studies Unit, Universiti Pertanian Malaysia.

Ng, C. (1987b). 'Agricultural Modernisation and Gender Differentiation in a Rural Malay Community 1983–1987'. In C. Ng (ed.), *Technology and Gender: Women's work in Asia*. Serdang: Women's Studies Unit, Universiti Pertanian Malaysia.

Ngaosyvathn, M. (1989). 'Lao Women Today, More Equal but Maybe Not a Monk'. Paper presented at the Workshop on 'Research Methodologies, Perspectives and Directions for Policy in Women/Gender Studies in Southeast Asia', KANITA/UNESCO, Penang.

Ofreneo, R. P. (1987). 'Women in the Electronics Industry in the Philippines'. In C. Ng (ed.), *Technology and Gender: Women's Work in Asia*. Serdang: Women's Studies Unit, Universiti Pertanian Malaysia.

O'Harrow, S. (1986). 'Men of Hu, Men of Han, Men of the Hundred Man'. *Bulletin de l'Ecole Française*, d'Extrême-Orient, Vol. 75:45, 249–66.

O'Harrow, S. (1989). 'Understanding Women in Southeast Asia the Southeast Asian Way: The Case of Vietnam'. Paper presented at the Workshop on 'Research Methodologies, Perspectives and Directions for Policy in Women/Gender Studies in Southeast Asia', KANITA/UNESCO, Penang.

Ong, A. C. (1987). *Spirits of Resistance and Capitalist Discipline: Factory Women in Malaysia*. New York: State University of New York Press.

Ortner, S. (1974). 'Is Female to Male as Nature is to Culture?' In M. Z. Rosaldo and L. Lamphere (eds), *Women, Culture and Society*. Stanford: Stanford University Press.

—— (1981). 'Gender and Sexuality in Hierarchical Societies: the Case of Polynesia and Some Comparative Implication'. In S. Ortner and H. Whitehead (eds), *Sexual Meanings: The Cultural Construction of Gender and Sexuality*. Cambridge: Cambridge University Press.

Ortner, S. and Whitehead, H. (eds) (1981). *Sexual Meanings: The Cultural Construction of Gender and Sexuality*. Cambridge: Cambridge University Press.

Oorijitham, K. S. S. (1984). 'Indian Women in Urban Malaysia'. In Hing Ai Yun, Nik Safiah Karim and Rokiah Talib (eds), *Women in Malaysia*. Kuala Lumpur: Pelanduk Publications.

Palmer, L. H. (1960). *Social Status and Power in Java*, London School of Economics Monograph No. 20. New York: Athlone Press.

Papanek, H. and Schwede, L. (1988). 'Women are Good with Money: Earning and Managing in an Indonesian City'. In J. Bruce and D. Dwyer (eds), *A Home Divided: Women and Income in the Third World*. Stanford: Stanford University Press.

Pasuk Phongpaichit (1980). *Rural Women in Thailand: From Peasant Girls to Bangkok Masseuses*. Geneva: ILO World Employment Programme Research Working Papers.

Peletz, M. G. (1988). *A Share of the Harvest: Kinship, Property and Social History among the Malays of Rembau*, Berkeley: University of California Press.

Potter, S. (1977). *Family Life in a Northern Thai Village: A Study in the Structural Significance of Women*. Berkeley: University of California Press.

Pramoedya Ananta Toer (1983). *Bumi Manusia*. Melaka: Wira Karya.

Pudijiwati Sajogyo (1983). *Peranan Wanita dalam Perkembangan Masyarakat Desa*. Jakarta: C.V. Rajawali.

Razha, Rashid (1993). 'On the Subjects of Malay Kings: a Study on the Bases and Processes of Legitimacy and Legitimation of Leadership in a Malay Village'. University of Toronto Ph.D. Thesis.

Reiter, R. R. (1975a). 'Men and Women in the South of France: Public and Private Domains'. In R. R. Reiter (ed.), *Towards an Anthropology of Women*. New York: Monthly Review Press.

Reiter R. R. (ed.) (1975b). *Towards an Anthropology of Women*. New York: Monthly Review Press.

Richards, A. I. (1950). 'Some Types of Family Structure amongst the Central Bantu'. In A. R. Radcliffe-Brown and D. Forde (eds), *African Systems of Kinship and Marriage*, London: Oxford University Press, pp. 207–51.

Rodenburg, J. (1983). *Women and Padi Farming: A Sociological Study of a Village in the Kemubu Scheme*. Amsterdam: Anthropological – Sociological Centre, Dept. of South and Southeast Asian Studies, University of Amsterdam.

Rogers, B. (1979). *The Domestication of Women: Discrimination in Developing Societies*. New York: St Martins Press.

Rosaldo, M. Z. (1974). 'Women, Culture and Society: A Theoretical Overview'. In M. Z. Rosaldo and L. Lamphere (eds), *Women Culture and Society*. Stanford: Stanford University Press.

—— (1980a). 'The Use and Abuse of Anthropology: Reflections on Feminism and Cross-Cultural Understanding'. *Signs*, 5(3): 389–417.

—— (1980b). *Knowledge and Passion: Ilongot Notions of Self and Social Life*. Cambridge: Cambridge University Press.

Rosaldo, M. Z. and Atkinson, J. (1975). 'Man the Hunter and Women: Metaphors for the sexes in Ilongot Magical Spells'. In R. Willis (ed.), *The Interpretation of Symbolism*. Malaby Press: London.

Sack, K. (1974). 'Engels Revisited: Women, the Organisation of Production, and Private Property'. In M. Z. Rosaldo and L. Lamphere (eds), *Women, Culture and Society*. Stanford: Stanford University Press.

Sansom, B. (1978). 'Sex Age and Social Control in Mobs of the Darwin Hinterland'. In J. S. La Fontaine (ed.), *Sex and Age as Principles of Social Differentiation*, ASA Monograph 17. London: Academic Press.

Siegel, J. T. (1969). *The Rope of God*. Berkeley: University of California Press.

Sitisoemandari Soeroto (1984 [1977]). *Kartini: Sebuah Bibliografi*. Jakarta: Gunung Agung. (First published 1977.)

Solichin Salam (1981). *Arti Kartini dalam Sejarah Nasional Indonesia*. Surabaya: Surya Murthi Publishing.

Sri Subakir (1978). *Seribu Burung Layang-Layang di Tanggerang*. Jakarta: Gaya Favorit Press.

Stivens, M. (1981). 'Women, Kinship and Capitalist Development'. In Young, Wolkowitz and Mc Cullagh (eds), *Of Marriage and the Market*. London: CSE Books.

Stoler, A. (1977). 'Class Structure and Female Autonomy in Rural Java'. *Signs*, 3:1, 74–89.

Strange, H. (1981). *Rural Malay Women in Tradition and Transition*. New York: Praeger Publishers.

Strathern, M. (1987). *Dealing with Inequality: Analysing Gender Relations in Melanesia and Beyond*. Cambridge: Cambridge University Press.

Sukanti, S. (1986). 'Domestic Workers in Seven Cities on the Island of Java'. Paper Presented at the UNU Workshop on 'Women's Work and Family Strategies', Kathmandu.

Sumardjo, Jakob (1981). 'Rumah Yang Damai: Wanita dalam Sastra Indonesia'. *Prisma*, 7, July, 44–53.

Sundaram, J. K. and Tan, P. L. (1985). 'Not the Better Half: Malaysian Women and Development Planning'. In N. Heyzer (ed.), *Missing Women Development Planning in Asia and the Pacific*. Kuala Lumpur: Asian and Pacific Development Centre.

Sutan Takdir Alisjahbana (1963). *Layer Terkembang*. Petaling Jaya: Zaman Baru.

Suryakusuma, Julia I. (1981). 'Wanita dalam Mitos, Realities dan Emansipasi'. *Prisma*, 7, July, 3–14.

Sutlive, V. H. (ed.) (1991). *Female and Male in Borneo: Contributions and Challenges to Gender Studies*, Borneo Research Council Monograph Series Vol. 1. Williamburg, Virginia: Dept. of Anthropology.

Swift, M. (1963). 'Man and Women in Malay Society'. In B. Ward (ed.), *Women in the New Asia*. Paris: UNESCO.

—— (1965). *Malay Peasant Society in Jelebu*. London: Athlone Press.

Tam, N. (1972). 'The Impact of Modernisation on Women'. Paper presented at a Seminar on 'Modernisation in Singapore', Singapore National Academy of Science, June 16 – 17.

Tambiah, S. J. (1970). *Buddhism and Spirit Cults in North-East Thailand*. Cambridge: Cambridge University Press.

—— (1976). *World Conqueror and World Renouncer: A Study of Buddhism and Polity in Thailand*. Cambridge: Cambridge University Press.

Tanner, N. (1974). 'Matrifocality in Indonesia and Africa and among Black Americans'. In M. Z. Rosaldo and L. Lamphere (eds), *Women, Culture and Society*. Stanford: Stanford University Press.

Tham, S. S. (ed.) (1972). *Modernisation in Singapore: Impact on the Individual*. Singapore: Singapore Education Press.

Tidalgo, R. L. P. (1985). 'The Integration of Women in Development and Philippine Development Planning'. In N. Heyzer (ed.), *Missing Women: Development Planning in Asia and the Pacific*. Kuala Lumpur: Asia and Pacific Development Centre.

Turton, A. (1972). 'Matrilineal Descent Groups and Spirit-Cults of the Thai-Yuan in Northern Thailand'. *Journal of the Siam Society*, 60: 217–56.

Van Esterik, P. (1982a). *Women of Southeast Asia*, Center for Southeast Asian Studies, Occasional Paper No. 9. DeKalb: Northern Illinois University.

—— (1982b). 'Women Meditation Teachers in Thailand'. In P. Van Esterik (ed.), *Women of Southeast Asia*, Center for Southeast Asian Studies, Occasional Paper No. 9. DeKalb: Northern Illinois University.

—— (1982c). 'Lay Women in Theravada Buddhism'. In P. Van Esterik (ed.), *Women of Southeast Asia*, Center for Southeast Asian Studies, Occasional Paper No. 9. DeKalb: Northern Illinois University.

Vreede-de Stuers, C. C. (1965). 'Kartini: Feiten en Ficties'. *Bijdragen TLV*, 121:20.

Walker, A. (ed.) (1975). *Farmers in Hills*. Penang: Universiti Sains Malaysia Press.

Wang, A. (1975). *Women in Modern Singapore*. Singapore: University Education Press.

—— (1976). 'Women as a Minority Group'. In R. Hassan (ed.), *Singapore: Society in Transition*. Kuala Lumpur: Oxford University Press.

Ward, B. (1963). *Women in the New Asia*. Paris: UNESCO.

Webster, P. (1975). 'Matriachy: A Vision of Power'. In R. R. Reiter (ed.), *Towards an Anthropology of Women*. New York: Monthly Review Press.

White, C. P. (1989). 'On the Cash Nexus and Gender Relation: Vietnam in an Era of Market Liberalisation'. Paper presented at the Conference on 'Rural Southeast Asia in Transition: Village Society in Economic, Political and Gender Perspectives', Lund.

Wijeyewardene, G. (1967). 'Some Aspects of Rural Life in Thailand'. In T. H. Silcock (ed.), *Thailand: Social and Economic Studies in Development*. Durham: Duke University Press.

—— (1977). 'Matriclan or Female Cults: A Problem in Northern Thai Ethnography'. *Mankind*, 11: 19–25.

Wilder, W. D. (1970). 'Socialisation and Social Structure in a Malay Village'. In P. Mayer (ed.), *Socialisation: The Approach from Social Anthropology*. ASA Monograph 8. London: Tavistock Publications, pp. 215–68.

—— (1982). *Communication, Social Structure and Development in Rural Malaysia: A Study of Kampung Kuala Bera*. London: Athlone Press.

Winzeler. R. (1974). 'Sex Role Equality, Wet Rice Cultivation and the State in Southeast Asia'. *American Anthropologist*, 76: 563–7.

—— (1976). 'Ecology, Culture, Social Organisation and State Formation in Southeast Asia'. *Current Anthropology*, 17:4, 623–31.

3

Gender at the Margins of Southeast Asia

Otome Klein-Hutheesing

The Marginal Female and Male as Model

As comparative data on instances of a sexual symmetry on the Southeast Asia scene keep filtering through the literature, the notion of a typical gender stratification pattern for the region seems to be gaining more ground. A survey of research findings in this context indicates an absence of a pronounced male dominance complex in the cultural realm, while gender relations are more likely to be apprehended in terms of multiple, unstable codes (Ong 1989). Another appraisal of sexual roles, based on more than thirty agrarian societies in this part of the world, has given substance to the thesis of a relative sexual equality (Winzeler 1982: 211). Winzeler's resultant 'more or less egalitarian' model for the sexes was derived from an evaluation of economic–political variables and cultural practices (inheritance rules, kinship systems and the like). The author hinted that the peculiar non-hierarchical positioning of female and male status may be an outflow of a long-established pattern of local organisation, initially supported by low-density populations and weak state penetration. What appears remarkable is that the generalisation of egalitarian relations among the sexes seems to hold for wet and dry farming areas and for state as well as non-state communities. In an earlier critique on the causative factors of irrigation culture which engender sexual symmetry in Southeast Asian family systems, Winzeler made the suggestion that a more in-depth comparison should be made between peasants and swidden farmers. This comparison could result in an adequate assessment of a universal social organisation pattern of Southeast Asia with demonstrable elements of egalitarian gender relations (Winzeler 1974: 563–7).

It is with the above considerations in mind that an exploration of the sexual stratification of marginal farming areas is given attention. This study first tries to show the extent to which female–male relations at the periphery of a number of Southeast Asian societies constitute a specific case of relative sexual equality. The periphery is illustrative of those borderline communities that cover the so-called indigenous or tribal enclaves in forest interiors or the migrant hill farmers who move along the frontiers of different nations. Their swidden economics combined with hunting–gathering activities and simple trading encourage the development of a fluid social system, of power, prestige and property dimensions. The typical features of an early gender system will be highlighted through an interpretation of material activities and ideological configurations of female and male. It will include the ways in which *both sexes* have been apprehended, and as such attempt to fill a gap in research on gender at the margins. A surprising observation in this context is that most studies in this field have given focus to the marginal male.[1]

Secondly, the study examines the theme of relative sexual equality from a dynamic viewpoint, i.e. the context of development strategies emanating from a dominant political centre. The effects of these modernising influences will be analysed for four selected areas; the Semai of Peninsular Malaysia, the land Dayak of Sarawak, the Negrito of the Philippines and the Lisu of Northern Thailand. Here a supposition is made that the sudden and very incisive penetration of state-oriented power concepts into the left-over 'hinterland' will be conducive to a greater juxtaposition of the marginal[2] female and male. Viewed from this perspective the margins provide suitable study areas to test local precepts relating to female–male worth. Changes at the periphery reflect on the macro, the remoulding of gender relations in simple economies, bombarded with interventions from state bureaucracies. Money markets also invade indigenous organisation and belief systems. A scrutiny of the factors associated with changes in gender relations at the periphery could then provide a processual framework of understanding the way in which gender is subject to reinterpretation from within and how shifts in notions of sexual equality might occur.

The Marginal Female and Male at Work and Worship

At the margins, ethnic minorities labour and move in ever-changing scenes of work fields and residence. As long as their environments are not redeveloped by their respective power centres, they can continue to maintain their economic autonomy and develop strategies to overcome cultural colonisation. However, large-scale commercial undertakings under the sponsorship of national governments place them in the reversed situation as the 'despoilers' of the land, justifying their resettlement. (For the Hmong in Thailand, see: Radley 1986: 103; Tapp 1990: 154; for the Batak and Tinggians of the Philippines: Eder 1988: 38; Dorall 1990: 43; for the Orang Asli/West Malaysia: Hood Salleh 1990: 147; for the Dayaks[3] of Sarawak: Hong 1987: 30–2).

The Lisu, Semai, Negrito and Dayak show a similar pattern of ecological adaptation despite their cultural diversity. Uniformities relating to their sources of livelihood are predominantly centred on a combination of subsistence activities (rice, cassava) in cleared forest areas and the hunting of game and gathering of jungle products. Cash-crop agriculture may involve a variety of grown commodities for sale. The 'native' economy has also exhibited century-long trading patterns with outside communities. A review of the relevant literature reveals, for the Semai of Peninsular Malaysia, that a cash economy has long been practised from the sale of jungle fruits and commercially grown crops (rubber, oil palm, cocoa), while increasing reliance on outside wage labour can be observed (Gomes 1990: 12–36). Among the various marginal groups of Sarawak (collectively called the Dayak) who are primarily swiddeners, foragers and hunters and traders of forest goods, new work arrangements have emerged within the context of logging jobs, town employment and the sale of cash crops (Hong 1987). For the mountain people of Thailand, among the so-called 'farmers in the forest', shifting cultivation (at times in conjunction with irrigated rice) has always been combined with cash cropping related to opium, maize and tea. Currently seasonal wage work is becoming increasingly noticeable (Kunstadter and Chapman 1978: 3–23). Irrigated rice terraces, swidden plots and a cash economy conducted through the sale of homegrown and forest produce are the main characteristics of the Philippine Negrito frontier societies, of the so-called Batak and Agta groups (Sajise 1989: 507–13).

For the last three decades or so, these communities have adapted to a diminishing forest environment, which necessitates continuous changes in the indigenous economy. In terms of an earlier division of labour for the sexes, the patterns indicate that the hunting of large game, the felling of trees and the collection of forest goods such as rattan are male activities. Women are basically concerned with weeding the swidden plots, the gathering of forest plants and the care of small domesticated animals. Within this setting of shifting cultivation, ideas on female and male status do not lend themselves to fixed definitions. The work distribution and its associated sex roles among the marginal groupings does not seem to imply that the male activities are imbued with power or more prestige on account of their involvement with tasks that are considered to be perilous or require greater physical strength.

Within an emic interpretative framework there is little inclination to evaluate labour according to criteria of economic remuneration or the power of decision-making. This was pointedly illustrated in a remark of a male Lisu elder when asked about the old days and whether there was a difference in esteem between female and male work. He replied: '. . . A Lisu man and woman worked the same, a man's work we did not say, a woman's work we did not say. The man did a little heavy work, he went out more, (but) no one had more . . .' (Klein-Hutheesing 1990: 134). Typical for the peripheral peasant economy is that female and male activities for a large number of studied cases appear to fit and fellow the general patterning towards egalitarianism as indicated by the absence of authoritarian leadership and strategies of individual exploitation or appropriation. In these marginal communities the swidden rice patches were operated under loosely defined principles of usufruct – the communal or lineage ownership of gongs, silver, trees – that did not imply a gender bias. On account of shifting cultivation practices (initially) on sufficient land, these peripheral groups have produced some noteworthy concerns regarding female and male value. Within the setting of the male as hunter and the female as cultivator, gender relations were viewed as complementary or in a state of balance. Such interpretations were based on various theoretical approaches and the choice of particular indicators, at times laced with romanticised notions on the part of the ethnographer.

Anthropological studies of the Thai hill tribes have so far exhibited little specific focus on the gender issue. In a few cases, the concern with sexual inequality has been folded into the larger analytical framework of cosmological constructs or kinship structures. Thus we read that gender among the Akha mountain dwellers is primarily perceived as a cultural elaboration, with symbolic assignments to gendered space in which the male appears to represent the higher, more powerful domain. Yet in the spiritual realm a complementarity of the sexes is observed. While referring to the area of sex roles greater significance is reserved for the male role as orator, as public debater; Akha women however are bestowed the ultimate cultural value as creators of life, and as elders function in the role of important initiators of the family's ancestral offerings. In doubt of the nature–culture, private–public dichotomy of gender an observation is made of female and male images as both reciprocally relational (Kammerer 1986: 308–63). A study among the Hmong hill people presents a sceptical review of their women's exclusion from valued rituals and their symbolic devaluation with regard to menstrual blood. Sexuality of the female which is both valued and feared, a powerful 'vessel in which souls of the lineage continue the cycle of life', demonstrates the ambiguity of the gender system in a cosmological and ideological sense (Symonds 1991: 159–60). Using another perspective, Cooper noted for the Hmong that although in the pre-opium economy the female and male were meted out equal respect as elders in ritual performances, this equality made way for a more manifest male superiority on account of their appropriation of women's labour towards the opium cash crop (Cooper 1984: 237). This finding of a decrease in women's economic power due to the introduction of the poppy economy is not borne out in another opium-cultivating tribe like the Lisu. On the contrary, the control of money during the long phase of this illicit cash crop was firmly placed in the hands of Lisu women, while both sexes were equally competent in performing rituals, though rituals directed to different spiritual universes (Klein-Hutheesing 1991: 14–16). Another twist to the findings regarding gender equality is provided in the example of the Yao mountain minority in Thailand. Here the analytical framework focuses on their descent units. Initially under the Chinese Han the Yao gave the males the right to transmit descent under a system of patrilineality.

Among the Yao swidden cultivators at the Thai border, however, bilaterality prevailed through commoditising the right of any spouse to reside (Miles 1990: 140–2). For another swidden population in the hills of Burma, Lehman noted that among the Chin an almost equal participation of the sexes existed in the agricultural field. Also, when considering the inheritance or exchange of prestige goods which are passed between the sexes, no clear division of female and male goods can be ascertained (Lehman 1963: 128–9).

Turning to the Negritos in West Malaysia, mention is made of a sexual division of labour in which women gather food, plant crops, collect rattan and construct wind shelters, while men hunt and clear the forests (Carey 1967: 80–5). No evaluation is however attempted of these activities: for instance how the commercial endeavours of the Negrito male relating to the sale of rattan, charms and medicinal herbs imply greater economic power for the male. It has also been suggested that older men have more prestige because they are involved in political decision-making processes, but little reference is made to who decides in which matters and in which context – outside or behind the scenes of the female wind shelter? Little social weight is also attached to the fact that both female and male own trees.

Data on the Iban longhouses in Sarawak show a broad consistency towards sexual equity when rights of residence and inheritance are taken into consideration. In the early 1950s Freeman concluded that the equal treatment of the sexes, also exemplified in the prestige allotted to female and male 'leaders' (*pun*), was the main operating principle of the longhouse social organisation. Inequality in work participation or in sharing of consumption goods does not seem to occur with a particular advantage to one sex (Freeman 1971: 15–52). Research of a more recent date (1981) on the Iban longhouse substantiates the traditional idea of gender balance, which is primarily demonstrated in the value attached to male warriorhood and female weaving activities, with each sex deserving respect in their own right. From the perspective of the control over social and ritual space, no incidence of male dominance can be discerned (Mashman 1987: 233–55).

Along the line of bilaterality the same rights for female and male are observed for the Gaddang Hill farmers in the Philippines, which coexist with a mutual respect for each other and the practice of joint decision-making (Wallace 1970: 42). Other non-Christian minorities in the Philippines are known who attach equal value to both female and male issue, as shown in the lack of a marked preference for boys, while inheritance is equally divided among children of both sexes. In the sphere of political decision-making, however, women's authority is seldom acknowledged (Infante 1969: 60, 61, 159). Among Filipino minority women like the Negritos, of whom the Agta are a subgroup, the female seems to exercise considerable influence in the sex act, but less in the settlement of disputes, though some may attain the position of headwoman (Rojas *et al.* 1978: 242–6). From anthropological fieldwork conducted on selected communities at the rim of Southeast Asian societies, certain inferences can be drawn that point in the direction of a fair treatment of the sexes with reference to customary rights and property.

Another distinguishing feature of the rim societies appears to be the cultural underpinning of status within the context of honour, prestige and respect, which however does not carry the connotation of one sex being more honoured than the other. An evaluation of differences in gender roles demonstrates an ideology where personhood or self follows different gender paths. Among the Lisu of Northern Thailand the achievement of each sex is evaluated by the respective tasks which the female and the male set out to do. These surface in metaphors of repute, which are different for men and women. In Lisu language, it cannot be known if female repute is higher or more valuable that male repute. Respect is meted out in equal fashion depending on the adherence to cultural norms – the male, as skilful hunter, the female, as industrious weeder in swidden areas, both having the potential to acquire prestige, except that the female should know more about shame in order to be honourable (Klein-Hutheesing 1990: 100).

In the ideological spheres of these marginal groups, hierarchies of deities, female witches, male demons and bisexual guardian spirits can be observed. Cosmological spheres are carved up along female and male principles, following gender-dualisms of sun–moon, East–West, up–down and light and dark (Benjamin 1979; Alting von Geusau 1985). Supernatural beings have their sex-linked preoccupations: female medicine or rice spirits, male thunder gods, joint lord and lady deities that oversee the land. Although these genderised cosmological realms carry a resemblance of hierarchy, with the male deity's 'soul stuff' being higher (in the sky) and bigger, this should not be associated with real-life dominance or subordination according to sex. The male spirits are imagined to be stronger and more potent; these beings, however, are not seen as the rulers of the spiritual universe, overpowering and suppressing enfeebled, female spiritual forces of the earth. One would have to conceive their religion as consisting of a constant flow of discourse and negotiation between the supernatural and the human world. Persons who communicate with the outside ethereal forces are often men who chant with special language expertise; but women have their own religious duties, to propitiate hearth and household spirits with soul-calling ceremonies, while female shamans or mediums are also known as communicators with the supernatural. In mythical representations the productive capacity of the female is invariably associated with rice fields.[4] Ceremonies centring on rice are focused on female officiants, at which 'the male praxis is marginal' (for the Temoq in Malaysia see: Laird 1984: 59–60). The symbolisation of the highest sky god as Big Mother/Big Father in the minds of the Sumba Islanders (Onvlee 1980: 47) and the greater superiority which is given to female-inside domains among the equations of the Tetum in Timor (Hicks 1984: 8) seem to belie the cosmologisation of male power as being the strongest. Moreover, inconsistencies of gender anthropormorphisms associated with water deities also appear to surface, as is shown in the case of the Torajas, where female lord crocodiles coexist with male river gods in the shape of gigantic eels (Nooy-Palm 1979: 116).

The people at the margins appear to live in fleeting universes, as they move their altars or designate auspicious spots. Their fluctuating worldviews are symbolic of malleable lineage structures and gender relations which are susceptible to redefinition. The worldly power of the village headman or the conventional council of elders is equally tenuous and temporal, as it can be easily disbanded (Harrison 1987). Though this type of decision-making is frequently placed in male hands, women have their input as well. Decisions are made as the situation arises. Thus within the supernatural, as well as in mundane political contexts, male spokesmen appear to be heard; but women speak their minds in other contexts (wedding negotiations, for instance). Each sex has its own contribution in the maintenance of the cosmological and social order, which oscillates between seeming hierarchy and a halfway fixity. Complementarity of activities between the sexes is not weighed nor measured; each gender provides a share depending on female and male time. This kind of swaying from female and male 'bigness' according to specific occasions has for the Akha mountain periphery of Thailand appropriately been phrased a 'shifting of gender asymmetries' (Kammerer 1988).

Fission of Gender at the Fringes (Four Cases)

Minority cultures have at times been portrayed as the original affluent societies, on account of their ideal farming economies, in which optimal game and favourable trading relationships prevailed. However, when modern affairs of state (conducted on the basis of a close relationship between bureaucracy and capitalism, often in cooperation with the military) invade, these idealised communities experience imbalances between the natural resources and population needs. As new grounds are opened up and lands under state supervision developed, the margins of Southeast Asia are drawn into commercialised farming areas. Ancestral hunting grounds are turned into estate enterprises with marketable commodities such as cocoa, coffee, corn, rubber and tea. Licences and leases are distributed to multinational companies. Roads are carved for timber extraction or used by army units, who destroy illegal crops (opium). Evacuation by force of tribal settlers from other margins (the Burmese Akha in Thailand for example) is also a phenomenon of the new polity. So pervasive is the presence of officials in the marginal hamlets that one member of a Thai mountain group remarked: 'In the old days we knew only two tribes who were our neighbours; nowadays there is a new tribe with different spirits: the government people.' Technology accelerates development with the help of bulldozers, electric saws and insecticides, which inevitably inflict material and social hardships on minorities. Under the name of progress, procedures become legalistically embroiled when land deeds, national registration cards and contracts are required. What are the implications of these intrusions on the gender constructs of marginal people?

Before answering this question, one should distinguish between different forms and levels of penetration into the ecology. It then becomes apparent that several adaptation responses exist, varying from an environmental, isolated niche to a social symbiosis. Applying this idea to the Philippines, Sajise noted that for a number of minorities, diverse coping strategies unfolded. Some stayed autonomous, using the natural environment for daily sustenance, while others had adopted commercial farming of vegetables. Adaptation to commercial farming has in turn transformed local institutions of leadership and organisation. Some communities have acquired legal ownership of land, while simultaneously regaining a base in the traditional structure of their natural economy (Sajise 1989). But, in general, where trade transactions have intensified without buffer mechanisms, the change from hunter–gatherer *cum* subsistence farmer to sedentary cultivator has resulted in lopsided exchanges for forest dwellers. A number of asymmetries have been noted, namely between upland minority and lowland majority, between ethnic groups and within the marginal group itself (for the Negrito of the Philippines see: Eder 1988: 37). There no longer seems to be any 'merit of the margin', on account of the unequal exchange relationships with the centre, which commands greater structural weight in terms of its formal and legal knowledge of land acquisition and development.

Similar conflicts are reported for Thailand and Malaysia when the fringe communities become incorporated into a larger state context via commercialised farming. Tensions of a political–ecological nature between lowlanders and highlanders and within the marginal groups themselves due to land use have been documented for the North-West of Thailand (Anan Ganjanapan 1987: 511). Many marginal areas of Malaysia show similar disquieting events in cases where rubber and oil palm estates are developed (Gomes 1990: 73–4; Colchester 1989: 55). Even when their crafts become evaluated in terms of money as amongst the Jah Hut of Western Malaysia, tensions develop in the sharing of the end product. (Couillard 1980: 85). The dramatic impact of logging companies (hand in hand with politicians) on the livelihood of the Penans of Sarawak is the most acute illustration of how bourgeois-state power can eliminate nature and the traditional livelihood of its people (World Rainforest Movement, SAM 1989).

Below an assessment will now be made of the scenarios which have unfolded with regard to the Lisu of Northern Thailand, the Semai of peninsular Malaysia, the Dayaks of East Malaysia and the Negritos (Agta) of the Philippines. Each study has elicited a different trajectory in terms of female and male activities, although the changes which have been noted all point towards gender fission between the sexes.

Lisu Gender and Crop Substitution Policy

One pattern is increasing gender differentiation, and this has been observed among the Lisu (Klein-Hutheesing 1990, Ch. VII). An ethnic minority of Thailand (consisting of 25,251 people in 1990), the Lisu have, since the beginning of this century, drifted towards the Thai and Burmese borders. While combining traditional swidden agriculture with hunting and gathering, they have for over a century also been growers and traders of opium. An intensive village study of the Lisu highlighted the fact that their money-economy was enacted in a vernacular environment, i.e. the local community of dispersed hamlets, where the sale of opium was carried out 'on their own turf'. Both female and male were equally proficient in the weighing and negotiating of the opium bundles with outside merchants, while cash was invariably controlled by the women. Besides the cash crop of opium, other crops were sown, such as maize, ginger, peppers and potatoes, whenever the price of opium was too low. Subsistence production was carried out, according to 'female and male soul capacity', in an interlocked fashion, without wondering what the weight of each task was in terms of prestige.

The Lisu work environment became completely transformed as a result of a more active government development policy based on the argument that they practised an inefficient method of cultivation (slash-and-burn agriculture) and that their opium involvement was detrimental to tribal welfare. Moreover, the homesteads of these immigrant populations were defined as security areas, rife with Communist infiltrators. Policies were primarily directed towards providing welfare and economic growth in stable environments, which would guarantee an identification with the Thai nation. Cash crops which would replace poppy planting were designed to broaden hilltribe employment and 'reorganise their lifestyles' (Bhruksasri 1989: 13–22). The slowness of the centralised bureaucracy in issuing landrights, together with the ignorance of suitable cash crops to substitute for opium, however, bred alienation and resentment among the tribal hill farmers (Vienne 1989: 54–5). The lack of any assistance from the authorities concerned to guide them towards modern agricultural production methods proved disastrous for the Lisu. The effects that the replacement of opium policy had on gender will be spelled out for the Lisu in particular in forthcoming sections. In general it can be stated that hill women in Thailand have remained less in touch with the modernisation trends of the lowlands and have not been able to contribute to self-development, the organisation of women's groups or income-generating projects (Panyacheewin 1990: 29). The concept implied in government policies places minority women in the supposed traditional corner of home-bound roles: a concept which underestimates the vital contribution of the Lisu female towards agriculture and trading in concert with the male.

The building of a road (for the military and the forestry agencies) and the introduction of identity and residence cards were other new events which affected the lives of the Lisu. Inequalities between the sexes became noticeable, in that fewer girls went outside to further their education, although equal numbers of boys and girls attended the village school. The big incursion into their socio-economic practices occurred when in the early 1980s opium eradication was enforced on a dramatic scale, and households had to search for a substitute cash crop. The first fissure between the sexes became apparent when the new crop of tomatoes had to be sold in lowland markets. The Lisu male, traditionally more liable to travel to foreign terrains, became a fulltime trader, which meant a greater control of cash. Consumption transferred into male hands. Other modernisation trends involved the introduction of a coffee plantation near the village grounds on which Lisu women were paid for their labour as weeders. Girls became dependants of the large-scale enterprise, while the elder females practised a kind of patchwork subsistence economy on diminished swidden and jungle land. Lisu men (young and old) having lost their hunting grounds turned into growers of commercial crops and independent traders. Their work roles detached themselves from the rice-growing swidden scene and jungle reliance, while land for subsistence became scarce, on account of land sales to the plantation and the greater need to convert land for the new cash crop. The earlier gender equilibrium became unhinged with the more frequent involvement of the Lisu male in the lowland markets. Gender conflicts arose about the sale and use of land, the pawning of silver (women's bridewealth), the growing heroin habit of the Lisu male, the taking of brides from other tribal communities or marriages of Lisu daughters to Thai men. The outcome of this double marginalisation process (economically and culturally) in terms of costs and benefits for the status of each gender is still too precarious to conceptualise. What can be ascertained, however, is that with the widening of outside dependent networks, the work-worlds of the Lisu female and male have become dissociated, and that new methods of economic control have frittered away the power base of women.

Spotty Development Tendencies among the Semai

The Semai of West Malaysia, who number 18,327, became firmly entrenched in national government policies after the Emergency (1948–1960) – policies which initially were aimed at protecting their economic and political interests and at a later stage included the provision of medical and educational facilities, in this resembling similar Thai policies towards minority people. The idea of national integration was the main motivation behind the government's approach, to deal with the security threat that the Semai posed. The development of the Orang Asli in general was based on an improvement of their living standards through modification of their agriculture and linking their incomes to a market economy. For the Semai this meant to be engaged in simple commodity production, where in principle they have access to their own means of production as 'wage labour equivalents', although the control of their land is under the jurisdiction of the State, and more specifically of the Office of Tribal Affairs, which regroups and allocates the lands. Intrusions from non-Semai into their original environment to appropriate its produce are frequently reported. The increasing dependency on a buyers' market which offers low prices has led to instances in which the Semai have returned to their traditional economy, moving deeper into their communal lands (Nicholas 1990: 70–80).

Within the context of government development ideology and business intrusions instances of recent gender segregation can be observed among the Semai, traditionally known for gender-shared decision-making activities (Dentan 1968: 68) in a relatively closed economy. The Semai are now engaged in cash crops, the collection of forest products and wage employment (Gomes 1991: 164). Commercialisation of economic activities relating to the sale of fruits, rubber and fish became a pronounced phenomenon in the 1980s. A diversified cash economy emerged, with part-time gathering of jungle produce and intermittent wage work. Dependence on fruit trees as a means of production has entailed an increasing specification of ownership rights of trees and control of land – more so than among the Lisu, who rely on a looser concept of land use. Though the idea of private property is gaining recognition among the Semai and is replacing their concept of communal and sibling rights, the old custom of bilaterality regardless of sex is still practised. It is clear that wives and sisters are given their share from the sale of fruits, despite the fact that the Semai male is spending more time on 'the production line' than the female (owing to the hazardous nature of the task of picking the fruits from tall trees). On the other hand, woman's autonomy is being threatened on account of the decline of the subsistence economy. An incipient sexual inequality, replacing an earlier flexible division of labour, may start to operate when land for subsistence needs diminishes, thereby jeopardising the Semai woman's economic position in their society. Outside employment of Semai men as officials in development schemes has encouraged women's retreat into activities of lesser value (house sitting), while waiting for their share of the commodity production sales. A report on a Semai community mentions increasing incidences of prostitution, carried out in the village or in a neighbouring township (Leong 1991: 37–8). Gender differentiation among the Semai is mostly apparent from the perspective of a dissimilar involvement in the commoditisation process, in which the female has lesser work input. But what differentiates them from the Lisu is that the latter have known a far longer history of cash-crop agriculture, while the Semai are still caught in networks of localised trading relationships with a heavy reliance on individual *tawkeys* (Chinese middle men). Male confrontation with big market centres (where spending becomes a major source of temptation) is thus less likely to happen with the Semai.

In sum, Semai involvement with small commodity production did not shortchange the female Semai and bilateral gender relations, while concepts of group ownership remained embedded in the social system.

The Onslaught on the Iban Longhouse Economy

The Iban of Sarawak, along with other minorities, are particularly affected by state policies over land development schemes. Native customary land rights are in this process being whittled away, owing to policies of commercialised agriculture, the lucrative timber industry and the construction of dams (Hong 1987: 60–3). The Iban ancestral land is being developed by means of opening up estates or plantations, with the effect that the hill farmers abandon their shifting cultivation practices and become liable to being resettled. They are made to become dependants, who no longer have a voice in the kind of crops that they will grow.

The cash crops of rubber, cocoa, and oil palm intended for resettled Iban smallholders undid their earlier subsistence economy, while the pattern of single-family homesteads proved incompatible with their traditional longhouse way of life. Growing poverty was noted on account of the fluctuations in world market prices. For those who became workers on the estates a new inequality could be observed, with higher pay rates for male workers in comparision with female (Survival International

1992: 85, 92).

This abrupt introduction of large-scale development programmes, monocrop plantations and gigantic logging enterprises has apparently created significant fissures in the communal and gender relations of Dayak groups (particularly reported among the longhouse Iban) in East Malaysia (Sarawak). The sexual equality of the Iban was embedded in a society which did not espouse a clear hierarchical structure (Freeman 1981). The Iban longhouse organisation and work patterns associated with rice swidden cultivation on dispersed plots in cleared forest areas was characterised by equal access to rights to land and its use, irrespective of sex. Each female and male contributed to the hunting–gathering and swidden process, while filiations to the longhouse room were practised on a very nearly 'equal incidence' of virilocal or uxorilocal principles (Freeman 1971: 47).

Certain observations made among the Iban indicate that individual profit has replaced the earlier concept of recycled communal wealth, a process which was primarily instigated by a marketing of surplus outside Iban villages (Colchester 1989: 45). With the increased emphasis on individual status generated by value systems of the dominant political economy, other re-evaluations of the gender system are taking place. References have been made to an erosion of Iban women's traditional egalitarian relationship with men, primarily on account of development agencies' policies, which paid compensation for land to male heads of households irrespective of historical concepts of joint ownership. Both female and male have become dependants as labourers/wage workers on resettlement schemes. It may be inferred, however, that the lack of autonomy is more deeply felt among Iban women, who in a symbolic as well as a realistic sense have lost their rice lands and their traditional activity of collecting jungle produce (Colchester 1989: 61). The failure of the new policies to secure a stable income has provided an impetus towards urban migration in search for jobs as labourers. According to one report a large number of Iban women have become prostitutes in a Sarawak town (Hong 1987: 200). Changes in the Iban cosmology, where gods and godesses coexisted and where the rice soul originated from a mythical grandmother, must inevitably evolve around an obliteration of the cosmic forces if rice rituals are no longer carried out or if the Iban become more susceptible to conversion to Christianity. The Iban woman as the prototypical female creator and the 'handler of rice seeds, the pace setter for its sowing, the opener of rice bins' in real life, and the Iban man as the follower of the agressive male god of warfare (Sutlive 1979:

73) will both tend to go their separate ways in a growing class context where everything is purchased and cash earnings become essential for survival.

The Agta (Negritos) of the Philippines: Commercialisation of Hunters–Gatherers

Yet another pattern of restructuring sex roles has been reported for the Negrito (the Agta) of the Philippines. As mountain dwellers they have known a history of internal migration and geographical mobility due to external trade relationships (Peterson 1977: 63). In this long-drawn-out process of colonisation via trade, in which deer meat and skins were exchanged for salt, sugar and rice and casual work on the farms of lowlanders ensured some money to purchase other durables, hunting and gathering activities eventually declined. The exchanges of game against carbohydrates between the Negritos and the peasants have in one instance been interpreted as advantageous to both groups involved. An interesting aspect of this type of trading pattern is the observation that it was carried out between two individuals who were 'not always male and married' (Peterson 1977: 68). The economic dependencies that were described as 'efficacious' and mutually beneficial to both highlanders and lowlanders, however, have also produced an increasing inequality, in which the Negrito becomes a victim of price-control by the dominant Filipino. One by-product of this exploitation is the growing indulgence of the mountain people in the acquisition of consumer goods, and a visible trend towards alcohol addiction among the males. According to Eder (1988: 45), the greed of multinationals, which results in land shortage, has led to a number of tensions between different parties and between the sexes. Gender conflict seems to be a concomitant of the commercialisation process, as husbands and wives become embroiled in arguments about the purchase of goods. An important observation is the more extensive time-periods spent by the Negrito to supply goods and collect payments, which can no longer be devoted to subsistence. If the growing involvement with lowland markets and administrative centres is more male-oriented, leading to a retreat of the female into subsistence activities, then this development could eventually spark off a further marginalisation of Negrito women and a loss of autonomy in the management of household cash. The Filipino Negrito female would then show a poignant similarity to her Lisu counterpart in the Thai hills.

An Overview of State Policies and Their Effect on Gender and Personhood

Besides instances of structural differentiation between the sexes, with their implications for a more lopsided distribution of economic power favouring the male, the four cases studied also refer (though sporadically) to the cultural repercussions of the closer contact with modern state policies and capitalist endeavours. National integration efforts that aim at incorporating the marginals into a mainstream of modernisation have led to a process of deculturation, illustrated among other things by a greater frequency of cross-cultural marriages and other cross-cultural heterosexual encounters. Though references are made in the four case studies to the general meaning of loss of culture in terms of customs and crafts, very little attention is given to the meaning of deculturation for the marginal female and male, nor to a differential evaluation of each gender from the vantage point of cultural selfhood as a value. One by-process of this adjustment to the values of the dominant society is that the various tribal marginals each lose their specific cultural identity and ethnic labels (see Eder 1988: 48 for the Filipino hunting–gathering groups). In several instances they are 'heaped together' under one name, not only censuswise but also in common parlance. Interestingly, the lowland Thai usually call the members of the six different hill tribes 'Meo', which for one thing is a derogatory word for the Hmong, and secondly also carries the connotation of referring to those marginals who, besides being successful in trade, are also rebellious trouble-makers. But in this 'heaping together' process, the degree of deculturation of each gender has seldom been a research focus. Increased trade with the outside has first affected the male relationships between minority and majority groups, in which the former become acquainted with processes of accounting (pawning, selling, cheques, receipts) and official language use. Foreign songs of the outside culture are being introduced by the marginal males into their own local culture more often. Besides the sale of goods, in which he acquires ideas of exchange value, he also becomes engaged in the flesh trade, developing an alien concept of sex for money. With the introduction of venereal diseases in the tribal settlements, the tendency can be noted of marginal women's blaming the outside women, thereby creating an animosity and unequalness, couched in ethnic terms, between the 'inside' and the 'outside' female.

There are no hard data to testify to this growing moral segregation of female honour and virtue among tribal and non-tribal women. I can only allude to remarks made during fieldwork among the Lisu, where the lowland Thai women were portrayed as shameful, customless, and 'like animals'. Philandering adulterous Lisu men who on the other hand had sex with women of their own kind could always expiate their 'sins' by arranging a forgiveness ceremony with offerings, while the female victim concerned and her child would be reintegrated in the community. Lisu women, who have invariably been described as 'powerful in custom' (Klein-Hutheesing 1990), are now fearful of losing that power together with their reproductive role when the men lose themselves to loose foreign women. In an ironic twist, the marginal female has been given the disparaging epithet of being 'bad and wild' when men from the dominant society want to practise illicit sex. In a material and moral sense she is branded as 'cheap'. The marginal male, in his greater exposure to a dominant society, may gain more from a detribalisation process in terms of a prestige evaluation which ultimately could lead to a further cultural split of the gender structure into unequal parts: i.e. a majority-acculturated tribal male versus his ethnically-minoritised and ethically degraded female counterpart.

Summary and Conclusions

As was mentioned before, the margins provide important 'laboratories' for testing the germination of power complexes under modern state influences. In communities at the edge of Southeast Asian societies, a clear differentiation of economic sex roles has become apparent; but whether this has led to a hierarchical differentiation of the 'male' and 'female' is unclear. New semantic indices of hierarchised differentiation have not emerged, although the observer might be tempted to provide his or her own personal reference-point of 'domesticity': the greater confinement of women to the home, owing to loss of cash earnings, as in the case of the Lisu.

It is speculated that as long as rice swiddening land can be allowed to go on and forest spaces can be left for women to carry out gathering and horticulture, female and male productivity may remain equal. This in turn encourages a continuity of gender bilaterality. Values which produce intersexual dependency and a reluctance to name either sex as 'superior' still remain for all groups. The impact of increasing competition and the loss of economic autonomy of each sex are still difficult to ascertain. With the increasing destruction of the environment the first to suffer with certainty is the male. A thinning of hunting grounds results in the loss of the male hunting role. This loss affects the male concept of honour and the male's prestigious position as distributor of game. Within the modern labour market, the male of the margins is the prime mover, ironically helping to destroy his natural work environment as a hired labourer or contract labourer. Male journeys into newly found 'development' work may be seen as an extension of an earlier role as wandering bachelor or hunter, except that this modern role implies greater dependency on alien agencies. Does this new exposure make them more domineering towards their women, with greater ability to subdue them? In encounters with the modern state authorities or big bosses the marginal male is the underdog: the first to be arrested for felling trees on his/her (customary) land, the first to be searched for illegal drugs, and the first to be imprisoned for having an unlicensed gun in his possession. His earlier prestigious role as hunter has become a liability. His alienation from local customs is more pervasive and intense compared with that of the female who has stayed back in the interior. The man's entitlement to land deeds and national identity cards does not bear much fruit if there is little land or if excessive bribes are required to process official documents. His diminished position in society and greater exposure to the outside state may be more harmful than the changes facing the marginal female, who continues to maintain some form of subsistence swidden environment. Her involvement with the market economy is closer to home when it concerns local sales of forest produce (rattan, medicinal herbs, grasses for brooms) or the bartering of small livestock.[5] Though wages on nearby estates are lower for women (because of job descriptions according to 'light' and 'heavy' work and the reservation of lighter work for women), they are at least more often assured of receiving wages. Male work tends to be more transitory or seasonal (building a road, cutting jungle growth, picking durians or transporting oil-palm fruits). But once the commercialised activities of the city impinge upon the younger female of the margins she becomes a more permanent victim of the power of the male majority population. One example of this is the path to prostitution (see Hong 1987: 209). She becomes exploited by male brothel owners, who scan the fringe areas for the supposedly more exotic sexual pleasures that the 'tribal' female can provide. Marginal women also become victims of rape by lowland Thai soldiers who raid their villages in search of opium.

The breaking-point of sexual equality is when female and male prestige systems undergo a mutation of meaning. It is when the males have access to consumer goods markets and class-associated symbols that male honour becomes a more pervasive symbol of power than female honour. The power of possession may make men more powerful than the females, who become seemingly more illiterate as they fail to acquire the language and symbols of industrialised modernity. Although the changes in acquisition are not overtly demonstrated, male encounters with the modern centre are growing, and they could ultimately be resocialised into understanding power as access to goods and services. Gender differentiation may be articulated in different ways, such as the awareness of women as a precious resource (Karim 1993: 189) or in terms of the loss of women to outside men, or of access to and participation in technological production, or of the acquisition of symbols of class and mobility generated from the 'centre'. However, these changes only have implications for new meanings of 'power'.

Notes

1. The ethnography on the Mnong Gar Montagnards of Vietnam by Condominas shows for instance a preference for detailed descriptions of male activities (also exhibited in the larger number of photographs of men). No doubt buffalo sacrifices executed by the male represent more spectacular aspects of culture in comparison with the weaving of blankets and preparation of beer done by the female, but the functional importance of the women's work on which these feasts of prestige depend ought to deserve greater focus. The impression is given that Mnong Gar men 'eat the forest' for livelihood; it is the women, however, who consume its soil'. See Condominas, Georges, '*We have Eaten the Forest*': The Story of a Montagnard Village in the central highlands of Vietnam (English translation, 1977).
2. I follow here the designation of 'marginal' for the groups in question in accordance with Swift who preferred its use over and above such concepts as 'indigenous, minority, tribal' (Swift 1978: 3, 4).
3. The Dayak people comprise a number of ethnic groups in Sarawak, of which the Iban constitute the largest group. With a total population amounting to about 44 per cent of the State they numerically could not be termed marginal. However, within the larger political framework of Malaysia and an economic peripheralisation in view of the exploitation of their resources, a large number could be defined as marginal. The materials in this paper particularly refer to those Dayaks who live in the interior, along rivers, and who have also been referred to as Land Dayaks.
4. In a listing of divinities worshipped by the mountain people of Vietnam a telling slip was made regarding the deity who rules the paddy. *Yang Sori* was mistranslated as 'God' of the rice field, whereas in the explanatory text 'he' was referred to as 'her': 'the Montagnards praise her' (Mole 1970: 22–3).

5. An earlier exchange pattern of forest products like rattan against commodities or cash among the Temiar of West Malaysia demonstrates a balanced gender involvement. The latter tends to be disrupted when households move to settlements near oil-palm estates on which Temiar men predominantly are employed, resulting in incomes which are considerably lower than those collected during the trading of rattan. See Amir Haidi Bin Samion, 'Pengaruh Kapitalisme terhadap Perkembangan Masyarakat Orang Asli di Perak'. Unpublished Academic Exercise, Universiti Sains Malaysia, Penang (1991).

Bibliography

Alting von Geusau, L. (1985). 'The Dialectics of Akha *Zang*: Interiorizations of a perennial Minority Group'. In John McKinnon and Wanat Bhruksasri (eds), *Highlanders of Thailand*. Kuala Lumpur: Oxford University Press, pp. 241–78.

Anan Ganjanapan (1987). 'Conflicting Patterns of Land Tenure among Ethnic Groups in the Highlands of Northern Thailand: The Impact of State and Market Intervention. In *Proceedings of the Third International Conference on Thai Studies*, ANU, Canberra, 3 – 6 July, pp. 505–11.

Benjamin, G. (1979). 'Indigenous Religious Systems of the Malay Peninsula'. In A. Becker (ed.), *The Imagination of Reality*. Norwood, New Jersey: Ablex, pp. 9–27.

Bhruksasri, W. (1989). 'Government Policy: Highland Ethnic Minorities'. In J. McKinnon and B. Vienne (eds), *Hill Tribes Today. Problems in Change*, pp. 5–33. Bangkok: White Lotus-Orstom.

Carey, I. (1976). *Orang Asli. The Aboriginal Tribes of Peninsular Malaysia*. Kuala Lumpur: Oxford University Press.

Colchester, M. (1989). 'Pirates, Squatters and Poachers. The Political Ecology of Dispossession of the Native Peoples of Sarawak'. London and Petaling Jaya: Survival International Report in Association with INSAN.

Condominas, G. (1977). *We have eaten the Forest. The story of a Montagnard Village in the Central Highlands of Vietnam*. New York: Hill and Wang.

Cooper, R. (1984). *Resource Scarcity and the Hmong Response*. Singapore: Singapore University Press.

Couillard, M. A. (1980). *Tradition in Tension. Carving in a Jah Hut Community*. Penang: Universiti Sains Malaysia Press.

——— (1989). 'The Pangs and Pitfalls of Development for Malay Women: From the Rule of the Domestic Sphere to its Downfall'. *Kajian Malaysia*, Vol. 8, No. 2, pp. 68–92.

Dentan, R. (1968). *The Semai: A Nonviolent People of Malaya*. New York: Holt, Rinehart and Winston.

Dorall, R. F. (1990). 'The Dialectic of Development: Tribal Responses to Development Capital in the Cordillera Central, Northern Luzon, Philippines'. In Lim Teck Chee and A. G. Gomes (eds), *Tribal Peoples and Development in Southeast Asia*. Kuala Lumpur: University of Malaya, pp. 37–68.

Eder, J. (1988). 'Hunter–gatherer/Farmer Exchange in the Philippines, Some Implications for Ethnic Identity and Adaptive Well-being'. In T. Rambo *et al.* (eds), *Ethnic Diversity and the Control of Natural Resources in Southeast Asia*, Michigan Papers on South and Southeast Asia, No. 32. Ann Arbor: University of Michigan in cooperation with E. W. Center, Environmental and Policy Institute, Honolulu, Hawai.

Freeman, D. (1971). 'The Family System of the Iban of Borneo'. In J. Goody (ed.), *The Developmental Cycle in Domestic Groups*, pp. 15–52. Cambridge: Cambridge University Press.

—— (1981). *Some Reflections on the Nature of Iban Society*, Occasional Paper. ANU, Canberra: Dept. of Anthropology, Research School of Pacific Studies, ANU.

Gall, P. L. (1977). 'Temuan Socio-economic Exchange: An Ecological Model'. In W. Wood, (ed.), *Cultural Ecological Perspectives in Southeast Asia*, pp. 102–12. Athens: Ohio University.

Gomes, A. G. (1990). 'Confrontation and Continuity: Simple Commodity Production among the Orang Asli'. In Lim Teck Ghee and Alberto G. Gomes (eds), *Tribal Peoples and Development in Southeast Asia*. Kuala Lumpur: University of Malaya.

—— (1991). 'Commodification and Social Relations among the Semai of Malaysia'. In N. Peterson and Toshio Matsuyama (eds). *Cash Commoditisation and Changing Foragers*, National Museum of Ethnology, Osaka, Japan.

Harrison, R. (1979). 'Where have all the Rituals gone? Ritual Presence among the Ranau Dusun of Sabah, Malaysia'. In A. Becker (ed.), *The Imagination of Reality*, pp. 55–73. Norwood, New Jersey: Ablex.

Hicks, D. (1984). *A Maternal Religion: The Role of Women in Tetum Myth and Ritual*, Monograph Series on Southeast Asia, Special Report, No. 22. DeKalb: Northern Illinois University.

Hong, E. (1987). *Natives of Sarawak. Survival in Borneo's Vanishing Forests*. Penang: Institut Masyarakat.

Hood Salleh (1990). 'Orang Asli of Malaysia: An Overview of Recent Development Policy and its Impact'. In Lim Teck Ghee and Alberto G. Gomes (eds), pp. 141–9. Kuala Lumpur: University of Malaya.

Infante, T. (1969). 'The Women in Early Philippines and among the Cultural Minorities'. Manila: University of Santo Thomas.

Kammerer, C. (1986). Gateway to the Akha World: Kinship, Ritual and Community among Highlanders of Thailand, Ph.D. thesis, University of Chicago, Illinois.

—— (1988). 'Shifting Gender Asymmetries among Akha of Northern Thailand'. In N. Eberhardt (ed.), *Gender, Power and the Construction of the Moral Order: Studies from the Thai Periphery*, University of Wisconsin, Center for Southeast Asian Studies, Monograph. Madison: Wisconsin University Press, pp 33–53.

Karim, W. J. (1993). 'With Moyang Melur in Carey Island: More Endangered, More Engendered'. In D. Bell, P. Caplan and W. J. Karim (eds), *Gendered*

Fields. Women, Men and Ethnography. London: Routledge.

Klein-Hutheesing, O. (1990). *Emerging Sexual Inequality among the Lisu of Northern Thailand. The Waning of Dog and Elephant Repute.* Brill: Leiden.

—— (1991). 'Strategies of the Lisu in the Ordering of Spiritual Universes'. In *Spirit Cults and Popular Knowledge in Southeast Asia,* 15th International Symposium, National Museum of Ethnology, November 1991, Osaka, Japan (in press).

Kunstadter, P. and Chapman, E. C. (1978). *Problems of Shifting Cultivation and Economic Development.* In P. Kunstadter, E.C. Chapman and Sanga Sabhasri (eds), *Farmers in the Forest.* Honolulu: University Press of Hawaii.

Laird, P. (1984). 'Ritual, Territory and Region: the Temoq of Pahang, West Malaysia'. In B. Kapferer (ed.), *The Power of Ritual: Transition, Transformation and Transcendence in Ritual Practice, Special Issue, Social Analysis,* pp. 54–81. Adelaide: Dept. of Anthropology, University of Adelaide.

Lehman, F. K. (1963). 'The Structure of Chin Society. A Tribal People of Burma Adapted to a Non-Western Civilization', Illinois Studies in Anthropology, No. 3. Urbana: University of Illinois Press.

Leong, R. (1991). 'Kesan Modenisasi ke atas Masyarakat Orang Asli Semai di sebuah Perkampungan di Perak Selatan'. Academic Exercise. Penang: Universiti Sains Malaysia.

Mashman, V. (1987). 'Warriors and Weavers: A Study of Gender Relations among the Iban of Sarawak'. In V. Sutlive (ed.), *Female and Male in Borneo. Contributions and Challenges to Gender Studies,* The Borneo Research Council Monograph Series. Vol. I. Williamsburg: Dept. of Anthropology, The College of William and Mary in Virginia, USA, pp. 23–271.

Maznah, Mohamad (1982). 'Status of Rural Women in Relation to Labour and State Modernization Processes', Kanita Paper. Penang: Universiti Sains Malaysia.

Miles, D. (1990). 'Capitalism and the Structure of Yao Descent Units in China and Thailand: A Comparison of Youling (1983) and Pulangka (1968)'. In G. Wijeyewardene (ed.), *Ethnic Groups across National Boundaries in Mainland Southeast Asia.* Singapore: Institute of Southeast Asian Studies.

Mole, R. (1970). 'The Montagnards of South Vietnam. A Study of Nine Tribes'. Tokyo: Charles E. Tuttle.

Nicholas, C. (1990). 'In the Name of the Semai?. The State and Semai Society in Peninsular Malaysia'. In Lim Teck Ghee and Alberto Gomes (eds), *Tribal Peoples and Development in Southeast Asia.* Kuala Lumpur: University of Malaya, pp. 68–89.

Nooy-Palm, H. (1979). 'The Sa'Dan-Toraja. A Study of their Social Life and Religion'. *Verhandelingen van het koninklijk Instituut voor Taal-, Land-, en volkenkunde.* The Hague: Martinus Nijhoff.

Ong, A. (1989). 'Gender, Periphery, and Hierarchy: Gender in Southeast Asia.' In S. Morgan (ed.) *Gender and Anthropology: Critical Reviews for Research and Teaching.* Washington D.C.: American Anthropological Association, pp.

294–312. Kanita Research Programme, Penang 12–15 Dec.

Onvlee, L. (1980). 'Mannelijk en Vrouwelijk in de sociale Organizatie van Soemba'. In R. Schefold *et al.* (eds), *Man, Meaning and History. Essays in honour of H. G. Schulte Northolt. Verhandelingen van het koninklijk Instituut voor Taal-, Land-, en volkenkunde.* The Hague: Martinus Nijhoff.

Panyacheewin, S. (1990). 'Hard Lesson in the Hills. Learning How to Help Hilltribe Women Help Themselves'. *Bangkok Post*, 7 June 1990, p. 29.

Peterson, T. J. (1977). 'Merits of Margins'. In W. Wood (ed.), *Cultural Ecological Perspectives in Southeast Asia.* Athens: Ohio University, pp. 63–73.

Radley, H. (1986). 'Economic Marginalization and Ethnic Consciousness of the Green Hmong (Moob Ntsuab) of North Western Thailand', Ph.D thesis, Oxford University.

Rojas, I. A. T. E. C. (1978). *A Profile of Filipino Women.* Manila: Philippine Business for Social Progress.

Sajise, P. (1989). 'Culture and Environment in the Philippines. Some Perspectives', Paper for *Symposium: Culture and Environment in Thailand.* Bangkok: The Siam Society, pp. 507–13.

Survival International (1992). 'Plantation Failure, Dissent and Repression'. In INSAN *et al.*, *Logging against the Natives of Sarawak*, 2nd edn. Kuala Lumpur: INSAN, The Institute of Social Analysis, Vinlin Press.

Sutlive, V. H. (1979). 'Iban Folk Literature and Socialization: The Fertility of Symbolism'. In A. Becker (ed.), *The Imagination of Reality.* Norwood, New Jersey: Ablex, pp. 105–23.

Swift, J. (1978). 'Societies at the Frontier: Vulnerable Peoples in Asia and the Arctic'. *Development and Change*, 1978, 9:1, 3–21.

Symonds, P. (1991). 'Cosmology and the Cycle of Life: Among Views of Birth, Death and Gender in a Mountain Village in Northern Thailand', Ph.D. thesis, Brown University, Rhode Island.

Tapp, N. (1990). 'Squatters and Refugees: Development and the Hmong'. In G. Wijeyewardene (ed.), *Ethnic Groups across National Boundaries in Mainland Southeast Asia.* Singapore: Institute of Southeast Asian Studies, pp. 149–73.

Vienne, B. (1989). 'Facing Development in the Highlands: A Challenge for Thai Society'. In J. Mackinnon and B. Vienne (eds), *Hill Tribes Today: Problems in Change.* Bangkok: White Lotus-Orstom, pp. 33–61.

Wallace, B. J. (1970). *Hill and Valley Farmers. Socio-Economic Change among a Philippine People.* Cambridge, Mass.: Schenkman.

Winzeler, R. (1974). 'Sex Role Equality, Wet Rice Cultivation and the State in Southeast Asia'. *American Anthropologist*, 76: 563–9.

—— (1982). 'Sexual Status in Southeast Asia: Comparative Perspectives on Women, Agriculture and Political Organization'. In P. Van Esterik (ed.), *Women of Southeast Asia*, Center for Southeast Asian Studies, Occasional Paper No. 9. DeKalb: Northern Illinois University.

World Rainforest Movement, Sahabat Alam Malaysia (1989). *The Battle for Sarawak's Forests.* Penang: World Rainforest Movement.

PART II

Ethnography and Culture

4

Modern Malay Women and the Message of the 'Veil'

Judith Nagata

Orientalism, Feminism and Islam: The Need for a Reciprocal Dialogue

The intellectual challenge thrown down by Edwards Said in his now legendary volume *Orientalism* (1979) was sufficiently provocative to cause a number of stereotypes and assumptions to be re-examined in a new light. Some Western scholars have gone so far as to take up the gauntlet and run in new academic directions (for example, Inden's approach to Indian history (1986)), while others have now circumspectly tried to incorporate his lessons in their construction of the 'other'. For many anthropologists too, to whose profession the problem of representation of 'other' has long been central, the last decade (the 1980s) has unquestionably seen a renewed sensitivity to the potential political implications of the powers of metaphor, style and genre in communication across cultures (cf. Marcus and Fisher 1986).

Carried to its logical extreme, however, the *angst* of possible misrepresentation can lead to an abandonment of any attempt to find an ultimate truth or reality, acceptable to a universal audience. It can also lead to a proliferation of multiple cultural narratives, each speaking only to its own particularistic audience, or finally, to complete academic immobilisation, in which it becomes impossible or politically unacceptable to presume to speak for, or on behalf of, an 'other' in any language. Such a deadlock is of course implicit in the basic paradox hitherto not always fully appreciated in scholarly communities, namely that the very fact and act of social science are Western constructs, albeit often appropriated by non-Western practitioners using Western languages, who purvey these ideas as a universalistic science and body of knowledge.

The situation becomes uncomfortable when the 'other' (for example, the non-Westerner) rejects the established concepts and framework and 'conventional wisdom', and, on grounds of discrimination or mis-representation, speaks out and back, as did Said the disaffected Palestinian. The question of reciprocity in scholarly discourse was never fully resolved by Said, although it seems to suggest directions worthy of further exploration in forms of intellectual cooperation between Westerners and non-Westerners. Western-trained scholars in anthropology can then draw on its tradition of cultural critique and engage in a fruitful discourse, even a productive debate, in which subject/object distinctions are less discretely opposed. Here, the focus would be on a more promising and sustained interaction and dialogue (personal or textual) between Asian and non-Asian, and the sharing and comparing of concepts from both traditions, as has been attempted in the subaltern histories of India (for example, Prakash 1990). In this context the original orientalist 'knowledge and information as power' differential would thereby be removed under mutual critical scrutiny. However, this does not solve the problem of the power difference between the field anthropologist and the object of 'study'. The anthropological enterprise can only go forward, therefore, when it is sensitive to the meanings, metaphors and languages of its target populations, attempting to draw them into reflective dialogues and exchanges of ideas, which may eventually detach researchers from cherished formulae and categories built into their discipline.

In this frame, the rise of feminist literature and ideology has had a mixed reputation. In a zeal to discover, represent and even plead a case for certain universals in the female condition, much attention has been directed towards the subordination and exploitation of women as a generic, global 'fact' in a positivistic sense. This has sometimes been done at the expense of losing sight of the differences in women's situation in particular cultures, and feminist debates have continued to replay some of the same issues rehearsed since the days of Mead. Feminists (especially such Marxist feminists as Gough and Reiter), striving to dissolve social boundaries (between oriental, occidental or other), have tended to portray stereotypes in a manner reminiscent of the orientalist framing of the world, without allowing for equal and reciprocal dialogue in each case.

More recently, however, many feminist anthropologists have redis-covered the spirit of their discipline, applying their cultural awareness and communicative skills to recognise and represent 'other' women in their own terms and to enter into a meaningful exchange of problems and ideas. Among the methodologies appropriate in such interactional approaches are biographies, life-histories and other extended case studies capable of reflecting a quality of communication confounding easy stereotypes or cross-cultural universals.

It is proposed here to reflect once more on some aspects of the impact and expression of the recent *dakwah* movement on Malay women in Malaysia. In what follows, I attempt to avoid a culture-bound and often dogmatically naïve kind of Western feminist reaction aroused in connection with women's place in fundamentalist religious movements generally, especially in Islam (but also in Hinduism, Orthodox Judaism and fundamentalist Christianity). Some of the rhetoric displays a less than adequate understanding of the wider social frame into which certain behaviours fit. The representation of such highly visible behaviours as style of dress, resistance to certain types of career or to Western patterns of gender relations in public by such terms as 'retreating behind the veil', 'losing opportunities', 'moving backwards' or 'regressing', 'being anti-modern' and so on, is both provocative and prejudges the situation. Attitudes to and about gender roles and other ideas about 'liberation' are but arbitrary elements of a Western package of feminism. Such views also perpetuate an artificial opposition between 'traditional' and 'modern', together with their accompanying value judgments, and convey a sense of a reversal of the 'normal' ideals of progress (cf. Pastner 1978; Sayigh 1981), in which modernity is seemingly rejected.

Such apparent perversity may be perceived by some Marxist feminists as analogous to the situation depicted in Marx's *Eighteenth Brumaire*, wherein the unknowing victims (French peasants) have yet to arrive at a full consciousness of their oppressed condition, candidates for an enlightenment they have failed to recognise, even in their own apparent self-interest. An assumption that women themselves are incapable of perceiving their own interest within their personal, social and cultural milieu is therefore somewhat presumptuous. To avoid this brand of cultural hegemony in the form of Western 'scientific' analysis there must be a niche for more than one kind of feminism, allowing for culturally appropriate interpretations, and informed by the views of the subjects themselves, thus becoming the product of an interactive exercise. The material which follows is all drawn from extensive personal interaction by the author in the 'field' in Malaysia, and from an exchange of ideas between the anthropologist and many Malay Muslim women, rural and urban, conducted in the Malay language.

Finally, attention must be drawn to the often neglected fact that gender is not an undifferentiated category *sui generis*. Womanhood in any society and culture is also inextricably attached to other constituencies of class, status, age, generation, occupation, residence and ethnicity, any of which may modify the basic gender role substantially. It is thus crucial to unravel how the above are reflected in cultural meanings and ideals in Malay-Muslim society, as elements in female identity. Given this internal variability, it should not be expected that any perfect consensus about women's roles, ideal or actual, will exist even within a single society, and this appears to include also the Malay case.

Muslim Resurgence in Malaysia

The recent religious revival in many parts of the Muslim world, including Malaysia, has caught the attention of Western media and observers. In particular, the image of the 'oppressed' Muslim women has taken on a new and perplexing cast, particularly for the apparent voluntariness of women's participation in veiling and other highly visible religious activities, which seem to reduce their educational, career and other opportunities. The apparent contradiction in the fact that many of these much-publicised 'veiled' women, whether in Egypt or Malaysia, are also often prominent in the middle class seems to escape the attention of many outside commentators. They are highly-educated, and foreign-exposed, and actively involved in their career development. Rather than being passive, they are usually articulate about their own motives in pursuing a religious world-view and lifestyle.[1]

In Malaysia, the strongest manifestation of voluntary veiling and commitment to Islamic values and lifestyle has occurred within that cohort of women who underwent their secondary and/or tertiary education between 1970 and the mid-1980s, and whose principal social networks revolved around educational and professional institutions, both in Malaysia and overseas. For the pre-1970 generation of Malay women, by contrast, their most formative years coincided with a society still very much influenced by the spirit of colonialism and Western modernity. Their support groups and social networks were formed well before the take-off of the *dakwah* movement, and some of the urban women had already embarked upon successful careers as secretaries, teachers, clerks and so on, or else had become politically active in the then *Kaum Ibu* (Wanita UMNO) (cf. Manderson 1980), or in other voluntary associations. Such women had few reservations about public involvement and exposure, especially after marriage. They managed to balance the requirements of their domestic and public lives. The duties of the latter were performed in a suitably modest Malay style, often in separate cohorts parallel to, but not in direct competition with, their male colleagues.

For most of these women, Islam was just one part of a composite Malay identity, complementing Malay ideals of femininity without dominating them, and without creating undue anxiety as to their identity as females or their position *vis-à-vis* men. The preferred attire was usually a *batik sarung* and *kebaya* (closely fitted blouse) with a loose headscarf (*selendang*), or sometimes Western dress. These were the women who subsequently found it most difficult to accept the more extreme forms of *dakwah* and strictures on dress and public entertainment which developed later.

A feeling for the sentiments of this cohort can be inferred from events at the 1975 annual meeting of the *Pertubuhan Kebajikan Perempuan Islam* in Kuala Lumpur. At a time when their younger sisters were immersed in the full swing of the *dakwah* movement at school and in university or college, the older women were prepared to question publicly some of the more extreme dress styles being adopted in these institutions, which they found excessive. As a result, some of the more conservative *ulama* attending the conference responded by challenging the women delegates to demonstrate their commitment to Islam by appearing on the third and final day of the conference in a *selendang* in keeping with the spirit of the times. However, most of the delegates disagreed and were prepared to resist, and when, on the final day, no one had made any adjustment in her attire, one even declared that she would not 'go to hell for not wearing a *kain selendang*'. She even went on to intimate that women had many more important concerns, having to do with divorce, alimony and status as second wives, to be resolved (*Utusan Malaysia* 22/3/75).

Meanwhile rural women of this era continued to express their religiosity in the traditionally tolerant Malay style, with its unique blend of *adat* and Islam (see Karim 1992). The personal exposure entailed in open, outdoor peasant life, and the bilateral orientation of the kinship system with tendencies towards uxorilocality and easy divorce, imposed few limitations on public activities and appearances within accepted bounds of Malay propriety (*budi bahasa*). In contrast with the youthful *dakwah* followers, visible religiosity is greater in the older members of the senior generations, part of a life process of social–religious maturation and progression, culminating ideally in the pilgrimage (*haj*) and possible retirement in the *pondok* school of some locally revered religious teacher or *Tok Guru*.

A new generation of Malay women arose out of the confluence of events, internal and external, that charted new directions for Malaysia after independence. The country's most serious ethnic conflicts to date, in 1969, coincided with the emerging political ascendancy and economic power of the Middle East and the new assertiveness of Islam.[2] At home, the NEP (New Economic Policy) conferred upon young Malays of both genders, who had never known colonialism, an array of substantial and new educational occupational and political opportunities.[3]

For the first time, girls from the village were entering boarding schools and institutions of higher learning in considerable numbers, both in urban Malaysian centres and overseas. Malays of the NEP generation were schooled to litanies of 'uplifting their race', and providing the appropriate educational resources to vindicate themselves *vis-à-vis* their non-Malay compatriots. For this pioneering cohort of Malay students and intellectuals of the 1960s and 1970s, the Malay language was the symbol around which they rallied; but this was soon to be replaced by an even more potent symbol, that of religion. Its particular potency arose from its capacity to link Malay youth to a more universal, transnational religious community (*ummah*), which at the time was itself undergoing a period of ferment and renewal. Participation in international Islamic networks and activities gave Malays a new sense of their own identity in a global perspective, which, when transplanted back into the parochial (Malaysian) context, carried with it a more spirited sense of ethnic confidence, but also separateness from the local non-Muslim communities. Several new religious movements, collectively known as *dakwah*, such as Angkatan Belia Islam Malaysia (ABIM),[4] Darul Arqam and Tabligh, blossomed during the decade of the 1970s, and it is probably not irreverent to suggest that some of the leaders of these associations, particularly ABIM's Anwar Ibrahim, became the romantic heroes of the younger generation, replacing Western pop stars and idols.

At this point, the academically mobile young Malays, being groomed for roles and occupations for which they had no models or precedents, in a technocratic and secular world obsessed with Western ideas of 'progress', were faced with conflicting messages. The technocratic ideologies of modernity were challenged by the growing acceptance of a newly discovered 'older' identity more deeply rooted in the larger Islamic community, and this inspired Malays to review their recent history under colonialism and to create a new vision of their place and purpose in life, within and beyond Malaysia.

Educated young women, in particular, were caught in uncertainties as to acceptable behaviour between these two worlds, and increasingly uncomfortable and intimidated by what they often perceived as the 'excesses' of strident Western feminism. Having experimented with parties, movies, jeans and miniskirts, they saw in Islam a clear and unambiguous set of rules. Adherence to these, moreover, helped to vindicate their reputations as females in public places, especially in the eyes of young men and potential marriage partners.

The Message of the 'Veil'

Among women dress is one of the most powerful images and symbols of identity, conveying messages at many levels, conscious and subliminal. Highly visible, it can also be superficial or misleading in its message, obscuring a multitude of subtle cues, as well as the body. In a very literal sense, clothing is a cover for a plurality of possible motives and intentions, and has no necessary or predictable connection with actual behaviour or beliefs, as commonly assumed *a priori* by non-Muslim outsiders. For the general public in Malaysia and overseas, a connection between women's attire and *dakwah* participation is entrenched to the point that assumptions as to personal behaviour and religiosity are often based on it alone. However, the donning of the so-called *dakwah* style of dress, in Malaysia, may be subject to more than one interpretation. This attire, or *tudung* as it is known in contemporary Malaysian circles, usually involves a loose-fitting two-piece Malay dress (*baju kurung*), together with a shoulder-length head-covering resembling a nun's wimple (*mini-telekung*), or a voluminous headscarf, and sometimes a more extensive face veil (*purdah*), and even gloves and ankle-covering or socks. Frequently, adoption of the *tudung* style is the end-product of a graduated series of steps, representing events and decisions in a woman's personal, social and spiritual career, as responses to specific life crises or under certain social pressures. Outwardly, these are marked by increasing degrees of concealment or moves in the direction of modesty: from *sarung* and *kebaya* to *baju kurung*; from scarf to *selendang* or *mini-telekung* or *purdah*.

In the school and university environments where so many of these 'veiled' women are found, the commonest crises revolve around health problems and the cycle of examinations and academic achievement. Many women will make a vow (*niat*) to the effect that if they are successful in these goals they will be more observant in matters of dress, as a way of showing their thanks to God (*syukur kepada Allah*), and ultimately of dedicating their work and services to God, and as a test necessary for further success. It may appear as if such connections, directed towards specific goals, are essentially instrumental. The act of changing one's attire is either a means of achieving certain ends, a form of meritorious behaviour to be rewarded, or an expression of gratitude once achieved.

However, such reactions to crisis situations also require the appropriate mediating environment and social support groups, where sensitivity to the practices, attitudes and popular discourse of friends and colleagues help to shape the form of the response. In the intensity and initimacy of cloistered dormitories, women encourage each other to make verbal declarations of their vows and intentions, so that reneging is difficult, but going forward is socially rewarded. One of the most severe sanctions against signs of recidivism is the accusation of apostasy (*murtad*) or of being an unbeliever (*kafir*); but it is also a betrayal of friendship. Within these networks, the effective action takes place within small solidary groups (*usrah*) of from six to twelve women, whose constant presence and interaction, in residence, class and recreation, in the intimacy of ablutions for pre-dawn prayers, adjusting each others' hair and veils, reinforces a commitment once given voice. One effect of such intense interaction is that certain phrases of explanation and vindication are repeated like a refrain: 'for the sake of God' (*kerana Allah*); 'we who love Islam are returning to God' (*kita pencinta-cinta Islam, kita kembali mengingat Allah*); 'we are more conscious . . . to show that we are moral, right-minded and disciplined' (*kita lebih sedar . . . menonjolkan akhlak yang mulia dan berdisiplin'*); 'we are an example to society' (*contoh kepada masyarakat*).

Yet all of these women are swift to deny any suggestion that they are in any way under pressure. All claim that theirs is an individual decision (*secara individu*), and that dress behaviour is a matter of personality (*cara berpakaian dan berkelakuan, itulah personaliti*), without the influence of anyone (*saya melakukan tindakan ini bukan kerana pengaruh dari mana-mana pihak*), thus retaining a sense of their own personal and intellectual rationality and integrity.

Women wearing the *tudung* are also aware that, in the eyes of some observers, they are labelled as '*Orang dakwah*', which is popularly synonymous with 'narrow-minded, fanatical, orthodox' (*berfikiran sempit, fanatik, ortodoks*), and that they are being judged on the basis of this appearance alone. Any actual or anticipated criticisms from the public often meet with an active and vigorous defence of their style from the women concerned. Many of these have to do with image and efficiency, especially in the public, professional or government work sector, to which most students eventually graduate. Today, an increasing number of Malay women are employed in these sectors, as teachers, nurses, doctors, lawyers, executives; and the *tudung* has become a customary mode of attire. Although some come under pressure from their superiors not to convey too extreme an image in the interests of progress and modernity, they regard *tudung* as entirely compatible with their work: 'veiled women can be as creative and successful as any other; *tudung* is no obstacle to work'; 'wearing *tudung* doesn't mean I am not presentable . . . it's cleaner and more tidy'; while a nurse comments: 'in eight years of experience in the operating room, nothing has ever happened as a result of my wearing *tudung*'.

It should be apparent that a Malay woman's dress and external appearance provide no certain guide as to her other qualifications, or to her personal qualities and interests. Regularity of prayer observance, forms of preferred entertainment, and even discreet friendships with the opposite sex, occur somewhat independently of visible attire, just as there seems to be no direct correlation between dress styles and willingness to pursue a public or professional career. Even women who joined the now defunct *Darul Arqam dakwah*[5] movement, and adopted full *purdah* were permitted to engage in outside occupations, usually in female-oriented vocations relating to teaching, nursing and child-care. Some of them were also university and college graduates, and had substantial skills, some of which they contributed to public as well as religious pursuits. Other *Arqam* affiliates did not reside in the community, but merely make weekend or vacation retreats to it. In such cases, they contributed their skills (legal, medical, accounting and so on), on a part-time basis, as a form of 'tithe' to the movement. In either case, *Darul Arqam* women made the best of both worlds in setting their own priorities, in whatever proportion they prefer. Such arrangements provided religious legitimation for those who wished to place family (wife and mother) roles ahead of other work, yet without forsaking the latter entirely. This was satisfyingly supported by many Qur'anic statements affirming the obligation of women to serve men, and in the process, resolves potential guilt or conflict arising out of the choice. *Darul Arqam* women displayed much confidence (given the 'extremist' stigma attached to the movement nationally), in making virtues of their situation as women who practise polygyny and full *purdah*. They had flaunted the advantages of having the assistance of co-wives available in times of illness or trouble, without the need for non-familial paid labour. In the polygynous household, time-sharing arrangements between wives enabled those with small children to engage in a career outside the home, without the full and onerous double load of most working wives. *Arqam* women also played leading roles in many of the small entrepreneurial activities of the community, by running sewing and craft shops, canteens and food-processing and book-publishing concerns. They regularly accompanied teams of *Arqam* males on *dakwah* journeys, often outside Malaysia, to such new *dakwah* destinations as Europe, China and Uzbekistan, as emissaries of their way of life. Moreover, in the security of the women's quarters, they enjoyed their private irreverent jokes, for example, over the men's curiosity as to 'how pretty?' are the faces behind the veils. It is known that *Arqam* males were consumed by the mysteries of women (other than their own wives), whom they could not see, and women relished the tantalisation. The combined traditions of the Qur'an and Malay *adat* still allow women to maintain a privileged domain within the household, as 'queen of the household' (*suri rumahtangga*), without closing off other options completely. In their own words they can realise themselves as people, while honouring their responsibility to husband, children and society.

There was, however, a small minority of more deeply committed women, who see their religious obligations as a form of 'struggle' (*perjuangan*) against opposing pressures and institutions. They were proud to be labelled *solehah* (pious), and were prepared to wear full *purdah* with face veil, gloves, socks, all in uniform black. Not all of these women were members of 'extremist' groups such as *Darul Arqam*, but their presence often excites controversy in places of education and employment. In many government and private offices and in all Malaysian universities, including the International Islamic University, full *purdah* has been forbidden. Understandably, this regulation has resulted in some self-righteous responses to the effect that 'wearing *purdah* does not hamper the process of learning', and many remarks as to the irony of forbidding women in a Muslim country from observing the full letter of the divine law[6] to cover their modesty.

One particularly determined married woman in her mid-thirties, who had been dismissed from her job as a government legal clerk for wearing full *purdah* to work, in contravention of a government circular regulation, even took her case to court. Interestingly, she elected to have her case heard in a civil as opposed to the Islamic religious (*syari'ah*) court, and was defended by a non-Muslim lawyer, while her case was presented as one of violation of her constitutional rights, that is, freedom to practise her religion. After several appeals, the Supreme Court finally ruled that her dismissal was lawful, on grounds that wearing *purdah* was against occupational regulations, and that her disobedience was an act of insubordination. Clearly, this woman's strategy was not one of a mindless, emotional zealot. Nor was she under the pressure of school peers or even office colleagues, nor yet a member of a movement such as *Darul Arqam*. Rather, the approach adopted was a calculated way of presenting her case to a wider public as a thinking citizen desirous of realising her personal potential and legal rights in both government service and private religion. Recourse to the civil courts was designed to avoid any embarrassment to religious groups or authorities, who might otherwise have felt obliged to make it a political issue. She was also concerned that a scriptural, as opposed to a constitutional defence, would reinforce a perceived bias in many quarters as to the 'backwardness' of the religion whose scriptures she follows. Hence her decision to invoke constitutional laws to defend her civil rights.

It has been widely recognised (Lyon 1979; Nagata 1984; Zainah 1987), that Islamic dress appears most commonly among middle-class women, as illustrated above. This pattern is also characteristic of women in Egypt (Williams 1979; El Guindi 1981; Rugh 1986; Hoodfar 1988; Abu Lughod 1990), where it is among middle-income, semi-professional women and government employees that a renewed attention to the 'veil' is most prominent. For Egyptian women, this choice of attire simultaneously relieves them of the financial burdens of maintaining a fashionable working wardrobe on inadequate salaries, and likewise of the undesired attention and sexual harassment directed towards less modestly dressed women in public places and transport. Thus a modified 'veiling' is both practical and also mark of a particular socio-economic status among urban Egyptian women.

In Malaysia, considerations of cost and symbolic protection may play a minor role in determining dress codes; but the association with a particular status and educational level emerges more strongly. Among Malay women, the element of a critical consciousness, arising out of a freedom of choice, is more evident, as reflected in the high level of participation in the activities of *dakwah* religious movements, attendance at religious lectures and so on. From these, women acquire the ingredients for a more thoroughgoing critique of society, especially in its moral capitulation to the decadent West and unbelievers (*jahiliyah*) in the pursuit of economic development. Many of these same women are also foreign-educated; hence their choices are based on a broader base of experience, and they are able to see issues in an international perspective. Theirs is a cultural response to avoid total engulfment by all the unwanted accompaniments of economic 'success'; a concern over means as much as the ends in themselves. In their view, it is not Islam that oppresses women, but human beings, and of all societies, those most 'developed' are the most guilty of the economic, moral and sexual exploitation of women. A retreat to religion and to the 'veil' is partly a consequence of the insecurities of the first generation of Malays confronted with new roles and high expectations in a secular society, for which they have no models or precedents.

In the uncharted new territory of occupation and urban lifestyle, Western exposure and economic temptation, many women in the 1970s and 1980s, and still today, have found a bewildering number of choices simplified by the religious option. Banished are the decisions whether or not to play tennis, whether or not to date boys, to go to clubs, all of which involve problems of dressing for the occasion. Questions of cost are less important than those of a personal place and meaning in the system. Just as dedicated environmentalists in other cultures make informed choices which deeply influence, even control, their lifestyle, Malay women have found a cultural solution. For them, the consumer world of fashion is reversed: 'having a good time is a sign of the (moral) stone age; the mini-skirt is of the dark ages'.

Increasingly in Malaysia, versions of more 'modest' Islamic dress are a sign of the times. This is an era less experimental in many ways than that of the past two decades, and it is now customary to stress religious propriety and greater public emphasis on religious forms. Even in the less cloistered circumstances of middle-class urban neighbourhoods, many non-working Malay housewives who regularly meet together for social or charitable activities mutually reinforce one another in graduated moves towards more Islamic dress as part of a pattern of group conformity, and now, wider societal and cultural norms. A kind of compromise between two styles of life and dress is more graphically portrayed in some women's fashion magazines, which feature designs for the modern Muslim woman, 'modest and suited to Islamic requirements'. The message is that *dakwah* fashions can be made compatible with more popular and foreign-influenced trends by means of clever colour co-ordination, selection of fine materials, and adorned by the discreet application of accessories, decorations and even jewellery. For some women such modified *dakwah* styles have become so much a part of the modern Malay scene that it is considered sophisticated and trendy, sometimes even described as 'groovy', and compatible with other areas of life and activity, such as sports and vacations: wearing *purdah* and covering one's modesty is now enjoyed by many, who consider it 'up to date'. In this more eclectic spirit, some women even find such dress styles liberating, in reducing some of the obsessive pre-occupation with hair and body shape in daily and public life – a freedom not afforded by Western dress. Undoubtedly, a form of Muslim attire is no more irrational than the bizarre body-image and eating problems suffered by some Western women in their 'free' and exposed world. In their own words, they are free of the 'tyranny of skirt and hair fashions . . . by which they are chained'.

Finally, now that access to the Holy Land by air and tour package is readily available, and with the affluence of the modern Malay middle class, many relatively young Malay women have performed the pilgrimage (*haj*), and this too, in the same spirit as among the older rural women of earlier years, often provides the incentive for some symbolic affirmation of their new religious status, in an adjustment of dress style to one more appropriate to a *hajah*.

In an ethnically polarised society such as Malaysia, forms of Islamic attire have also become one of the most visible symbols of ethnic identity, an instant medium of communication about status, readily perceived. On the international scene, some variant of Muslim dress, especially when combined with distinctively Malay touches, such as batik cloth, or the cut of the *baju kurung*, may function as a national costume, particularly in foreign student communities. In this capacity, it reinforces a newly-discovered solidarity with a global Muslim community. Through it, not only do Malays gain wider recognition beyond their homeland, but also a new and proud identity in an older, sacred tradition, beyond mere modernity.

Finally, to attribute all *dakwah*-related behaviour to a mindless conformity or to a naïve acceptance of the immediate social network would be to oversimplify, or worse, to come close to falling into the 'Orientalist' trap. Many of these women are thoughtful and articulate and quite capable of reflecting on their own condition, with its contradictory pressures and responsibilities, and on the vulnerability of the 'independent' or aggressive female in a Malay setting. Adopting a reverse view of 'Occidental' women, some perceptive young Malay women regard the more strident demands of Western feminism as counter-productive and distasteful (*tak elok*), risking a devaluation of the nurturant, wife/mother roles in the process. In the light of the above observation it seems less of a paradox that many of the first generation of so-called *dakwah* women initially adopted the 'veil' overseas in Western countries. Indeed there is a certain irony in this deliberate status reversal, encompassing a confident assertion of pride by the 'colonised oriental' woman. Similar views were also reported for some Iranian middle-class women following the Khomeini revolution (Afshar 1982). The visible sartorial response was thus but one manifestation of a more generalised sentiment of distaste for, and distancing from, the brazen Western environment. Finally, given that many female Malay university students with roots in rural Malaysia are suddenly thrust into the company of companions from urban and more privileged backgrounds, another appeal of a more uniform dress is its socially levelling effect in reducing the need for competitive display and consumption – one of the principal motivations of the professional Egyptian women.

It may also be noted that a rather more calculated and strategic use of the 'veil' has been made by some non-Malay Muslim women, principally those of Indian extraction, for whom it represents an expression of ethnic status which is as much a metaphor of social cohesion and sense of 'becoming more Malay' as a retreat from modernity.

The Class Factor

The connection between dress styles and commitment to *dakwah* social status or class appears quite strikingly among urban Malay women. The highest incidence occurs, as noted, among the cohorts of educated, upwardly mobile or younger professional women, and is conspicuous for its rarity within the growing contingent of young urban women factory workers. While such women are unquestionably involved in social cliques and peer pressures similar to those of the students, one critical difference lies in their lack of direct exposure to religious activism and alternate forms of role modelling with which they can readily identify. Their Islam is still of the more parochial, rural variety whence most of them have recently come, and less consciously associated with an international Islamic identity. They also enjoy less of the students' intellectual 'luxury' of introspection, debate and discussion or the opportunity to exercise options in the economic sphere, given the economic constraints which have forced most of them into factory life. During the 1970s and early 1980s some students were heard to deplore the unenlightened lifestyle and lack of religious commitment of their factory cousins, reflecting some of the popular Minah Karan and Kaki Joli[7] sentiments of the population at large. There were even attempts to send the ABIM and other *dakwah* lecturers to factories for more religious instruction – efforts usually thwarted by a suspicious management. On the other hand, factory girls were often to be observed in the audiences at public religious lectures of the general interest variety, as opposed to the more restricted *dakwah*-style events which attracted the university constituency. Invariably, the dress styles of the former tend to be more casual (*bebas*) and less influenced by male censorship than the latter. Many factory women still do not cover their hair, and are much more experimental with dress style and cosmetics. Thus the distinction between women of different status levels assumes a moralistic tone, of which the most visible and tangible marker is dress, and imputed associated behaviours. By implication too, the suitability of these respective constituencies of women as wives also becomes an issue. In the sexual politics of the university, where men have become highly sensitised to a more rigid and uncompromising Islam from outside Malaysia, their revised expectations of women's roles reinforces the ambivalence felt by the women themselves, from which one refuge is a retreat from bodily provocations. Working-class women are generally less exposed to such pressures in their day-to-day networks.

For women remaining in villages there is also less visible evidence of *dakwah* dress styles or behaviour, save from some returning or visiting students, who often eventually abandon efforts to sustain these in the open and generally more permissive social patterns of the village. Such styles are often regarded as urban affectations, inappropriate among the young. Religiosity for the rural women is expressed in the more typical '*adat/* Islam compromise' (of Karim 1992), whereby more conspicuous signs of religious expression are reserved for those of more advanced years or who have already made the *haj*.

Conclusion

From the foregoing, I conclude that many behaviours associated with gender may be substantially modified by such factors as social class and status, occupation residence, education, ethnicity and social network. All of these contribute in some measure to the response of modern Malay women to their faith.

Thus the peak of *dakwah* activity and obsession with dress forms seems to occur most prominently among the upwardly mobile and educationally 'privileged' sectors of the Malay female community and in part to reflect some confusion as to their career expectations and domestic roles, without succumbing to a Western feminist solution. It is thus a class as much as a gender issue. However, inferences by outsiders (including other Malays) do not necessarily correspond with insider perceptions. Surface evidence on the basis of dress alone does not provide an accurate indicator as to a women's eventual career intentions and involvement. Rather it represents an attempt to come to terms with two competing 'cultural hegemonies', from a Western technocratic educational and professional culture on the one hand, and a domestic ideal grounded in a larger sacred tradition with ethnic (Malay) and religious charters of legitimacy on the other. Instead of viewing Malay women's religious commitments and behaviour as anti-modern or retrogressive it might be more appropriate to place it in a larger historical–religious tradition, in which a new and more global sense of identity is sought, beyond mere 'modernity'. In some respects, the situation of Malay Muslim women reflects the moral dilemma that the Malaysian state is being presented with in its aggressive pursuit of modernity and full industrial development by the year 2020 by the Islamic religious opposition party, Party Islamic Se Malaysia (PAS). If only for party-political reasons, government policy-makers too have to pay heed to religious strictures, and to clothe their programmes in Islamic dress. In part, this is also a mechanism of distancing from the more blatant forms of Western decadence, and an attempt to find an appropriate Malaysian path to the best of both worlds.

By way of a comparative postscript, it may be noted that there currently exists in Malaysia some apparent parallels to the *dakwah* convert in other religions, which also attempt to chart for their followers a more predictable and orderly existence with unambiguous guidelines for life in an uncertain world. Here too the principal protagonists are young urban middle-class students and professionals, found in the vanguard of Theravada Buddhist and Christian revivals.

As members of minority faiths in Malaysia, the global reference community for Buddhists and Christians is largely external to the country. From a local perspective, these faiths are often viewed as ethnically antithetical to Islam in matters of gender behaviour and propriety.

As a generic category, Christians in particular (whether Chinese or Indian), are frequently identified with Western ideas concerning 'progress' and 'modernity', and this can result in further alienation from current local Islamic *mores*. In the realm of gender and sexual morality, the popular (Muslim) perception attributes greater liberalness of behaviour, sometimes to the point of unacceptability, to Christian women, and this is reinforced by the (often misplaced) emphasis on the evidence of dress and other highly visible behaviour alone. However, just as the attire of Muslim Malay women is not a certain predictor of personal motivation or beliefs, the moral or social status of Christian women cannot be judged by appearance alone. Even the apparent prominence of women in Christian organisations can be misleading. In fact, in most religious institutions, especially in positions of leadership, Malaysian Christian women still play subordinate roles, subject to male power and control in matters of decision-making and doctrine. Feminine initiative is invariably channelled into parallel, 'female-designated' activities, having to do with 'nurturant' catering, counselling, kindergartens, care of the aged and social work, which pose no direct challenge to male interests or authority. While Christian women may express a desire for travel or education in a

Western country, many explicitly do not identify with extreme Western brands of feminism, and would feel uncomfortable trying to assume male pastoral positions involving power over other men.

Likewise, Theravada Buddhist women, who claim to have shaken off the limitations of Chinese custom and the 'anti-intellectual' ritualism of Mahayana Buddhism for a more 'rational' and 'modern' practice, are nonetheless still subject to numerous gender proscriptions. The so-called Thai or Sri Lankan forms of Buddhism to which they often aspire also maintain rigidly separate or parallel religious institutions for females, whether in retreats or in social service activities, and deference to males on all matters of leadership and theology remains unquestioned.

Once the obfuscation of dress is removed, there may emerge stronger parallels between the patterns of religious re-intensification and 'inner conversion' of revivalist Muslim, Buddhist and Christian young women in Malaysia than is immediately or visibly apparent. For all, in large measure, are preoccupied with coming to terms with the disjunctive demands of an intrusive culture in daily material life, and an identity rooted in a social and religious community governed by different principles. The problem for all is one of asserting control over the external influences, without abandoning their fruits entirely.

Notes

1. In post-revolutionary Iran, by contrast, the most loyal followers of Khomeini in his call to women to return to their domestic roles and destiny were from among the women of the working class, who welcomed the possibility of a (religiously sanctioned) reprieve from their daily and menial toils outside the home (Hoodfar 1980).
2. Over the past few decades or so, the most recent of at least a century-long series of movements and changes has been sweeping the Muslim world. Some earlier movements, such as the Wahhabis, aspired to greater congruence between Islam and the 'modern' developments of the Western technical and economic order, as did the later variant known as the *Kaum Muda* among the Malays of the early twentieth century. The *Kaum Muda*, however was countered by its local antithesis, the *Kaum Tua*, representing a more traditional strand of Malay Islam (Roff 1967). Once again, Malays have responded to events in the Islamic heartland, such as the Iranian revolution, Libyan involvement in the Third World, and religious polarisation in Lebanon and

Israel.

3. The NEP (New Economic Policy) was initially launched in 1971, in conjunction with the Second Malaysia Plan, as part of a policy designed to reduce poverty generally, and in particular to propel Malays into a position of greater advantage *vis-à-vis* non-Malays, and so reverse the economic legacy of colonialism. This policy, which has been upheld until the present, incorporated a variety of favourable quotas or affirmative actions for Malays, including access to Division I Civil Service posts, education, scholarships, training and loan schemes, which were partly responsible for the creation of new occupational experiences and opportunities for young Malays.

4. One of the best known of the *dakwah* Movements, ABIM (Angkatan Belia Islam Malaysia), was also popular in university circles for its intellectual and political content and the quality of its lecturers, many of whom were fellow students. ABIM also encouraged activities and retreats which appealed to students and helped to reinforce their sense of solidarity. The peak of ABIM's success coincided with the leadership of Anwar Ibrahim, himself a student and leader of the earlier Malay Language Society. Some of ABIM's strength was lost with Anwar's unexpected departure to a political career in the party UMNO, where he is currently Minister of Finance.

5. *Darul Arqam* was another Muslim resurgent movement which arose in the late 1960s, and which flourished as a fringe group, based on a mostly young membership with high levels of education and skills. Members patterned their lives, often in separate communities, according to the example of the Prophet, with emphasis on economic self-sufficiency, redistribution according to need, and Islamically correct gender and family relations, which include polygyny, male dominance and full *purdah*. It was officially banned in late 1994 and the various Arqam communes are being gradually disbanded.

6. There is, however a solid theological basis for the veiling, irrespective of its idiosyncratic use by individuals in particular cases. Veiling comes under the rule of *aurat*, a notion of modesty, which can in extreme forms of interpretation extend to the use of the (feminine) voice.

7. *Minah Karan* is a derogatory popular reference term for factory girls, denoting a wanton, brazen kind of female, while *Kaki Joli* refers to someone, male or female who is always out looking for fun. The contrasting sexuality of the urban factory-girl migrant and the rural village nubile girl is deliberately evoked to demonstrate the negative effects of Westernisation in urban areas.

Bibliography

Abu-Lughod, L. (1990). 'The Romance of Resistance: Tracing Transformations of Power through Bedouin Women'. *American Ethnologist*, 17:1, 41–5.

Afshar, H. (1982). 'Khomeini's Teachings and their Implication for Women'. *Feminist Review*, No. 12:5.

Clifford, J. and Marcus, G. (1986). *Writing Culture: The Poetics and Politics of Ethnography*. Berkeley: University of California Press.

El Guindi, F. (1981). 'Veiling *Infitah* with Muslim Ethic: Egypt and the Contemporary Islamic Movement'. *Social Problems*, 28, 465–83.

Gough, K. (1972). 'An Anthropologist Looks at Engels'. In Nona Glazer-Malbin and Helen Youngelson Waehrer (eds), *Woman in a Man-Made World*. Chicago: Rand McNally.

Haddad, Y. and Haddad, E. F. (eds) (1985). *Women, Religion and Social Change*. Albany: State University of New York Press.

Hoodfar, H. (1988). 'Return to the Veil: Personal Strategy to 'Public' Participation in Egypt'. In N. Redclift and T. Sinclair (eds), *Working Women: International Perspectives on Labour and Gender Ideology*. London: Routledge.

Inden, R. (1986). 'Orientalist Constructions of India'. *Modern Asian Studies*, 20:3, 401–46.

Karim, W. J. (1992). *Women and Culture: Between Malay Adat and Islam*. Boulder, Colorado: Westview Press.

Lyon, M. (1979). 'The Dakwah Movement in Malaysia'. *Review of Indonesian and Malaysian Affairs*, 13:2.

Manderson, L. (1980). *Women, Politics and Change: The Kaum Ibu UMNO, Malaysia, 1945–1972*. Kuala Lumpur: Oxford University Press.

Marcus, G. E. and Fischer, M. (1986). Anthropology as Cultural Critique: An Experimental Movement in the Human Sciences. Chicago: University of Chicago Press.

Nagata, J. (1984). *The Reflowering of Malaysian Islam*. Vancouver: University of British Columbia Press.

Pastner, C. M. (1978). 'Englishmen in Arabia: Encounters with Middle Eastern Women'. *Signs*, 4:2, 309–23.

Prakash, G. (1990). 'Writing Post-Orientalist Histories of the Third World: Perspectives from Indian Historiography'. *Comparative Studies in Society and History*, 32:2, 382–408 (April).

Reiter, R. R. (ed.) (1975). *Toward an Anthropology of Women*. New York and London: Monthly Review Press.

Roff, W. (1967). *The Origins of Malay Nationalism*. Kuala Lumpur: University of Malaya Press.

Rogers, S. (1975). 'Female Forms of Power and the Myth of Male Dominance. *American Ethnologist*, 2:4, 727–56.

Rugh, A. (1986). *Reveal and Conceal: Dress in Contemporary Egypt*. Syracuse, New York: Syracuse University Press.

Said, E. (1978). *Orientalism*. New York: Pantheon.

Sayigh, R. (1981). 'Roles and Functions of Arab Women: A Reappraisal'. *Arab Studies Quarterly*, 3:3, 258–74.

Tabari, A. (1985). 'The Enigma of Veiled Iranian Women'. *Feminist Review*, No. 5.

Williams, J. A. (1979). 'A Return to Veil in Egypt'. *Middle East Review*, 11:3, 49–54.

Zainah, A. (1987). *Islamic Revivalism in Malaysia: Dakwah Among the Students.* Petaling Jaya: Pelanduk Publications.

5

Engendering Disquiet: On Kinship and Gender in Bali

Mark Hobart

How adequate are analyses of kinship and gender which rest upon supposedly universal features of the human condition? Are such analyses, for instance, sufficient to enable us to understand the actual diversity of human relationships in Bali? Universalist accounts tend to represent biology as processed into cultural units which separate and unite people at various levels into groups for activities associated with caste, gender and worship. If one considers gender as a kind of activity or practice however, how can this be best analysed in the context of Balinese society? It is clear that, beyond a certain point, kinship theory does not help one understand 'gender' either as a construct or as an activity. This is because kinship theory is usually derived from a Western discourse of the relationships between biology and affinity, a discourse which is steeped in Eurocentric assumptions about such relationships being 'basic', 'natural' and 'primordial' to Man and best appreciated in the context of primitive social systems. So, all 'primitive' societies were said to contain kinship systems, which became a criterion of the authenticity of the 'primitiveness' of a particular culture.

In this paper I question how useful it is to try to reduce practices to do with kinship and gender to general biological or sociological explanations. I suggest first that kinship does not have the kind of reality usually attributed to it. Second, I shall argue that, if we are to try to understand relationships between men and women in Bali, in the first instance these are best understood through Balinese ways of talking about and arguing over such relationships. Ideas do not exist in the abstract, but attain their social reality in situated practice. And much of this practice is in a dialogal mode which contradicts most 'grand theories' that set out to explain interpersonal and group relationships. Third, I shall suggest that there are quite different ways of talking about male–female relationships, which

Western academics commonly link to biology, affinity and territoriality, without needing to engage in any formal reconstitution of kinship theory in Bali.

Perilous Presuppositions

Stipulating a cross-cultural reality to kinship is to equate discourses upon the imaginary with factuality. The unkindest cut of all is the way Western scholars treat kinship among non-Western peoples as something primordial to which they are bound (consider Lansing's vision of Balinese as *kaiket*, 1974), a state of affairs which 'the West' somehow transcends. What is commonly called kinship is a chimera, a mythical monster with a face of folk categories and a tail of metaphysical assumptions. Needham has challenged the validity of prevailing principles and modes of classification (1971, 1975). Schneider has sought to sever the cultural constructs from a heterogeneous social conglomerate (1968, 1972); while Inden has pointed out that people elsewhere may make quite different assumptions about how humans are related (1976). Yet kinship continues to be discussed as a 'social institution' in anthropology. This may be because anthropology is heir to a strongly essentialist (and substantialist) intellectual tradition.

Unless we are quite clear what kind of 'thing' kinship is, we may find that we have a problem of translation and comparison. How do we know that what we call kinship denotes something comparable in other usages? Also, there is the question of what statements about kinship are about. Are we dealing with descriptions about the world? Or is it more a matter of what various classifications of relationships may be used, for particular purposes, to assert, claim, challenge or deny? Finally, there is the metaphysical issue of what at any historical moment, other peoples recognise, explicitly or implicitly, as existing in their world. How does the classification of relationships relate to what is held to exist? I would suggest that using the notion of kinship, even as 'an odd-job word', tends to cover up the difficulty in knowing how we translate; what uses of language may exist; and whether, or in what senses, other ways of classifying are remotely comparable. Anthropological determination to find a fixed and easily identifiable object of study has yielded a particular jural, moral and ontological package we call kinship. It would be a startling example of what someone once delightfully called 'RUP' – Residual Unresolved Positivism – were we to fail to consider the full implications of the fact that anthropologists' ideas about other peoples' kinship are no simple truths about the world, but affected by our changing assumptions. It is not an issue of how to compare facts but of how, using one epistemological model, to talk about others – or perhaps better, the problem of talking about one discourse using another.

As the issues are complex, I shall highlight some of the points most relevant to a discussion of kinship. In its easiest formulation the problem of radical translation (between unrelated languages where there has been little, or no, cultural contact) is an extreme example of the hermeneutic issue of how to interpret texts or statements. For 'the special problem of interpretation is that it very often appears to be necessary and inevitable when in fact it never is. This appearance of inevitability is a phantasm raised by the circularity of the interpretive process' (Hirsch 1967: 164). The reason is that one is dealing with a system of signs which '. . . must be construed before it furnishes confirmation of an interpretation. Furthermore, the manner in which the signs are construed is partly predetermined by the interpretation itself' (Hirsch 1967: 165).

Why can one not simply translate by finding out what native words or expressions correspond with the facts? In order to understand the difficulty, it is useful to look at the theory of truth, and meaning, which is required for such an approach. This is the classical 'Correspondence Theory', in which truth, and so true meaning, consists in some form of correspondence between facts and ideas, and which has a very ancient European pedigree indeed. Or, as we shall see, the kinds of schemes used to classify kin relations rely on culturally specific metaphysical assumptions of particular things' or people's having essential properties, by virtue of which they may be definitively classified.

There are serious problems in any 'Correspondence Theory'. Three are relevant here. First, many of the words critical to a translation, such as logical connectives, do not correspond to any facts. Second, as Gellner (1970: 25) has observed, in effect introducing 'reality' as a stage in translating one language into another merely adds a further language and compounds the difficulties. Why this should be so is clear in the light of my last objection, namely that there is an indeterminacy in translation, such that more than one scheme may make sense of what has been said.

There is no simple way of climbing out of one's translational scheme to ask even the best-informed native informant whether one is correct without having to translate him or her. The catch is that 'there can be no doubt that rival systems of analytical hypotheses can fit the totality of speech behaviour to perfection, and can fit the totality of dispositions to speech behaviour as well, and still specify mutually incompatible translations of countless sentences insusceptible of independent control'

(Quine 1960: 72). In other words there is no way of knowing whether the ethnographer's translation of words like kinship, family, or father are in fact what people aim to express in their speech behaviour. Once the ethnographer gets going on her or his scheme, however shot-through with one's own cultural presuppositions, it tends to become self-confirming, because many of the key notions are mutually defined and sufficiently far away from statements for which there is empirical evidence. How do we know that the comfortable-seeming similarity of ideas about kinship round the world is not a result of the observers' sharing similar preconceptions which they invest in their translational systems? Consider, for instance, how radical would be the difference were common notions like 'soul' or 'spirit' to be rendered as 'identity' instead, and how hard it would be to invalidate either (see Hobart 1987: 37–44).

Leaving aside the difficulties in translation, what in fact are we comparing? The problem is that, whatever their purported basis in biology, as with gender, kinship relations are not natural facts. What the anthropologist conventionally goes by are native statements held to describe the social relationships of a particular kind in which humans are engaged, so to speak. Now statements differ from 'facts' by being asserted by people on particular occasions, rather than, in some sense, being 'out there'. 'Being someone's brother' is construed from the 'facts', whatever they might be in any instance, in terms of cultural categories, which include ideas of taxonomy, logical operations and much else besides. Anthropologists' statements about kinship are therefore, among other things, applications of classificatory principles to the actions, events and so forth from which relationships are inferred. It is not evident *a priori* that other peoples either use similar procedures or treat practices so idealistically as instantiations of ideas or categories.

There are other grounds too on which to question whether statements about kinship could ever be neutral propositions about the world. Words do not just say things, but do things at the same time. In speaking one does not simply make propositions but also presents that proposition, if such it be, in different ways or with differing force, which may further have effects in the world. Even this formulation is perilous, because propositions are a fine example of dubious mental entities. People tend to speak in utterances, commonly in dialogue with others (Bakhtin 1986a,b). I shall try to show later quite how dangerous it is to think of statements about kinship as descriptions. It fits better with ethnographic evidence to treat these as situated practices of prescribing, asserting, denying, questioning or any of the other ways in which people may use language on different occasions for particular purposes. Endless confusion is created by mistaking claims for descriptions.

These difficulties seem to pale in the face of the hurdles involved in comparing ideas cross-culturally. Evans-Pritchard (1965) has made the point that comparison easily leads to a circularity. To compare things one requires criteria, but how does one establish the criteria in the first place without comparison? Our notions of comparison are highly conventional and subsume learning 'similarity relations' (Kuhn 1977: 307–19, on 'finitism'). Matters are worse still when dealing with the classification of jural or moral relations which are widely argued to be key aspects of kinship (see for example Fortes 1969). For a start on what grounds could we assume that ideas of 'law' and jural notions such as person, obligation, or prohibition are sufficiently commensurable as to be worth the exercise, when they have changed so much in the West? The assumption that the moral dimension of kinship is important does tend to presuppose that ideas of morality have equivalence cross-culturally, which rather flies in the face of the evidence. A great deal of anthropology consists in closing one's eyes and hoping the world will go away.

What then are Balinese ideas about the material base of kin relations? Significantly, what Balinese say depends on the context in which the issue arises, the occasion and the textual knowledge of the speaker. How they approach the notion of 'matter' is complicated. They stress the transformation of appearance or the causation of events instead (see below). More specifically, theories of conception famously tend to involve differing social claims. Many accounts stressed the complementary fluids males and females brought to making the child, with determination of gender depending on whether the man or woman was the stronger party in the union. That said, detailed inquiry with eighty adult women and men in the research village, yielded eighty rather different accounts. To overgeneralise, members of the élite, in suitably essentialist spirit, tend to put more weight than peasants on pedigree, which is not unconnected to claims to political legitimacy. They also put more stress on ideas of partly innate purity, which is thought to be transmitted by fluids at the time of conception. Just what purity is is a complex and debated issue; and the ostensible evidence of procreation may be overridden where other factors intervene – as when a low-born man attains power or acquires the attributes of a prince. As I discuss below, the realm of 'kinship' may well be, for Balinese, that which makes humans similar or different, in which many considerations combine. Balinese do not identify family resemblances just by referring to inherited traits. Besides the doctrine of *karma pala*, villagers recognise the disparities between 'kin' as much as the congruences. Part of the inquiry about new-born children is finding out from a spirit-medium the identity of which forebear has manifested itself. Quite different kinds of situational factor come into play too. In Balinese accounts of causation, personal identity is partly determined by the circumstances of birth, including time and space, and it further remains inextricably linked with the fate of a child's four mystical siblings (the *kanda 'mpat*, the ejecta at birth). So there is no mechanical theory of the natural basis of kinship. Rather, personal identity and domestic relations are decided by various factors operating within a causal field.

One way of approaching my opening question about how one might set about understanding human relationships in Bali is to consider briefly – and necessarily somewhat simplistically – Balinese uses of words for causation. Instead of stressing a deterministic biological 'basis' to kinship and gender, Balinese often stress the events which made things and people what they are. When inquiring about how something came to be what it is at that moment, its *karana*, 'cause' or, perhaps better, 'condition of being', Balinese widely use a cluster of six related terms. The first is the species or personal name, *adan*. Indeed, *adan* literally glosses as 'the being of'. Names may be used just as conventional labels, but they must be appropriate to the object or person in question. Persons may change their names if their circumstances change. The vital act of naming humans or species (Hobart 1990) requires the participation and approval of Divinity in some form. The second condition is *lakar*, the constituents of a thing or person, what inheres in its being at any moment. This cannot be reduced to simple matter. What inheres in the being of a person in Bali and makes them what they are arguably includes the *kanda 'mpat*, which survive their initial existence as the ejecta of birth and remain important aspects of a person. A third condition of being is the form or shape of something, its *rupa*. It is this, for instance, which distinguishes males, females and *bancih* (hermaphrodites) from one another. Form is not fixed. Where women in Bali regularly work ricefields, their *rupa* is said to become more like men (see below), and their behaviour may change accordingly.

A vital fourth condition of being is the instrumental cause of something, its karana (*nimittakáraÑa* in Indian Nyáya-Vaioe∞ika thinking, Potter 1977: 56–8). This term is sufficiently central that it often doubles for 'cause' in a more general sense. *Karana* is the act or event that makes something what it is. The act of manufacturing a motor-cycle is its *karana*, as the act of coition of parents is the *karana* of a child. Fifth, things and people have more or less *guna*, use, or use value. Without this condition, whatever it is is gravely defective. A motor cycle which cannot be driven, rice which cannot be eaten, an adult who cannot carry out the appropriate work of a woman or man lacks the appropriate *guna*. Finally, things and beings have their conventional or fitting place in the world, *genah*. If a being or thing is too long outside its usual place, its *guna* changes. For instance, if a domestic cat runs feral for longer than a few weeks, it is thought of as having gone wild and therefore becomes edible. A man who lives in his wife's compound on a permanent basis becomes in one sense a woman (see below). So, in contrast to what is ultimately the biological determinism of much academic writing about kinship and gender, Balinese stress a range of partly changeable and interrelated conditions of being.

A final point should be made about my reference to metaphysics. By this I mean the kinds of idea, category, logical operation, ontological commitment or whatever which Balinese appeal to, explicitly in speech, or implicitly by inference or reflection on discourse. Such a metaphysics-in-the-buff, as I have called it (1983), is more common than anthropologists often allow (cf. Evans-Pritchard 1937, 1956; Lienhardt 1961; Inden 1976; Vitebsky 1993). Certainly in a literate civilisation like Bali, texts and traditions of philosophical discussion abound; and philosophical terms and ideas are used in daily life unselfconsciously, with enthusiasm and aplomb, to explain actions and account for the nature of the world. It is one thing for Balinese to interpret matters this way; but to what extent does my approach claim to explain why humans do what they do? The short answer is that it does not claim to do so. My concern is simply to look at the empirical conditions – which include Balinese statements involving metaphysical terms – under which action takes place, and, given the particular sets of circumstances, to piece together the ways in which Balinese talk about what is happening in different contexts.

There is no way in which we could ever know which of the possible sets of constructs, if any, is the one in fact responsible for the events. This modest constraint on my aims follows directly from arguments such as the one noted above, about the underdetermination of theory by experience. If such a caution has any validity it is the death-knell for anyone who purports to establish that any scheme can, in principle, explain events. There is an unstated step in many cultural analyses. After positing a theoretical framework which, with luck, bears some relation to the ethnographic evidence, there is a surreptitious assumption that, given the best and richest conceptual scheme, a causal or rational account could be read off on demand. These general remarks about the questionably substantive status of 'kinship' can also be argued from the ethnography of gender.

Temples and Shrines as Centres of Activity

Among many kinds of temple congregation in Bali are those known as
pamaksaan, *dadiya* or, more specifically, as *soroh*, followed by the name
of the worship group. The terms are found in different parts of the island
with somewhat different usage. The folk etymology is interesting.
Pamaksaan is usually held to derive from the root *paksa*, force; and refers
to those who are expected to worship at (*maturan*, to give offerings, and
muspa, to pray), or who are obliged to support (*nyungsung*), a temple.
Balinese often link *dadiya* to *dadi*, to grow or become, but also, to allow.
So it may be read either as those who have grown from one origin,
kawitan, or those between whom certain acts or exchanges are permitted.
Soroh is the general word for class or kind. So it denotes a class of people
linked to a temple, and so place. In common with almost all temple
associations in Bali, the main function of its members is to perform
calendrical rituals to the incumbent deity (usually known by a title, Batara,
which indicates divine status, followed by the name of the temple or
worship group – most Balinese taxonomy stresses terminal classes in
nominalist fashion). The principles of incorporation of different groups
in principle differ mainly in the range of functions and the criteria of
eligibility. In practice matters are not always so clear-cut. The grounds
for formal association, however, are worth brief consideration.

   The criteria for inclusion in such worship groups may be expressed in
several ways. A key, but difficult, term is *purusa*. In Sanskrit it is often
translated as 'male' (Gonda 1952: 73; Inden 1976: 13), but also as 'seed-
man' (Inden and Nicholas 1977: 30) or as part of the 'cosmic
manifestation of the primal Superman (*purusa*)' (Long 1980: 58). The
notion of *purusa* is variously interpreted in different Hindu philosophical
traditions: as an aspect of deity (Gonda 1970: 16ff.), as self opposed to
substance (Potter 1980: 263), as consciousness beyond matter, 'sheer
contentless presence' as against 'awareness (which) is active, intentional,
engaged' (Larson 1980: 308). It is not an easy word. At first sight matters
are much simpler in Bali. *Sakèng purusa* belongs to a contrast set with
sakèng pradana, 'from the male (side)' and 'from the female (side)'
respectively (see Gonda 1952: 173). Here *sakèng purusa* designates those
related to a male forebear. In this sense the worship groups mentioned
above may be read as having their principle of association defined by
descent – Balinese use the same metaphor, *turun*, as in English – here
agnation. *Purus(a)* also is used for 'penis': so does *sakèng purusa* refer
to socially recognised, or biologically conceived, connections? This is
not a quibble. Such ambiguities are critical to how Balinese interpret

group membership and explain action.

There is a subtlety here. After all, why not define 'kin groups' straightforwardly by who joins, and dismiss folk semantics as incidental? This is an easy way out, but it imports Western ideas of the relation of word and object. Defining *purusa* by denotation is woefully inadequate. Granted the range of implications, Balinese suffer from (or delight in) the dilemmas of what the senses of *purusa* are all about. Is *sakèng purusa* about conventional association or about acts of procreation? (Where descent is traced through women, it is referred to as *sakèng purusa*.) Is the stress on transmission or substantive qualities? Or is it about something else? Is it, for instance, sharing something with a given deity, considered as ancestral? Or worse, is it some shared attribute, or perhaps outlook, separate from the individual interests of those concerned? Such issues tend to arise when the ambiguous grounds of incorporation are highlighted, inevitably in disputes or changing circumstances.

It will be obvious that the interpretations Balinese may place upon the notion of *purusa* stem in part from reworkings of some of its many senses noted by Sanskrit scholars. This is equally true of the other terms mentioned so far. For instance, villagers in the settlement where I worked treated *dadiya* on occasions as deriving from *dadi*, as 'to allow'. Sharing a *dadiya* had the sense of being allowed to share things like food, so those who did not in fact do so were not of the same *dadiya*. By varying the defining attributes Balinese can, and do, give quite different slants to what terms should refer to, whom to include and exclude, and what such decisions might imply. Whether we like it or not, interpretation is not easily divorced from Balinese practice, nor translation from the task of the ethnographer.

Should it be thought I am splitting hairs, let us look at the other terms Balinese use to classify people with whom they live and worship. A common way of speaking about whom one regards as related is as *semeton*, the etymology of which is often given as *se-metu-an*, or roughly 'one exit' or 'from one source' (but also 'see the light', 'break through'). So, on one reading, the exit may be the mother's womb, as *metu* is a synonym in high Balinese for being born. As divorce is common, coming from one mother does not entail having the same father. So perhaps the two most used words to refer to criteria of membership in 'descent groups' are complementarily linked to the perceived functions of males and females in a rather loose way.

Metaphor plays an interesting part in how relationships are portrayed. So far the possible images are of a procreative penis and coming from a mother's womb. The other terms used of 'kin ties' may, significantly, also be given metaphorical associations. To refer to ties traced strictly through males (jurally?) the term is *saturunan*, of one descent, from *turun*: to descend, drop or fall. To cloud matters, however, there is another word, *katurunan*, the abstract noun from the same root, which designates all who can trace descent (filiation would be the less metaphorical anthropological expression) through males, females or any mix of the two. Under what circumstances, and with what care, Balinese distinguish between the two terms in actual use is a tricky question.

So far the images refer to sequence expressed spatially (descent), or perhaps better to causal juxtaposition (penis or womb → child, a relation sometimes described as 'metonymy'). Other words conjure up different associations. *Lingsehan*, from *lingseh*: a stalk of rice, refers to a bilaterally reckoned grouping. Perhaps the most widely used term in the region of Bali where I worked is *nyama*. As the noun denoting persons, *panyamaan*, its range is similar to *semeton*, if not broader still. When coupled with *beraya*, *nyama beraya* is used of fellow villagers (sometimes set against *panembahan*, those one prays to, or bows before, *sembah*, i.e. persons of high caste), and so suggests recognising a common link. In public meetings it attains a sense at times close to 'moral community'. *Nyama*, however, also refers to parents' siblings, genealogically or by age, and sometimes to all senior members of a *dadiya*. Again *panyamaan* and *nyama* are used interchangeably in many contexts. *Nyama* either comes from the root *sama*, or is its perfect synonym. *Sama* normally is used to indicate something like 'same' or 'similar', sharing some aspect of identity, being alike. The connection is not lost on Balinese. Whether etymologically or metaphorically these terms have precious little to do with 'kinship'. Nor would we be wise to infer that *nyama*, or *semeton*, which is equally used of 'non-kin', really denote kin and the other uses are just marginal, or ancillary, extensions. On what grounds can we be sure that the narrower use is not just one of a number of special applications? To argue the extensionist case is to impute a degree of essentialism to Balinese which there is no evidence that they have.

Balinese do not, as we have seen, speak of their relationships in simple kin terms. As with temples, local ties are defined commonly in terms of sites of worship, known as *sanggah* (shrines) or *sanggah gedé* (simply: big shrines), according to the perceived remoteness of the relevant forebears. Ideologically, inclusion is expressed in terms of *purusa*. However, one's place (*genah*) of worship affects the condition of one's being. For instance, it is not uncommon for people to be told, when illness is diagnosed by spirit mediums, that they are worshipping at the shrine of the wrong *purusa*, i.e. in the wrong place. This allows a play between social and biological paternity, contrasting ideas of wrong association, and situated practice. Also women, if they are not divorced or do not return home, become house shrine deities (gradually subsumed under the genderless title of Batara, deity, protector) in their husband's group as defined by *purusa* (and vice versa, of course, for in-marrying males). Activity in a place affects one's being. So it is not surprising that Balinese widely regard the work for, and worship at, house shrines as a critical means of distinguishing members of a group claiming shared *purusa* from others. At marriage women pray at both their natal, and their marital, shrines to state their change of residence: the same happens on divorce or return. When we look, however, at who actually turns up on such occasions, the results are rather unexpected if one regards *purusa* as simply agnation.

In some parts of Bali many people do not know, or choose not to pay attention to, the sites where they may worship their *purusa*. In what follows I outline the state of affairs in 1971 in the ward of Pisangkaja, which was part of the settlement of Tengahpadang in Northern Gianyar. (The figures I give below should be treated with suitable caution and are only intended as sighting shots. People are often related in several ways, so what constitute the data are simply the most common assertions of relevant relationship.) In Tengahpadang 88 per cent of householders claimed to know the site of worship of their *purusa*. Attendance at temple affairs being compulsory for its members, on pain of fine or expulsion, turnout is high. At domestic shrines matters are different and, while everyone claims that it is almost unthinkable for a person with proper *purusa* ties not to turn up, this is far from the mark in accounting, for example, for actual attendance in Pisangkaja. Help in preparing the substantial offerings was undertaken largely by the household, however constituted, of the compound heir (69 per cent of helpers), as this is regarded as the place of origin, *kawitan*, of families which have moved away. What is a little unexpected is that jural agnates accounted for less than half the remaining help. In all, 10 per cent of the workforce were affines, and a further 5 per cent just neighbours (from different worship groups), while several other people turned up who had been adopted into other groups and so had no formal link. So far, the pattern is interesting, but not perhaps very surprising.

When it comes to worship at house shrines, however, the picture is curious. Of those who came to worship only 33 per cent were agnates in any jural, or strict, sense. Close on 10 per cent were affines, who properly should not worship at another's shrine at all. There was also a smattering of political clients, where even caste category was in doubt. The largest single category were what one might term 'out-marrying agnates', that is men and women who have left the group on marriage or adoption. In the formal language of agnation therefore, those entitled, and indeed required, to worship at the shrine form a minority.

Agnates are still less evident in agricultural labour relations, the milling of rice and other general forms of work exchange or help. Here affinity, neighbourhood and friendship or political clientage predominate (see Hobart 1979: 338–44).

Obviously, one may allow a measure of idiosyncrasy in personal motivation. But on what grounds, one wonders, at least as far as worship is concerned, is it justified to impose our category of agnation, rather than say cognation, a general sense of shared origin or mutual concern, or other reasons yet to be discerned? It is inelegant to dismiss the exceptions as mere contingencies. The scientific ploy of moving from the nomological to the statistical does not apply in the same way where human intention or reflexivity is involved. It is also a moot point whether one can assume – as almost all anthropological analyses do – that the participants' interpretations are homogeneous; in other words that they all share the same ideas of what worship, *purusa*, and so on are about. Lastly, to claim that what is important is the jural, or ideal, model does not help at all. Words like *purusa*, *saturunan* or *nyama* do not denote unambiguous classes of person, any more than those who turned up can easily be pigeon-holed.

Of what value, then, is the technical language of kinship? To speak of agnates as a fixed jural category suitable for cross-cultural comparison is of questionable worth. On the one hand such categories do not fit easily with indigenous principles; on the other they do not even correspond with the 'facts on the ground' (whatever those be). Some terms are obviously more circumscribed in their reference; many are used more narrowly when actually deciding whom to include than when accounting for someone's presence to outsiders. Most of the terms Balinese use are sufficiently open to interpretation that they can be used to encompass almost anyone local who feels like turning up: *nyama* (*beraya*) can be used, for instance, of anyone with whom one wishes to declare relations of a certain warmth and equality. So, when they choose, Balinese can, with clear consciences, declare that those who work and worship together are all *nyama*! The significance of *purusa* may now be clearer. While it may be used to give ostensibly jural instructions (as in adoption, when the rule tends to read something like: when looking for an heir take the nearest person from the *purusa* – although low castes in fact tend not to), it may equally refer to different categories. It may be those who feel attachment to a place of birth, or to people they grew up with, or those with whom one shares something (still to be defined) in common and so forth. Might one however conclude with the trite comment that patrilineal systems in theory are always bilateral in practice? For reasons that will be discussed shortly, this is not an adequate answer either.

Marriage and the Relationship of 'Male' to 'Female'

It is sensible to look at marriage in the context of male–female relations generally. Humans are not the only class of beings, or things, which properly are found in complementary pairs. In fact, humans are not a very good example to take, because Balinese recognise a third class, of *bancih*, hermaphrodite, transsexual or transvestite, even if there are relatively few persons who allocate themselves or are allocated to this last. Be that as it may, according to various written and oral accounts, 'male' deities have 'female' counterparts, sometimes known, as in India, as their *sakti*, which is commonly translated from the Balinese as 'mystical power', but might more adequately be rendered as 'manifest potency or potentiality'. Female deities, like Durga or Uma (associated with destruction or witches, and rice, respectively), tend to be more immediately involved in Balinese life than do their male 'consorts'. It makes little sense, however, to treat the relation between non-manifest (*niskala*) and therefore largely unknowable agents as marriage. In many situations Balinese do not speak of deities as 'male' or 'female'.

As Balinese domestic and kin relations have been fairly fully outlined elsewhere (Boon 1977; Geertz and Geertz 1975; Hobart 1979), only a few remarks are needed here. Most commonly, after marriage a couple sets up its own home, except for the youngest child or designated heir. Usually a male assumes this role; but, failing sons, women are quite acceptable. As land has become increasingly short, sons tend to stay in their parents' compound, as may daughters. In the ward of Pisangkaja, on which the following account is mainly based, residence arrangements were as follows. In compounds with more than one household, 22 per cent are related by ties other than between males. This excludes female heirs, who are treated in effect as jural males. Significantly, they are said 'to be a man' (literally: 'to have the body of a male', *maraga lanang* in High Balinese), and their husbands are correspondingly designated female. This point will be discussed later. If the constituent compound ties are calculated, those not through males are nearly half. In many instances the exceptions, if they can be called that, are where people live with affines. As living with one's wife's family involves a double humiliation – one cannot afford to keep a family in one's own compound, and one's family cannot afford to keep one – perhaps it is surprising that the figure is so high. If one chooses to read *purusa* as a principle defining agnation however, the problems this entails emerge with horrible clarity.

The rite of *masakapan*, which is the normal cultural condition for forming an effective functioning human domestic unit, is also required similarly for other recognised pairings as diverse as pigs, drums or slit-gongs. The stress in each instance is upon parts forming a functioning whole. Priests must have female counterparts in order to undertake the full range of their religious activities, but these need not be their wives. In just the same way, a man or woman requires a member of the opposite common gender to form a viable household unit because of the sexual division of labour, but this need not in fact be a wife/husband – a sister/brother or another unrelated woman/man is acceptable. The Balinese emphasis on complementarity includes recognition that good cannot exist without evil, kings without peasants, mystic heroes without anti-heroes. It makes at least as much sense to regard the sexual and reproductive union of humans as an aspect of Balinese ideas about the complex relationship of parts to the whole they constitute, as it does to isolate from context one relationship and compare it with others taken out of context. If we wish to focus on marriage as such, should we not include pigs and slit-gongs, which pass through the same rite?

According to traditional accounts the Balinese practise preferential patrilateral parallel cousin marriage (since Bourdieu 1977, this should be a signal of trouble to come), or, failing that, at least marriage within the *dadiya* (Geertz and Geertz 1975), that is, traced by ties of *purusa*. The frequency with which such unions occur varies greatly. In the village of smiths studied by the Geertzs it was high, in the mixed-caste community of Pisangkaja (and equally in the other parts of the settlement) it was very low. As against actual father's brother's daughter marriage of 7 per cent in Tihingan, the equivalents in Pisangkaja were 2 and 1 per cent for high and low castes respectively, and sank lower still for second patrilateral parallel cousins. In fact more high-caste marriages between kin were contracted with non-agnates than agnates (66 per cent as against 33 per cent). For low castes the comparable figures rose to 7–8 per cent with non-agnates. This suggests that, whatever the ideals stated in the ethnographic literature, most cousin marriages tend towards other possibilities (the more so as notionally father's sister's daughter unions are avoided because they involve direct exchange, so the other three possible cousin unions are not equally open in theory). Quite what this implies will become clearer when we look at the overall pattern.

Not all marriages take place with the agreement of the families involved, or even the assent of the partners themselves. As the concern here is with the evidence that recognition of kinship in some sense affects positive marriage choice, I shall omit all those unions (22 per cent for unions between members of the same high caste, 44 per cent for all other unions) in which extraneous factors like being caught *in flagrante* or elopement in the face of disapproval were given as the predominant reasons. What is striking is the high proportion of kin marriages (28 per cent) where there is no agnatic tie at all among low castes. In fact, if one contrasts unions where agnatic ties are thought to exist (also coincidentally 28 per cent) with those where kin ties of some kind are (43 per cent), there is little evidence in favour of a bias towards agnation. The comparable figures for high castes show an equal balance of agnation as against kin ties. So far it is hard to detect from the figures a preference, especially among low castes, for agnatic unions. Were we now to rephrase matters, for the sake of argument, in bilateral terms, the picture is of an even spread with a slight bias, if anything, towards matrilateral kin. The evidence is sufficiently underdetermined to be capable of supporting several alternative hypotheses.

The discussion so far remains seriously incomplete. Almost half the approved marriages of ordinary villagers are between people with no kin tie of any kind in conventional terminology. Need we consider these? Villagers themselves offer an account which is of interest. There is tacit, and not infrequently explicit, agreement on the importance of wealth. Richer families try to avoid their children marrying into poorer families, while often trying to place their own offspring as advantageously as they can. Realistic Balinese remark that one tends to land up marrying those of one's own kind, by that referring not to *purusa*, *dadiya* and so on, but to family capital assets (or rarely, secure salaries). The results of testing this suggestion statistically are spectacular. Marriage is approved significantly more often where the partners come from households of equal wealth. The choice seems to be cash or kin. Or is it kith or kin?

How do wealth and kin connections compare as criteria for approval of marriage? In kin marriages, where unions are agreed to, the parties are closely equal in economic assets. In any case, for reasons to which I wish to turn, it is not necessarily useful to ask if the villagers of Pisangkaja contract ties with others for wealth or because of putative kin links. Wealth certainly seems to play as important a part as, if not more important a part than, kin ties in securing the approval of parents. As the evidence does not suggest a strong bias in favour of agnation as against bilateral kin, an intriguing possibility arises. Family fortunes do not, for the most part, change rapidly in one generation. So those who marry people of equal wealth in one generation may find their children in a position to marry the same people, now kin, in the next! Kin endogamy may be just another way of saying: marry people of like means.

'Aha!' might murmur a cavilling critic, 'for all your fancy footwork at the beginning, you see you cannot do without using kin terms yourself. Your argument is based as much on statistics as those of the rest of us, so you are just measuring your own mirages!' At the risk of disappointing the critic, I must demur and suggest that she or he is confused. First, all anthropological, and indeed all everyday, talk about other cultures involves translational schemes. The problems start when we confuse these with 'reality'. Second, my point has been just how inadequate the received categories of anthropological wisdom are; for they are self-confirming hypotheses, which can be turned against themselves.

'Surely', it might be countered, 'there is more order than you suggest. After all there is an organised system of prescriptions, preferences and prohibitions. There is an underlying system of rules.' For various reasons this reply is less adequate than might at first appear. For a start, the ontological status of rules is unclear: are they constitutive, regulative, ideal, expectations or observations of normal practice? Further, any positive rule in Bali is open to more than one interpretation. The preference for 'real' patrilateral parallel cousin marriage as sacred (Boon 1977: 132) is countered by Balinese who note that it is dangerous to the welfare of the partners (one reason given is that ties through males are hot, in contrast to those through females), and serves largely to consolidate wealth and ties within the *purusa*. (One might question whether it is sacred at all, for the nearest term in Balinese is *suci*, 'pure', and such unions are not generally regarded as *suci*.) Perhaps the most celebrated proscriptions involve what might be called a reverse in the flow of women, such as father's sister's daughter marriage (Boon 1977: 131) or sister exchange (1977: 138). Not only do both occur, but they are justified by alternative interpretations of what is desirable (here that ties through women are cool and so good; and that direct exchange avoids nasty overtones of rank difference). In other words, prescriptions, preferences and prohibitions tend to be re-evaluated in different interpretations. Recourse to rules, or worse pseudo-logical games (for example Boon 1990), are lures for the unwary.

A problem with most anthropological accounts is that cultural constructs are seen as having an independent reality and structuring action at other levels, such as the normative, psychological and so forth. The difficulties are several. It has not been established, for Bali at least, in what sense such levels in gender and kinship relationships are supposed to exist, or by whom they are recognised and under what circumstances. The notion that abstract ideas determine action and so, retrospectively, may be used to explain them looks to have more to do with the pervasive idealism of Western academic thinking than it does with Balinese representations or practice. Finally, postulating levels of reality involves an uncomfortable degree of essentialism. Almost any problem can be cleared up, as Russell tried to do with his paradox, by proliferating levels; but it is at the cost of making an ontologically cluttered world. The solution may also be spurious (see Hobart 1985: 48–9). The difficulty can be highlighted in the difference of Boon's ideals and the idea of metaphor touched on by the Geertzs, for example, that a village is a 'sacred space within whose bounds the fates of all residents are supernaturally intertwined' (Geertz and Geertz 1975: 167). It is one thing to suggest Balinese use a spatial metaphor of a centre and relative distance in terms of which to talk in a certain context. It is another to impute an abstract ideal in terms of which reality in fact is ordered. The former asks us to inquire seriously how people actually use and rework ideas in practice. The latter is not just a retreat into largely ungrounded speculation, it also continues the hegemony of a peculiarly Western vision, which is to perpetuate colonialism by other means.

Constructions of 'Male' and 'Female' in Bali

Constructions of female and male roles, in Bali at least, tend to be strikingly situational. This is less obvious than it might be, because it is easy to be distracted by stereotypes from the relationship between such ideological statements and contrary accounts and usage. More serious, it is still commonplace to impose alien categories upon what people say and do: underdetermination here underwrites facile explanation. Instead of perpetuating prevailing naturalist or semiotic assumptions about gender, it might be useful for a change to inquire into indigenous discourses. I shall suggest that Balinese make extensive use of *guna*, use or function, what a person can do, as a criterion of what makes a woman or man. No single frame of reference, however, is all-embracing. As *guna*, however important, is not the sole aspect of being, it could not be.

The most cursory glance at what Balinese say and do casts a critical light on monolithic academic theories. For a start, Balinese recognise transsexuals as a third distinct role or kind of being, which can only be reduced to a dichotomy by intellectual sleight of hand. While one could doubtless mock up a model to argue that women in Bali are perceived as somehow more natural and men more cultural, it flies in the face of what Balinese say on the subject. It commits the category mistake of imputing a nature:culture distinction *a priori*. Also, in conversations I have overheard, both men and women argue that males are more often prey to anger and lust; and that women bear the greater actual burden of learning and passing on the elaborate details of Balinese civilisation. Frequent disclaimers notwithstanding, debates on gender remain bedevilled by questionable European dichotomies and supposedly context-free 'transitivity' between them. As Errington noted, in writing about gender in Southeast Asia, it may be important not to assume gender to be dualistic. Balinese accounts of the conditions of being suggest humans differ among themselves at once by both degree and kind. So it may not quite be adequate to treat 'men and women as basically the same sorts of beings' (1990: 30).

Even such partly polemical points about academic and indigenous stereotypes run the risk of hypostatisation. They ignore what is actually said and done in different situations. Obviously there is no space here for a detailed analysis of situational use. So brief summaries of a few instances must suffice. On several occasions in Bali I heard males or females assert that women think about the short-term – and men the long-term – consequences of actions (*karma pala*). After fairly detailed research over a year, separately with different groups of women and men, what I learned suggests that in many circumstances one could as easily argue the reverse case. We are dealing however with attributed explanations. There is no simple link between what people say and what they do, what they may say afterwards, and what they say about what other people did. This makes global generalisations even more vapid.

Public pronouncements may well be contradicted in other settings. It is not uncommon to hear statements or witness behaviour, especially in formal public contexts, that implies that males rank superior to females. A popular theme among both women and men when chatting at home or in food stalls is how members of the opposite sex have a far easier time in life. I was rather surprised, therefore, to hear a group of men discussing in what form they would prefer to be reincarnated (rebirth is thought often to be within a few years). They agreed they would all prefer to be reborn as women. I raised this incident with various other groups of villagers and the theme was taken up with some relish. It transpired that almost everyone, whether females or males, took the same view. As several hastened to point out, they had no control over the matter, though! So much for the simplistic summaries and hypothetical questions on which so much anthropology relies!

Even if one allows for the highly situational and contextual nature of assertions about gender, another problem intrudes into anthropological writing on the subject. This is epistemological closure. Even those scholars who are wary of naturalist traps are liable to fall into their Western hermeneutic antithesis and assume that the body is regarded as a semiotic system. It is one thing to explore the analytical value of treating visible differences as potentially signifying (as does Errington 1990: 31–7); it is another to presume that other peoples necessarily do, or that valid conclusions stem from assuming so (for example Boon 1990: 224–33). (The Samoan practice of treating male offspring as daughters when a family deems there to be too few of the latter becomes a delightful instance of denying or overriding visible differences when they grow up muscular and hirsute!) Short of claiming a totalitarian epistemological supremacy, a minimal precondition would be an account of the semiotics of the people in question. That still leaves the question of the ways in which people do in fact evaluate that substantialised duality we call 'gender'. Elsewhere (1983), I have outlined a long discussion between Balinese about the difference between humans and animals. It was concluded by a well-known orator's stating that it depended on one's ability to carry out the full activities of a human. Women are expected not only to be able to bear children, but to engage in domestic tasks like cooking and make offerings, as well as to perform the appropriate female public duties. Equivalent expectations fall on men. Incidentally this accounts as well (and is certainly more faithful to Balinese discursive usage) for the opprobrium with which childless women and men are regarded, and the status of widows and widowers, as does the rather trite structuralist theme of deviation from the 'normal' complementarity between the sexes. Like the blind, they are unable to function fully by Balinese standards.

Earlier on I noted that form (*rupa*) – here the body (*raga*) – is part of a widely used scheme of causation or, perhaps better, what makes things what they are and delimits what they can do. The quite common practice of women's being designated heirs in the absence of a suitable male is interesting, because, as was noted, such women are said to '*maraga lanang*', to have the body of, or be, a man. This seems not to be a specious metaphor. For when Balinese are questioned how this could be, the usual answer is that the women are men for the purposes of inheritance. Furthermore, where there is substantial property, these women quite often behave as the dominant partner in the relevant domestic and sometimes public domains. Their role is quite compatible with their body's capabilities. A more striking instance is the custom of the womenfolk in the nearby village of Petulu of doing the bulk of the hard work of double-hoeing the rice fields. Unlike most Balinese women, they can be seen in the fields heavily smoking cigarettes!

Much writing on gender seems to me to impose unnecessary conceptual straitjackets on what people say and do. Western scholars usually wobble somewhere between a naïve realism that regards the complementarity of gender roles as distilled somehow from 'real' sexual difference and an idealism which treats it as a reflection of 'underlying' taxonomic principles. The problem of the former is that, apart from postulating the commentator's privileged access to reality, it says nothing about how classifications are used subsequently. The latter treats conceptual structures as homogeneous and as agents, of which humans in society are mere instruments. Both treat culture as a monologic system of thought or categories, rather than as involving heteroglossia (in Bakhtin's terms, 1986a) reworked dialogically in different situations. Where anthropologists regard this last possibility with suspicion, this is understandable, in so far as it threatens instant punditry and sweeping but doubtful generalities, and actually requires the commentators to learn the language properly and spend time actually listening to people.

Briefly I wish to explore the possible relevance of a dialogic approach to gender. Relationships are complicated, as is the connection between what people do and how they explain it, in that both are construed and reworked in different ways in different contexts. Appeal to the 'normal' suffices no more than to the 'ideal' (Hacking 1990: 160–9). Instead, one needs to ask who appeals to constructions of what is normal, ideal or whatever and in what situations? This raises the broader question of presuppositions of homogeneity and the monologic nature of language in anthropological explanation. On what grounds do we assume that there is a substance or class, 'gender', beyond dialogically constituted differences, that there is only one way of classifying such differences, that discourse on gender (or kinship) takes the form of a monologue, or that contradiction reflects a failing of the unreflective native mind?

Once one lets go of the vision of culture as some homogeneous monologue, other possibilities come to mind. Rather than gender's being the essential determinant of differential social behaviour, we need to consider when, how, and under what circumstances differences between women and men (however construed) are used as an explanation of action. Such differences widely seem to be sufficiently talked about in everyday life as not to be easily subject to simple regimentation. Certainly, on the occasions I have heard Balinese talk about them, they are fraught with contradiction and irony, and are even used recursively as a reminder of the contextual limits of encompassing schemes of explanation. When Balinese therefore refer to other aspects of social life by using the differences between females and males, this need not be a simple-minded attempt to domesticate deities, drums or what-have-you in a folksy, homespun way. It may offer far less comfortable constructions of the nature of relationships. Balinese may use attributions of male and female to a deity and its *sakti* respectively to suggest not just that the relationship is not simple, but that it is perilous for humans to talk about what is not manifest (*niskala*). Analogy, however, involves the mutual coloration of vehicle and tenor. So one should not assume that we are dealing merely with the extension of differences of sex. I have also heard the interlocking and shifting relationship of the large and small drum parts used to comment on the complex interdependence of husband and wife. Relations between women and men are distinguished *inter alia* in Bali by envy, distrust, antagonism and misunderstanding, as well as longing, care and attachment. This colours usage in ways which are not associated with other paired differences. If simple complementarity is all that is sought, it is unclear why Balinese do not use distinctions of day and night, sun and moon or countless others. There is, in short, no essential way of reading gender. Ascriptions of difference are recursive, situational and underdetermined by facts. Nor do we need *prima facie* to impose such a dichotomous substance when commenting on Balinese discourse in order to encompass the facts or 'collective representations'. On occasion Balinese may, of course, assert there to be essential differences between males and females. Others may question such statements. Assertions of overarching system by Balinese are themselves a distinctive aspect of heteroglossia.

This is not the place to elaborate the extension of Bakhtin's notion of dialogue as a theory of society. I wish, though, to note three points. Anthropologists have tended to ignore what people actually say – perhaps because it clouds the neat picture which is usually presented in academic monographs. Dialogue, however, in various senses has an obvious bearing on the topic of 'gender'. In Bali, relations between males and females form a recurrent theme in popular theatre. For instance, the problems of sexual attraction and unsated desire among the young and issues of status, power and propriety among the old, are represented with many misunderstandings and consequences. Balinese are far subtler commentators on their own usage than most Western anthropologists are. Further to this, the importance of theatre as a form of commentary by Balinese on their own practice makes dialogue central in two ways. Not only is the commentary elaborated in dialogue between actors, but, because the audience is actively involved in appreciating critically what happens, the relationship of troupe and audience is more dialogic than monologic. Finally, dialogue as an image of the differences between women and men is singularly appropriate for a subject which consists in no small part of women and men engaged in argument about such differences. The use of so complex, variable and dialogic a set of relationships as those between men and women does not entail dualistic closure. On the contrary, it suggests all sorts of possibilities, not least an argumentative world. Above all, it offers a vision quite different from timeless biological determinism. It implies that humans – and other forms of critical will – are capable, by the conditions of their being, of reflecting upon, and on occasion changing, those conditions.

Dialogue does not lend itself to the easy closure of monologue. The nature of relations between males, females, *bancih*, divinity and other beings is argued about and its significance rethought in public meetings, theatre, the market, coffee stalls and on all sorts of other occasions in Bali by interested participants. To subsume this diversity under some universal construct of gender or kinship, before inquiring whether Balinese actually talk in these terms, or need to presuppose them in order to talk, is hegemonic. They are arguably as unnecessary as a 'concept of time' is to talk about and appreciate processes of change. If this argument engenders disquiet, so be it. Dismissing the predilection in detective stories for unlikely, but titillating and marketable fantasy, Raymond Chandler once wrote of Dashiell Hammett that he 'gave murder back to the kind of people who commit it for reasons'. All too often it is a strange, truncated Bali that Western investigators serve up, severed from Balinese commentary on their own motives and practices. Perhaps it is time that Balinese were allowed back into the discussion about Bali.

Bibliography

Bakhtin, M. M. (1986a). 'The Problem of Speech Genres'. In C. Emerson and M. Holquist (eds), *Speech Genres and Other Late Essays*. Austin: University of Texas Press.
— (1986b). 'The Problem of the Text in Linguistics, Philology, and the Human Sciences: an Experiment in Philosophical Analysis'. In C. Emerson and M. Holquist (eds), *Speech Genres and Other Late Essays*. Austin: University of Texas Press.
Boon, J. A. (1977). *The Anthropological Romance of Bali 1597–1972: Dynamic Perspectives in Marriage and Caste, Politics and Religion*. Cambridge:

University Press.
— (1990). 'Balinese Twins Times Two: Gender, Birth Order, and "household" in Indonesia/Indo-Europe'. In J. M. Atkinson and S. Errington (eds), *Power and Difference: Gender is Island Southeast Asia*. Stanford: University Press.
Bourdieu, P. (1977). *Outline of a Theory of Practice*. trans. R. Nice, Cambridge: University Press.
Errington, S. (1990). 'Recasting Sex, Gender, and Power: A theoretical and Regional Overview'. In J. M. Atkinson and S. Errington (eds), *Power and Difference: Gender is Island Southeast Asia*. Standford: University Press.
Evans-Pritchard, E. E. (1937). *Witchcraft, Oracles and Magic Among the Azande*. Oxford: Clarendon Press.
— (1956). *Nuer Religion*. Oxford: University Press.
— (1965). The Comparative Method in Social Anthropology. In *The Position of Women in Primitive Society*. London: Faber.
Fortes, M. (1969). *Kinship and the Social Order: The Legacy of Lewis Henry Morgan*. London: Routledge and Kegan Paul.
Geertz, H. and Geertz, C. (1975). *Kinship in Bali*. London: University of Chicago Press.
Gellner, E. (1970). 'Concepts and Society'. In B. Wilson (ed.), *Rationality*. Oxford: Blackwell.
Gonda, J. (1952). *Sanskrit in Indonesia*. Nagpur: Academy of Indian Culture.
— (1970). *Visnuism and Sivaism*. London: Athlone.
Hacking, I. (1990). *The Taming of Chance*. Cambridge: University Press.
Hirsch, E. (1967). *Validity in Interpretation*. New Haven: Yale University Press.
Hobart, M. (1979). *A Balinese Village and its Field of Social Relations*. Unpublished Ph.D. thesis, University of London.
— (1983). 'Through Western Eyes, or How my Balinese Neighbour Became a Duck'. *Journal of the Indonesia circle*. 30: 33–47.
— (1985). 'Texte est un Con'. In R. H. Barnes, D. de Coppet and R. J. Parkin (eds), *Contexts and Levels: Essays on Hierarchy*. J.A.S.O. Occasional Paper No. 4. Oxford: J.A.S.O.
— (1987). 'Summer's Days and Salad Days: The Coming of Age of Anthropology'. In L. Holy (ed.), *Comparative Anthropology*, Oxford: Blackwell.
— (1990). 'The Patience of Plants: A Note on Agency in Bali'. *Review of Indonesian and Malaysian Affairs* 24, 2: 90–135.
Inden, R. (1976). *Marriage and Rank in Bengali Culture*. Berkeley: University of California Press.
— and Nicholas, R. W. (1977). *Kinship in Bengali Culture*. Chicago: University Press.
Kuhn, T. S. (1977). *The Essential Tension: Selected Studies in Scientific Tradition and Change*. Chicago: University Press.
Lansing, S. (1974). 'Evil in the Morning of the World: Phenomenological Approaches to a Balinese Community'. *Michigan Papers on South and Southeast Asia* No. 6, Ann Arbor: Center for South and Southeast Asian

Studies, University of Michigan.

Larson, G. J. (1980). 'Karma as a "Sociology of Knowledge" or "Social Psychology" of Process/Praxis'. In W. D. O'Flaherty (ed.) *Karma and Rebirth in Classical Indian Traditions*. London: University of California Press.

Lienhardt, G. (1961). *Divinity and Experience: The religion of the Dinka*. Oxford: Clarendon.

Long, B. (1980) 'The Concepts of Human Action and Rebirth in the Mahābhārata'. In W. D. O'Flaherty (ed.) *Karma and Rebirth in Classical Indian Traditions*. London: University of California Press.

Needham, R. (1971). 'Remarks on the Analysis of Kinship and Marriage'. In ASA11, R. Needham (ed.), *Rethinking Kinship and Marriage*. London: Tavistock.

— (1975). 'Polythetic Classification: Convergence and Consequences'. *Man* N.S. 10, 3.

Potter, K. H. (1977). *Indian Metaphysics and Epistemology: The Tradition of Nyāya-Vaiśeṣika up to Gaṅgeśa*. Princeton, N.J.: University Press.

— (1980). 'The Karma Theory and its Interpretation in Some Indian Philosophical Systems'. In W. D. O'Flaherty (ed.), *Karma and Rebirth in Classical Indian Traditions*. London: University of California Press.

Quine, W. V. O. (1960). *Word and Object*. Cambridge, Mass.: M.I.T. Press.

Schneider, D. (1968). *American Kinship*. New Jersey: Prentice-Hall.

— (1972). 'What is Kinship all About?'. In P. Reining (ed.) *Kinship Studies in the Morgan Centennial Year*. Washington.

Vitebsky, P. (1993). *Dialogues with the Dead*. Cambridge: University Press.

6

Buddhism, Merit Making and Gender: The Competition for Salvation in Laos

Mayoury Ngaosyvathn[1]

The Lao are so immersed in Buddhism that this religion has become an integral part of Lao national culture and identity. However, Buddhism was an imported religion, which was forced to coexist with a traditional cosmological order and an enduring belief in and worship of spirits. Women are partakers in both, for the Lao searches in animism for 'well-being and a system of terrestrial protection', while turning to Buddhism for response to 'essential problems of life, a way of temporal salvation' (Zago 1972: 380). The resulting experience of Lao women has been determined by traditional marginalised social status, within the limitations of which they have sought improvement of their earthly condition and a better after-life.

Women in Buddhism

Despite the general wisdom which asserts that 'the Buddhist religion mistrusts women' (Dannaud 1954: 30), Lao women were and are its devoted 'faithkeepers', who have ensured its survival throughout the turbulent history of the Lao state.

The spread of Buddhism into Laos and its institutionalisation as a state religion from the eleventh century heightened discriminating practices against women. In favouring men, the Buddhist religion introduced into Laos a notion of female exclusion which was previously less marked. Lao women, as were their peers in other Southeast Asia Theravadin countries, were forbidden to be part of the monastic male-oriented life (Van Esterick 1982: 4).[2] Women had no access to the most valued religious roles in society, since ordination to monkhood was exclusively reserved for men.

Social activity was rigidly segregated to protect 'female innocence' as well as to prevent monks from falling into 'evil temptation'. Hardship was the penalty when an offence had been committed. This situation masked a dialectical relationship between monkhood and womanhood: Buddhism was dependent on female devotees for its survival. Monks had to be fed and female devotees had to remain active in merit-making activities in order to justify for men their continuing role as monks. On the other hand, women needed religion for their salvation in future life. Moreover, if they were active as devotees they could at least gain some social recognition for their efforts.

From the past to the present, travellers have listened to the noise of women grinding rice in the small hours of the morning, as they were preparing the early-morning meal for the monks. Soon they were at work again, preparing the lunch meal for the monks. In the evenings of the numerous holy days they crowded the pagoda courts to listen to prayers. To mark these holy days, they contributed to the innumerable tasks to be performed, such as making beeswax, carving banana trunks, and garlanding flowers to adorn the pagodas and Buddha statues.

Aside from the rudiments of profane knowledge, pagodas provided instruction for those interested in art, literature, traditional medicine, and such important matters as the magic formulae to bless the construction of a new house, how to appeal to benevolent spirits, and how to expel malevolent ones to cure illness. Magical knowledge normally reserved for men and consolidated their power in society (Barber 1974: 52). Some women, however, succeeded in deciphering the manuscripts of latania-leaf written in sacred characters, and mastering a good command of traditional medicine (Aymonier 1885).[3] Some women headed communities of devotees to recite consecrated formulae in the pagoda before the monks began their prayers.

Although limited, such inroads into 'territory' normally recorded for men are not accidental. From generation to generation, Lao women have been reliable ritual specialists involved in merit-making activities. The ethos developed by Buddhism, that women need to acquire more merit than men (Kirsch 1982: 27) kept them busy in merit-making activities. Karim (1989: 25) has suggested that 'women deliberately penetrate the public ritual sphere of Buddhism by partaking in merit-making activities. Affordability even allows women to assume the position of patron or sponsor, extending their entrepreneurship in ritual.'

At all times, even after 1975 when Buddhism in Laos suffered from official displeasure, women doggedly continued to keep the faith alive

Figure 6.1   People making offerings to the monks

by offering rice to monks on their daily rounds. During these offerings, their posture emphasises their low status, for they kneel when holding the rice bowl. They have to avoid brushing against the yellow robe of the monk who presents his metal bowl (Lévy Phimmasone 1963: 257), while at the same time punctiliously avoiding eye contact with the monks (Breazeale and Smuckarn 1988: 209).[4] When encountering monks or novices, women sit respectfully at a proper distance in a position lower than that of the men, with their hands joined in front of their heads, even if the monk or novice is their own child. As representatives of the Buddha in the human world, monks or novices have to avoid any show of affection, which is viewed as unbecoming given the monastic ideal of equanimity (Zago 1972: 57). Such traditional rules are strictly adhered to in most regions of Laos. If a woman violates one of these, she will be in a position of demerit. Some anthropologists (Kirsch 1982: 27)[5] have contended that the ordination of a young child as novice is a ritual of initiation into adulthood, which simultaneously reaffirms a man's special position in Buddhism. However, it is obvious that it is women who keep the system together. They need men as monks to ensure their own salvation and because of that, women compete, as mothers or wives, to persuade their sons or husbands to become monks.

Mother and Son, Wife and Husband, in the Competition for Salvation

Buddhist doctrine emphasises the importance of filial piety by rewarding a mother for nurturing a child. A son who becomes a monk is in a particularly good position to reward his mother for her efforts in child-rearing. Similarly a father who has made sacrifices in bringing up his children derives merit when his son becomes a monk. Many parents are convinced that the ordination of a son will guarantee them a better place in their next lives; parents are said to be 'lifted into heaven on the yellow robe of their son' (Thitsa 1980: 18). The mother, in particular, can obtain enough merit through her son to achieve *nirvana* (Zago 1972: 34).[6]

While a son can help his mother achieve *nirvana*, a daughter can only pray for her parents to enjoy a good after-life. Thus Buddhism discriminates against females in a society which otherwise equally values boys or girls. A daughter obtains merit by caring for her parents when they are old and sick. Despite this, she is never able to earn for her parents the merit required for a better future life.

As a wife, a woman can also obtain merit through her husband, if he can be persuaded to become a monk. Through this ordination, she can cling to the fringes of her husband's saffron robe to be lifted into heaven when she dies. During the ordination, a man and his wife must go through a token 'divorce' in front of witnesses, and both have to ask pardon from their parents for all wrongdoing committed in the past. Those about to become monks must be purified. When the husband wants to become a layman again, another rite consisting of a token 'marriage' will be performed after the saffron robe is removed. After donning his layman's clothes, a virgin girl will give her hand to the former monk to help him cross the sacred space of the pagoda (which in a ritual sense implies that he has resumed a lay life). Such a man in traditional Lao culture, is a 'strengthened man' or a 'respected man and a responsible member of his village' (LeBar and Suddard 1960: 78). As a result, parents, particularly mothers, encourage their sons to become monks before their marriage, so they can acquire the maximum merit from them (Zago 1972: 54).[7] If a son becomes a monk after marriage, parents believe that their daughters-in-law will take away part of the merit which they deserve for caring for their son all those years. Hence women of different generations, with often conflicting social roles, as mother and wife must further compete out of necessity, willingly or unwillingly, to obtain the maximum merit from their sons and husbands. The marginalised have to struggle among themselves to achieve the narrow path to salvation for the sake of their souls.

Despite the relentless sacrifices women make to achieve merit, the burden of providing merit is as severe as the burden of achieving it. A man is socialised from a young age to repay his debts to his parents. If he chooses not to do so, he experiences the guilt of not providing his parents with sufficient merit to acquire a good rebirth in a future life. A woman, on the other hand, has to depend on her son or husband to provide merit for her, and will do her utmost to ensure that she gets her due share. However, in order to achieve these favours she has to perform sacrifices in feeding and preparing for ritual celebrations.

The system thus operates like a prayer wheel. Women and men go around in circles to fulfil the requirements of merit for the self and the 'other'. But it is a wheel only male hands may turn. A woman must get a monk to turn the wheel for her. Only thus can she manipulate the system to her advantage (Karim 1989), without being a monk or nun. As monks, men also manipulate the system to their advantage, by living off the labour and toil of women. For both parties, however, it is a necessary *quid pro quo*.

Women in Myths of Origin and the Foundation of Cities

As in many countries in the world, the Lao today come from many cultural and ethnic backgrounds. They embrace two main belief systems: the Buddhist religion, and forms of animism comprising beliefs in a multitude of spirits. The role of women in this second religious domain is very important within the community, for they are responsible for the rituals linking the sky and the earth. Such a role has deep historical roots. Already in the Lao myth of origin, it was a woman *Mae Nya Ngam* or *Nya Nyeu* (grandmother *Nyeu*)[8] who sacrified herself with her husband, *Pu Nyeu* (grandfather *Nyeu*) in cutting down *kheua khao kat*, the gigantic and baleful liana, which links the earth to the sky. This liana had grown so vast, it covered the planet so completely, that it blocked out the sun. After hacking away at the liana so that human beings could enjoy sunlight again, the couple were crushed to death when the giant vine collapsed. From that time on, both were venerated as *devada luang*, guardian deities of the kingdom (Aijmer 1979: 737). An altar was built for them in the garden of the pagoda Vat Aram, and year after year, till 1975, tribute was paid by the Lao king and court to these ancestors during the New Year ceremonies in the royal capital of Luang Prabang. Nowadays, in remembrance of this couple, most Lao people, and particularly the Lao of Luang Prabang, will, before they eat, invoke *ma nyeu, kin nyeu*! (come *nyeu*, eat *nyeu*!).

In times past, Lao towns were guarded against danger through voluntary human sacrifices by women whose spirits, upon their death, returned to protect the city. These spirits were known as *phi meuang* (i.e. 'city spirits') 'a relic of what may be the oldest form of religion in Southeast Asia' (Davis 1984: 273).

An example of such a pillar spirit is *Sao Si* (Lady *Si*), commonly known as *Nya Mae Si Meuang*. She was a young woman, several months pregnant, who sacrificed herself as described. Her name was given to the pagoda Vat Si Meuang.[9] This was the first pagoda established during the foundation of Vientiane by King Saisetthathiraj, as the new capital of Lan Xang in 1564. People in Vientiane recount that when Vientiane was being established as the capital of the kingdom of Lan Xang, and when the central pillar of the capital was about to be planted, this inspired a pregnant woman, *Sao Si*, to throw herself into the pit to be buried alive by the city pillar. This action gave her the status of spirit of the new capital. Nowadays, an annual ceremony, performed on the eve of the most important traditional celebration of the year, the *That Luang* festival, which is consecrated to the Lao national stupa, pays tribute to this woman.[10] The belief in the power of Lady *Si* is widespread, and even the Lao settled overseas require their parents in Laos to solicit her assistance to overcome protracted problems encountered in a new country.[11]

Nang Thiam, A Link Between Death and Human Beings

In daily life, women mediums commonly known as *Nang Thiam* (Lady in trance) or *Mo Thiam* (Doctor in trance),[12] equivalent to shamans in other civilisations,[13] play an important intermediary role between the world of human beings and that of the spirits.[14] When possessed by a male spirit, the *Nang Thiam* dresses as a man. This often happened in Luang Prabang.[15] Their activities are extensive, ranging from diagnostic and curing rituals to exorcism and putting loved ones in touch with dead kinsmen. They also act as oracles foretelling the future of the harvest or events of the coming year. Another popular activity relates to the solving of personal problems, particularly those relating to the family and marriage. For instance, if a child is drowned, it is of the *Nang Thiam* that the parents enquire of the child's whereabouts. The *Nang Thiam* is able to locate the corpse along the river. By the same process, people consult her on the identity of the thief who has stolen a precious necklace or the outcome of an important investment that has just been made.

Another important dimension to Lao supernaturalism is the intensively personal mode in which it is reproduced. Spirit-mediums are strictly non-hereditary. Anyone has an equal chance of becoming a medium, though the majority of women selected to be the *Nang Thiam* are young, and generally pretty (Pottier 1973: 101).[16] A *Nang Thiam* may expect a daughter or niece to succeed her, only to find that another person has been inspired to take over. A *Nang Thiam* must have the ability to withstand pain and suffering. Furthermore, the agreement of the guardian spirits of the village or the city has to be obtained, and a person who is 'disapproved of' by the guardian spirits for the purpose of being their 'vehicle', 'horse', 'seat', or 'body' will not get their cooperation in shamanistic perform-ances.[17] Generally then, the non-hereditary mode of perpetuating the *Nang Thiam* stands in sharp symbolic contrast to the predestination of fate through Buddhism. It is as egalitarian as Buddhism is hierarchical, explaining human fate through chance rather than destiny.

Spirit-mediumship is so important in folk society that Lao woman have become the symbol of supernatural authority. Possession of supernatural power is one of the most effective strategies demonstrating their social worth in society (Zago 1972: 55). In other Lao ethnic minorities, women

Figures 6.2 (a) & (b): *Nang Thiess*

play an important role as priestesses. For example, among the Black Tai, who are non-Buddhists, women are the officiants at the *baci-sukhuan* or the soul-fastening ceremony, so pervasive in the way of life of the Lao (Ngaosyvathn 1990), and are called *Mae Mot*. The same priestess role is found among the Red Tai, or the White Tai (Lafont 1959: 817–40).[18] Among the Brou minority,[19] a priestess called *Arak* is the medium and officiant at the *baci-sukhuan* ceremony (Matras 1973: 80–3).

Symbolically, women as spirit mediums and ritual specialists insured the community against all risks (Hours 1973: 59). Psychologically, they perform the therapeutic role of softening the blows of poverty, misfortune and calamity. In a world where *karma* and *nirvana* make individuals fatalistic about life, these women help people to obtain a sense of purpose and direction in the present and future. In other words, their spirituality is oriented towards developing personal powers in the public sphere, through contacts with the spirit realm, and access to the linkages between this world and the hereafter. These activities give the Lao a sense of control over life which Buddhism denies. Through women, the link between the past, present and future is articulated in clearer terms, democraticising a life process which is otherwise autocratic in its predeterminism. The Lao are a people fundamentally superstitious, and women are the most ardent followers and keepers of superstition. By controlling rites and practices linked to the past, women provide the Lao with a sense of calculated assurance about the continuity of interpersonal and communal relations in the future.

The Supernaturalism of Women Metaphorised in Their Images as Goddesses

As in other countries practising Theravada Buddhism, in Laos the New Year occurs in April,[20] and surprisingly enough ceremonies are placed under the aegis of a woman called *Nang Sangkhane*. Such a woman embodied a goddess. For the day, she is adorned with the most brilliant finery, and is paraded on a float lavishly decked with flowers. She is taken around the town to conjure away bad influences, and at the same time to bring prosperity to all inhabitants. Women and fertility are connected, which serves to counter the low status reserved to them in the Buddhist religion. Furthermore, goddesses also preside over daily life. The seven days of the week are named after different goddesses. Sengsai Giai (Giai 1981: 48)[21] wrote that 'the Lao as their neighbors the Thai, give a great importance to the days of the week and attribute to them a peculiar quality.

Each day carries a name of a goddess.'

Women maintain the symbolic attributes of goddesses in other contexts, such as rice-cultivation, which allows them to participate intimately in the supernatural world (Halpern 1964: 26–9). Seidenfaden (1958: 94–6) has explained how 'the Lao believe in a soul of the rice, a female spirit who dwells in the last sheaf to be gathered. This superstition seems formerly to have had a wide extension both in Southeastern Asia and in Europe where it was also found in the Nordic countries.' The rice-soul rite is unfailingly performed among the people inhabiting the valley of the Mekong, as well as among the minorities living in the mountains, the Lao Theung (upland Lao) and the Lao Sung (highland Lao).[22] The same belief is found in Thailand.[23] Women dominate these rituals as goddesses, priestesses and participants. Before the ricefields are tilled, women appeal to the goddess of rice, commonly called *Phosob Thevi* (*Phosob* Goddess) or *Mae Phosob* (*Phosob* Mother). This ritual ceremony is aimed at obtaining blessing for a prosperous harvest and to prevent natural calamities from destroying the crops. As goddesses and priestesses, women assume total responsibility over the continuity of the agrarian cycle, and the fate of the community. They especially had control over the invisible universe, crowded with spirits, over which human beings otherwise have little influence. They were thus required to conciliate the spirits to ensure survival and to prevent their animosity and wrath. After 1975, political campaigns were launched against superstitious beliefs to eradicate such despised 'old-fashioned' and 'pernicious' behaviour. Some impact was noticeable in urban as well as in rural areas. However, this was very transitory, for since 1980 the old rituals have gained new ground and new strength in the face of general economic deterioration.

Conclusion

Since 1975, women have been given new roles befitting the new political environment. Their responsibilities are wider than before, and they are expected to fulfil multiple, demanding and often conflicting roles: wife, mother, housekeeper, farmer, faithkeeper, member of the local branch of the party, the Lao Women's Unions, the Lao People's Revolutionary Youth Union, the Federation of Lao Trades Unions, the Lao Front for National Construction, the local militia, and the administration. With increasing demands to assume a more public role, their secondary position in Buddhism seems less important. Increasingly demanding, however, is the need to balance economic with public activity. In this respect women's

Figures 6.3 (a) & (b): *Boun Bang Iai*

continued interest in spiritual activities associated with animism and merit-making activities within Buddhism is part of an attempt to integrate the future in the present and the present in the future. Spiritualism and merit-making exist in a dialectical relationship of complementarity rather than conflict, engendering social and public activity in such a way that each sex becomes a specialist in events in different spaces and times.

Notes

1. I am indebted to Wazir Jahan Karim, Convenor of the Unit of Women's and Human Resource Studies, School of Social Sciences (Universiti Sains Malaysia) for this article. She has constantly encouraged and helped me in editing and rewriting it. I also would like to thank gratefully Otome Hutheesing, School of Social Sciences (Universiti Sains Malaysia), for editing two earlier versions of this paper. My grateful thanks also go to Dr Martin Stuart-Fox (University of Queensland, St Lucia), and Dr Pheuiphanh Ngaosyvathn (Griffith University, Queensland) for reading it again.
2. Kabilsigh 1984: 74; Keyes 1984: 233, 1986: 68; Breazeale and Smuckarn 1988: 209.
3. Lévy Phimmasone 1963: 248.
4. Dannaud 1954: 50.
5. Keyes 1986: 75–6.
6. Barber 1974: 50.
7. Breazeale and Smuckarn 1988: 171.
8. There are also other couples among of Lao ancestors, such as *Pu Thav Lay, Mae Mot; Pu Sang Ka Sa, Nya Sang Ka Si; Pu Pheum, Nya Ka Leum.* They became protector spirits of the royal capital Luang Prabang at the time of its establishment (Archaimbault 1959: 386–93).
9. On the pagoda of *Si Meuang*, see Deydier 1954: 90–2.
10. *That Luang* is the national shrine where official cultural ceremonies were annually performed during the period of the waxing moon of the twelfth Lao month, equivalent to the fourth week of November. According to the new Lao Constitution, it is recognised as a national symbol.
11. This tribute comprises a couple of fresh coconuts, bananas, fresh white flowers, candles, jossticks and money if one wishes. In 1989, the Lao community in Hawaii claimed that *Nya Mae Si Meuang* (Lady *Si Meuang*) had become incarnated in a *Nang Thiam* in Hawaii.
12. See Wijeyewardene 1981: 2 for details on a 'trance'.
13. For instance, in Malaysia, see Karim 1990: 21–63; Rashid 1990: 64–95;

Nasuruddin 1990: 142–58.

14. It is also true of the Lao resettled in the United States of America, where the shaman's role is to provide a link with life back in Laos (Tenhula 1991: 98).

15. Doré (1972: 76, 80, 83, 84, 88–9; 1973: 115, 116, 119) mentioned a woman of 23 who as a medium dressed in male clothes four times a day when she was in a trance brought about by a spirit. Four male spirits were incarnated in her for about two and half hours. Similar observations come from Thailand, see Irvine (1984: 320–1). However, Pottier (1973: 106) notes that in Vientiane 'We observed some cases where male mediums received the name of *Nang Thiam*, the term *nang* meaning "lady".' In Crete, if the male medium is possessed by a female spirit, he must dress as a female (Bernard 1985: 24).

16. Doré 1979: 14, 19; 1987: 76; Long 1993. A similar situation was found in Thailand, see Wijeyewardene 1981: 6.

17. Pottier (1973: 100) noted that the contender was designated by the community, and then the election was consented to by the spirits.

18. Pottier 1973: 103.

19. These groups have the same Austroasiatic language; most of them live near the Khmer–Lao border (Matras 1973: 71, 74).

20. In April, the traditional New Year parade led by the seven daughters, *Nang Sa:ngkhane*, of Kapila Brahma, is celebrated annually in Luang Prabang. See Nginn 1967; Viravong 1974; Channignavong 1974 for the story of *Nang Sa:ngkhane*. A similar celebration of the Tai Lu in Sipsong Panna, China, dedicated to seven daughters of the goddess (Zheng Lan 1983).

21. See Viravong 1974; Channignavong 1974; Giai 1981 for details on the name of goddesses of the week days.

22. Manola, S. (1985) 'Great Family of the Lao Nation: Ethnic Minority Khamu, Traditions and Culture' (in Lao), *Vanndlin*, May, 67: 6–7.

23. This ritual ceremony was also practised at the beginning of work in the ricefields in the central plain of Thailand: see Rajadhon 1961: 39; Seidenfaden 1958: 94–6. And Kajiwara (1983: 72) noted 'the spirit cult is presided over by an elderly female of the household as its specialist'. For more details, see Hubert 1981.

Bibliography

Aijmer, G. (1979). 'Reconciling Power with Authority: An Aspect of State Craft in Traditional Laos'. *Man*, 4:14, 734–49.

Archaimbault, C. (1959). 'La Naissance du Monde selon les traditions lao'. In *La Naissance du Monde*. Paris: Seuil.

Arvon, H. (1973). *Le Bouddhisme*, Que-Sais-Je? Paris: Presses Universitaires de France.

Aymonier, E. (1885). *Notes sur le Laos: Impressions et Souvenirs sur les Moeurs,*

Coûtumes, Traditions, Religions et Superstitions des Habitants des Diverses Régions du Laos. Saigon: Imprimerie Coloniale.

Barber, M. (1974). 'Urbanization and Religion in Laos: A Comparative Study'. In Barber and Doré (eds), *Sangkhom Khady San*. Vientiane: Pakpasak Press.

Bernard, J. L. (1985). *La Femme dans les Sociétés Secrètes*. France: Henri Veyrier.

Breazeale, K. and Smuckarn S. (1988). *A Culture in Search of Survival. The Phuan of Thailand and Laos*, Southeast Asia Studies, Monograph Series 31. New Haven: Yale University Press.

Channignavong, K. (1974). *Khanob thamniam lae hit sib sohng khohng sib si* (Traditions and Customs. The Twelve Rites and Fourteen Traditions). Vientiane: Latsabandit Sapha Lao.

Condominas, G. (1968). 'Notes sur le Bouddhisme Populaire en Milieu Rural Lao'. *Archives de Sociologie des Religions*, January–June, 25: 81–110.

Dannaud, J. P. (1954). *Indochine profonde*. Saigon: Revue Indochine, Sud-Est Asiatique.

Davis, R. B. (1984). *Muang Metaphysics*. Bangkok: Pandora Press.

Deydier, H. (1954). *Lokapala*. Paris: Plon.

Doré, P. S. A. (1972). *De l'Hibiscus à la Frangipane*. Paris: Centre d'Etudes de Documentation et de Recherches sur l'Asie du Sud Est et Monde Insulindien.

—— (1973). 'Notes sur les rites à l'autel de Lak Man'. *Asie du Sud est et Monde Insulindien*, 1(4): 111–32.

—— (1979). 'Profils Médiumiques Lao'. *Cahiers de l'Asie du Sud Est*, 5: 7–25.

—— (1987). 'Aux Sources de la Civilisation Lao: Contribution Ethno-Historique à la Connaissance de la Culture Louang-Phrabangnaise', Mémoire presented for the dissertation, Faculté Es-Lettres et Sciences Humaines, Paris.

Giai, S. (1981). 'La Semaine Lao'. *Sudestasie*, 13: 48.

Halpern, J. M. (1964). *Economy and Society of Laos. A Brief Survey*, Southeast Asia Studies, Monograph Series, No. 5. New Haven: Yale University Press.

Hours, B. (1973). 'Les Rites de Défense Chez Les Lavé du Sud-Laos'. *Asie du Sud Est et Monde Insulindien*, 3:4, 31–60.

Hubert, A. (1981). 'Rites à Mae Posop en Thailande du Centre'. *Peninsule*, 2–3: 5–17.

Irvine, W. (1984). 'Decline of Village Spirit Cults and Growth of Urban Spirit Mediumship. The Persistence of Spirit Beliefs, the Position of Women and Modernization'. *Mankind*, 4:14, 315–24.

Jordt, I. (1988). 'Bhikkhuni, Thilasinh, Mae-Chii: Women who Renounce the World in Burma, Thailand and the Classical Pali Buddhist Texts'. *Crossroads, Southeast Asian Studies*, Northern Illinois's Center for Southeast Asian Studies, Special Burma, 1(4).

Kabilsigh, C. (1984). 'Buddhism and the Status of Women'. In *Buddhism and Society in Thailand*. India: The Catholic Press.

Kajiwara, K. (1983). 'Blessing and Display: On Northern Thai House-Warming

Ceremonies'. *Osaka University East Cultural Studies*, 22, 1–4.

Karim, W. J. (1989). 'Gender in Southeast Asia: Anthropological Perspectives in Feminism and Post-Feminism'. Expert Group Meeting Sub-Regional Workshop on *Research Methodologies, Perspectives and Directions for Policy in Women/Gender Studies in Southeast Asia*, KANITA Research Programme, Penang.

—— (1990). 'Prelude to Madness: The Language of Emotion in Courtship and Early Marriage'. In W. J. Karim (ed.), *Emotions of Culture. A Malay Perspective*, South-East Asian Social Science Monographs. Kuala Lumpur: Oxford University Press.

Keyes, C. F. (1984). 'Mother or Mistress but never a Monk: Buddhist Notions of Female Gender in Rural Thailand'. *American Ethnologist*, May, 11:2, 223–41.

—— (1986). 'Ambiguous Gender: Male Inititation in a Northern Thai Buddhist Society'. In *Gender and Religion: On the Complexity of Symbols*. Boston: Beacon Press.

Kirsch, T. (1982). 'Buddhism, Sex-Roles and the Thai Economy'. In P. Van Esterik (ed.), *Women of Southeast Asia*, Northern Illinois University's Center for Southeast Asia Studies, Monograph Series on Southeast Asia, Occasional Paper, No. 9. DeKalb: Northern Illinois University.

Lafont, P. B. (1959). 'Pratiques médicales des Thai Noirs du Laos de l'Ouest'. *Anthropos*, 54, 817–40.

LeBar, F. M. and Suddard, A. (eds) (1960). *Laos: Its People, Its Society, Its Culture*. New Haven: The Human Relations Area Files Press.

Lévy Phimmasone, B. (1963). 'Yesterday and Today in Laos: A Girl's Autobiographical Notes'. In Barbara E. Ward (ed.), *Women in the New Asia. The Changing Social Roles of Men and Women in South and Southeast Asia*. Paris: Unesco.

Long, D. L. (1993). *Ban Vinai: The Refugee Camp*. New York: Columbia University Press.

Manivanna, K. (1969). 'Modes de Production du Laos. Aspects Socio-Economiques du Laos Médiéval'. In *Le Mode De Production Asiatique*. Paris: Editions Sociales.

Matras, J. (1973). 'Possession et Procédés Thérapeutiques Chez les Brou du Cambodge'. *Asie du Sud Est et Monde Insulindien*, 1:4, 71–97.

Nasuruddhin, M. G. (1990). 'Dancing to Ecstasy on the Hobby Horse'. In W. J. Karim (ed.), *Emotions of Culture. A Malay Perspective*, South-East Asian Social Science Monographs. Singapore: Oxford University Press.

Ngaosyvathn, M. (1990). 'Individual Soul, National Identity: The baci-Sou Khuan of the Lao'. *Sojourn*, (Singapore), September 5:2, 283–307.

Nginn, P. S. (1967). 'Le Boun Pimay' (New Year Festivities), *Revue Française*, October, No. 203: 44–52.

Pottier, R. (1973). 'Note sur les Chamanes et Médiums de Quelques Groupes Thai'. *Asie du Sud Est et Monde Insulindien*, 1:4, 99–109.

Rajadhon, A. (1961). *Life and Ritual in Old Siam. Three Studies of Thai Life and Customs*. New Haven: Human Relations Area Files Press.

Rashid, R. (1990). 'Martial Arts and the Malay Superman'. In W. J. Karim (ed.), *Emotions of Culture. A Malay Perspective*, South-East Asian Social Science Monographs. Singapore: Oxford University Press.

Seidenfaden, M. E. (1958). *The Thai Peoples: The Origins and Habitats of the Thai Peoples*. Bangkok: Siam Society.

Tenhula, J. (1991). *Voices from Southeast Asia*. New York: Holmes and Meier.

Thitsa, K. (1980). *Providence and Prostitution. Image and Reality for Women in Buddhist Thailand*. London: Change Reports, Calvert's North Star Press.

Van Esterik, P. (1982). 'Introduction'. In P. Van Esterik (ed.), *Women of Southeast Asia*, Northern Illinois University's Center for Southeast Asian Studies, Monograph Series on Southeast Asia, Occasional Paper, No. 9. DeKalb: University of Northern Illinois: 1–13.

Viravong, S. (1974). *Hit Sib Sohng* (The Twelve Rites). Vientiane: Pakpasak Press.

Wijeyewardene, G. (1981). 'Scrubbling Scurf: Medium and Deity in Chiang Mai'. *Mankind*, 1:13, 1–14.

Zago, M. (1972). *Rites et Cérémonies en Milieu Bouddhiste Lao*, Documenta Missionalia, 6. Rome: Università Gregoriana.

Zheng Lan (1983). *Travels Through Xishuang Banna*, 1981. Reproduced in *Silapavatthanatham* (Art and Culture, Thailand), July, No. 9.

7

Vietnamese Women and Confucianism: Creating Spaces from Patriarchy

Stephen O'Harrow[1]

The Problem

It appears that in the personal lives of Vietnamese men, one of the most persistent areas of discontent is the contradiction between what men believe their relationships to the women in their families ought to be and what those relationships really are, between what the rightful place of the male should be in their eyes and what it is. This, in turn, plays itself out against the background of how Vietnamese women think their men are going to behave. Thus, it would be helpful to start out by asking how do Vietnamese men believe women should act? What is the history of that belief? In what way is that ideal different from how Vietnamese women really behave? And what do Vietnamese women think Vietnamese men are up to?

To begin, the Vietnamese uphold an eclectic moral theory which is a combination of three early traditions:

1. Confucian moral paradigms (with, for the Communists, a thin Marxist veneer in modern times);
2. Buddhist–Taoist *metaphysical* reflections; and
3. *practical* folkways, including animism, since it involves practical interaction with the world of local Vietnamese spirits, for the benefit of daily life.

For centuries, the Confucian and Buddhist–Taoist patriarchal ideal has infused Vietnamese practical life. While the Buddhist–Taoist ideology relates more to definitions of public and ritual power, it is Confucianism which permeates family, intersexual and intergenerational relationships in the most profound way. Generally, the Confucian conception of society is based on a series of idealised relationships:

a. those relationships linked to the 'macro' society,[2] i.e.,
   - between Heaven [whose will must be fathomed by the Emperor] and the Emperor
   - between the Emperor [setter of example to the idealised gentleman] and his mandarins
   - between the mandarin [for idealised gentleman] and *the people (those whom he administers)*

b. relationships on the 'micro' level, i.e.,
   - between husband [idealised gentleman] and *wife*
   - between father [idealised gentleman] and *children*
   - between elder brother [idealised gentleman] and younger *sibling*
   - between teacher [idealised gentleman] and student
   - between friend [idealised gentleman] and friend.

Marxist ideology has underplayed the importance of Confucianism on the level of macro society, finding greater usefulness in Buddhism, which through its institution of priesthood and ritual-making, maintains a clearly defined separate ideology from Marxism. Its strength is in ritual rather than politics, and the afterlife rather than current affairs. Confucianism, without a priesthood or public ritual, fails to complement State ideology the way Buddhism can, and remains a stronghold of the family. The metaphor of the 'male' in macro society, however, permeates family intersexual relationships, engendering the family system further.

This enables the husband to formalise his position as 'superior' by assuming the features of mandarin and teacher. He is responsible for commanding, guiding, teaching, nurturing, and protecting the 'inferior', who is here the wife. On another level she becomes the student and commoner, and is responsible for obeying and venerating the 'superior'.

One will immediately note that this paradigm is *holistic* in both content and style (it is *all-encompassing*, treats society as an organic *whole*, subject to a *single* mode of meaningful analysis); secondly that it is *normative* (it tells us what we *ought* to be doing); and thirdly that it focuses on the idealised gentleman and is *expressly patriarchal* (except for the roles in italics, there is little or no emphasis on roles that women can play, and those which might involve women are all subordinated to men). Women in this *Weltanschauung* are almost incidental, furniture on the stage rather than actors. Their function is to obey and to show proper (i.e., obedient) behaviour in word and deed, through chastity and submissiveness.[3]

In point of fact, while chastity [*trinh tiet*] was supposedly required of both men and women, in practice, male chastity was almost never emphasised from a moral point of view, but rather from a *metaphysical* or pseudo-medical standpoint: it was believed that in giving himself to a women, a man's sexual energies [*duong*] were drained, while a women gained power (by increasing *am*). In other words, women got their hold over men in bed.[4] In any event, since society permitted men multiple wives, they could theoretically be chaste within marriage and still enjoy variety, something quite forbidden to women. Widows were permitted to remarry, but it was considered more virtuous for them to remain faithful to their late husbands.[5] I shall return to this point about *moral chastity for women* versus *metaphysical chastity for men* a little later.

Submissiveness (commonly called the 'three submissions', *tam tong*) was usually thought of in terms of specific periods in a woman's life. In childhood, she was supposed to obey her father; as soon as she was married (coincidental with the transition point from childhood), she was to obey her husband; and when her husband died (the almost universal pattern was for older men to marry young women), she was to obey her eldest son. There was a series of sub-actors in this paradigm. Female children were theoretically submissive to all older males in the family (elder brothers, uncles, grandfathers), as well as to their mothers and grandmothers. Once married, the role of enforcer of submission fell as often to the husband's mother as to the husband himself (see Ngaosyvathn, this volume).

Social and Economic Realities

Now if a Vietnamese male were to believe in this system, which obviously seems to bring with it significant advantages for him *vis-à-vis* his womenfolk, what hopes would he have of seeing it carried out in practice, bearing in mind that Confucianism is essentially Chinese, imported into a family system which is Vietnamese, that is to say, part of a wider Southeast Asian social system where women's power is founded in the family? In other Southeast Asian cultures (see Karim, Chapter 2, this volume) it is also through the family that women gain economic and political venues of decision-making, blurring boundaries of the 'domestic' and 'public'.

Do males, in fact, control the most important features of daily life? Are they in control of their wives? Are Vietnamese women chaste and submissive? Do men uphold economic decision-making within their family? For answers, we must look to economics, history and folklore (the secret and not-so-secret sayings of the common people, which often have the force of customary law), and personal observation. Much of what is subsequently recorded here refers to my own personal relationships with Vietnamese men and women, which span many decades of my life.

It is worthwhile remembering that, in the fateful winter of 1945, two million peasants in northern Viet Nam starved to death, an event incomprehensible anywhere else in Southeast Asia.[6] Even today, for all intents and purposes, Viet Nam has no meaningful macro-economy – the largest significant transactions in the lives of the average Vietnamese are microtransactions. This is not only due to the fact that heavy industry and large-scale operations are not yet widely enough distributed to make important inroads into the economic lives of the peasantry, but also because, with a few exceptions, the state-run economy (centrally planned by a largely male bureaucracy) is nearly bankrupt. Furthermore (in addition to government-encouraged liberalisation), the cooperative farming system is falling apart, even in the North, where it has been the preferred structure for over three decades. The Southern farmers were never successfully collectivised in the first place, so that peasants now as always look to the local market for the margin that sustains life.

What this means in practice is that small businesses are the heart of the distributive economy of Viet Nam. What goes on in the village or city market determines to a large extent how well the average family lives. It is here that most farm surplus is sold and it is here that the most significant prices are negotiated: how much for some onions, for a pair of slippers, a piece of cloth, a bicycle chain, or a package of cigarettes.

At this most important crossroad of the Vietnamese national economy, Vietnamese women act as the arbiters quasi-exclusively. Nearly all market stalls are run by women. In the towns, there are few Vietnamese-run shops that are openly or discreetly controlled by women.[7] Not only do women form the overwhelming majority of all active merchants in the country, they constitute the mass of the customers as well.[8] I would not hesitate to assert that more than half (probably a great deal more than half) of all commercial transactions at the point of sale in Viet Nam involve no men on either side.

And it seems that this has been the case historically as well. In the eighteenth century, the Reverend Father Koffler noted (quoted in Poirier,

Marie: 'La Conquête de la femme indigène en pays d'Annam', *La Grande Revue*, 10 December 1913: 717–36)

> In this kingdom, it can be said in praise of both the men and women that, born to work, they flee from idleness as they would from pestilence. But the latter [i.e., the women] take the prize, due to their truly inborn skills at augmenting the family's patrimony. The men take care of public offices, they are soldiers, hunters, artisans, fishermen. The women, and not without considerable revenue, engage in commerce in the market, as well as in the markets of foreign merchants of all countries . . .

Understanding the economic life of women in Viet Nam is crucial to a general understanding of their position in society. In spite of the male role of provider which is implicit in the Confucian paradigm, Vietnamese mothers raise their daughters to understand, if not explicitly, then by example, that they should always have their own money, and cannot depend on men. That Vietnamese men are, in fact, as imbued with the work ethic as are the women, can be attested to by any observer of the economic activity of the Vietnamese refugee communities in the West, where Vietnamese men commonly hold two and sometimes three jobs at a time to support their families. But the popular notion persists, commonly abetted by male authors such as the nineteenth-century libertine Tran Te Xuong (1890) that the height of *machismo* is not some Mediterranean predilection to physical abuse of women, but rather a gentlemanly idleness at their expense:[9] 'Drinking and gambling till you're on over your head, but even if you out of money, your kid's mother is still out there selling her wares.'

Whether or not most of the money is brought in by the father, it is commonly the mother in Vietnamese households who handles the family finances, collecting her husband's wages and putting him on a sort of allowance. A kind of institutionalised cheating usually arises where the husband tries to hide to some extent the true amount of his earnings, lest he should not have enough money for cigarettes, tea and going out with his friends. The wife, similarly, dissimulates or secretly invests the earnings from her embroidery and selling cakes, so her husband will not think her rich and take advantage of her to spend his money on *les petites amies*.

The most commonly acquired commodity for this kind of female protective investment is jewellery, preferably in unalloyed gold or with recognisable gems. Young girls quietly watch their mothers' elaborate systems of boxes, jars, purses, hidden floor boards, furtive containers of every kind and dimension, never opened in the father's presence – they observe and they learn. The precious contents are considered the mother's property and will stay with her should she leave. The extraordinary interest which Vietnamese women appear to take in jewellery is commonly misunderstood by outsiders to be simple vanity; and, of course, no one is immune from human foible; but one must comprehend the Vietnamese folk tradition of female economic self-defence in order to put this fascination into its proper perspective.[10]

Home and the 'In-Law' Question

In addition to finances, another major question in everyday Vietnamese life is: Where is the family going to live? The anwer to this question is arrived at by a balance between idealised Confucian custom mentioned above, folk practice, and economic exigency. The last of these considerations, especially when the economy is not going well (before the 1990s economic boom in Southeast Asia), is probably the one which would carry the most weight. For this reason, the accepted practice of the wife's going to live with her husband's family is breached in many ways. In urban settings, among office and factory workers, where accommodations are scarce and individual lodgings impossible to find, one lives where one can; in these cases, live-in sons-in-law are not rare. In the countryside, there is not only a stronger tradition, but also more space in which to carry it out, so typically young wives still dutifully go off to live in or next to their husband's relatives, though families with no sons may wish that at least one daughter stay in their home with her husband.

The husband's family is chiefly concerned with male issue. If the wife's firstborn is a boy and the baby lives past the first month of infancy, the wife's place in her husband's family is greatly strengthened. If it happens that her husband is the eldest son, she can in fact come to exercise great power (as queens throughout world history have discovered), effectively fending off the aggressions of his female relatives. In the event she is childless or insists on bearing daughters (folk belief ignores the medical fact that the sex of offspring is genetically determined by the father), her fate can be less enviable.[11] If her husband has no sisters of his own at home, her presence may be still very welcome, for certain kinds of work, such as keeping a kitchen garden, are thought to be impossible for men to do well.[12] But at best, like most women in the Third World, she can still expect a very demanding work schedule, even if she is relatively well treated.

Under these circumstances, it is not surprising that a young wife goes back to her own mother's house for an extended visit after the birth of a child (other than a firstborn male). Another, though frequently unmentioned, reason for this behaviour is the fact that (especially in the case of rather young wives) these women do not really know how to take care of infants. Grandmothers, and particularly maternal grandmothers, are the fount of this kind of knowledge (Fishman 1985).[13] Once a woman's eldest daughter is over the age of about seven or eight, she has a tendency to confer as many of the child-care duties for younger siblings as possible to this eldest daughter, who then becomes a little substitute mother.[14] Some knowledge is passed on in this way; but younger daughters are less likely to be well instructed, and, in any event, do not care for the suckling infants.

Once back at home with her mother, the young wife is among her own. The maternal grandmother is thought of as a warm-hearted spoiler of the young. The Vietnamese often say, 'Your mother's sister loves you as her own child. If misfortune takes your mother, she can still be counted on.' A sense of sisterhood also prevails. One's own sisters may be a welcoming thought since 'one can cut the strings from gourds and melons, but not the bond between blood sisters'. However, life with one's female in-laws is traditionally seen as the worst burden life has to offer a woman. As the saying goes, even 'Chinese bandits cannot equal one's husband's mother and sister'.

The problem for the husband is one of divided loyalties, for the notion of filial piety [*hieu*] places him under his parents, and it obliges his wife by the same token. Saving his wife from the exactions of his mother is obviously an excellent place for arguments to begin. As the saying goes, 'I'm hungry and I eat a starfruit or a fig, then I take one look at your mother and I can't swallow a thing.' How long can these two women stand each other? The following song explains the relationship: 'Your mother is fierce, my darling! And who knows whether we'll make it through life together? Or, just as I have come, shall I also leave, causing me great suffering, causing you much pain.' For a young wife, the added jealously of her husband's sisters is almost taken for granted. A common Vietnamese saying goes: 'Bitter and piquant, but still blood kin, Sweet and smooth, and yet strangers; When the husband's younger sister lives with the sister-in-law, You'd better watch out or come one day they'll kill each other.' Indeed probably nowhere in the world's folk literature is there a richer mine of sayings than the one found in Viet Nam about mothers-in-law, and specifically regarding the hatred that arises between the husband's mother and the young wife. Tensions between the husband

and the wife's mother receive scant attention. For every mention of how good mothers-in-law should act, cherishing their daughters-in-law as their own flesh and blood, there are fifty evocations of the evils of the system. The end seems predictable: 'The girl in the straw hat, where is she going? I am a daughter-in-law going away; I am fed up with my husband's vicious mother, I can bare to stay no longer, I going back to my home.'[16] One is forced to conclude that what we have here is a system which is highly dysfunctional, but which is nonetheless maintained. If this is the case, there must exist certain powerful forces, psychological or social, which require the persistence of a massive hypocrisy – what can these possibly be?

History

It is fairly clear, for one thing, that theoretical male domination was not always the case among the Vietnamese: the archaeological evidence (with female figures playing prominent totemic roles in the decoration of bronze artefacts from the first millennium BC) leads us to believe that two thousand years ago, in the Vietnamese *urheimat*,[17] before the arrival *en masse* of the Chinese and the importation of patriarchal Confucianism and written documents, women played prominent roles in public life.

This interpretation is reinforced by legends of female warriors, which are not only part of Vietnamese folklore, but are also noted as part of the historical record that the Chinese kept of their first incursions into Vietnamese territory. Two well-known cases are today part of Vietnamese popular iconography, the story of the Trung Sisters, whose rebellion against the Chinese colonial administration in AD 41 is noted in the *Hou Han Shu* (a third-century text *digne de foi*), and the tale of Lady Trieu Au in AD 248, who is said to have headed her troops seated in shining armour on the back of a giant elephant (O'Harrow 1979). Once the Chinese were firmly in control of this southern border territory, if not earlier, Viet Nam was witness to a continued influx of ethnic Chinese immigrants. We know, not only from well-documented recent immigration patterns, but also from citations in contemporary Chinese annals, that the vast majority of these migrants were peasant-class males. They took local wives in Viet Nam and, once installed, seldom returned to China. Their progeny eventually formed the bulk of the lowland farming population. This Vietnamese-speaking progeny, reared by Vietnamese mothers, was at once the inheritor of the indigenous Southeast Asian social ethic which placed a high value on the role of women, as well as heir to the male-centred Chinese tradition.[18]

The stage was thus set very early in their national history for a peculiarly Vietnamese social dichotomy, in which the two layers of social ethic co-existed: the sinicised male ethic *chez les hommes* and the Southeast Asian female ethic *chez les femmes*. Hence, the seeds of social dysfunction were present from a very early period. I have argued elsewhere that a primary cause for the female-led revolt of AD 41 was a conflict between the traditional indigenous land-tenure system, which seems to have allowed for female land inheritance, and Chinese law, which favoured male succession (O'Harrow 1979).

Theory

Obviously a *modus vivendi* had to be arrived at, one involving a sort of two-tiered layering of external male domination and internal female primacy. The process of layering is a metaphor for many aspects of Vietnamese life. In temples devoted to the worship of heroes and heroines of the State (not a Stalinist 'cult of personality' invention in Viet Nam, but a very ancient practice) there is frequently an inner altar or even a series of inner altars, behind the one usually seen by the public (O'Harrow 1986). Here the priesthood venerates the heroes who preceded (and therefore watched over) the one worshipped at the outer altar. The notion that there is always a deeper meaning beneath the surface or events (or behind one's gestures and the words one utters) pervades Vietnamese psychic life.

To begin to understand the processes of male–female accommodation that take place in Vietnamese daily life one must look into the psychic life of Vietnamese women. If I could sum up the psychic structural concerns which haunt the traditional Vietnamese woman in a single word, it would be 'containment'; and I would prefer to work with three words, each of which are a facet of containment: *privacy*, *control*, and *re-integration*.

Privacy

I believe this is a quasi-universal phenomenon, and not limited to Viet Nam. Since I am not a woman myself, I do not think I can do more than give a sympathetic reading of the situation, but it is necessary, for the purposes of this paper, that I do so and try to place it in a Vietnamese context.

The need for privacy when certain physical needs arise is an obvious concern, but the degree of this need is to a considerable extent culturally dependent. In some cultures, particularly traditional Muslim communities for example, the woman may feel uncomfortable in the physical presence of any adult male outside her immediate family, even if she is swathed from head to foot. The problem in Viet Nam is less a matter of cultural or social inclination than it is of poverty and enforced contact. The simple fact is that the average Vietnamese woman gets very little of the physical privacy she very much desires. But she can frequently develop strategies to cope with the physical world: she bathes at night, goes to a faraway field or a hidden bush to tend to some urgencies; and she spends hours mending her clothes to keep herself modest.[19]

Always surrounded by people, her real problem, one of the most irksome of her life, is not physical but psychological privacy – freedom from prying eyes. Here she is often less successful. If it is not her mother-in-law and her husband's sisters, then it is the village neighbours, if not the neighbours then her fellow workers or the busybody Communist party cadre spying on her. It is incessant gossip, ceaseless criticism. 'Her hair's too short, her hair's too long, she takes too long when she eats, she takes too much fish and not enough rice, she lets her husband go around in unironed clothes, she talks too much, she's too quiet . . .'. The average Vietnamese woman is surrounded by judges who measure her every step and note down her every gesture.

The great secret yearning of the Vietnamese woman is for a private space of her own to which she can admit only those whom she pleases and when she pleases; but this personal psychological space can only exist in her mind. From a very young age, therefore, she develops a very rich imaginative life, one into which she withdraws more and more often when under pressure. She may wish to admit her husband or lover into this space, but because it is her unsullied last refuge, she often does not dare.

The only men who can come into that secret space are dream men who possess all the pleasing boyish qualities, sometimes playful, sometimes sorrowful, but always turning to her for love and consolation, never turning to the outside world, out of the reach of mothers, sisters-in-law or girlfriends. Inside this space she knows she is pure – those other women, as their criticism and spying proves, are not. In the end, the only male who can even come close to this ideal is the one male over whom she can possibly have dominion, the one male who can look upon no other woman in the same way he looks upon her: her son. But if her son grows up and marries, he will leave her private space, betray this most intimate connection for another woman, his wife, who must now become her archrival. And so the wheel turns.

But there is much more to be said about this private world than simply describing its enemies.[20] Women sometimes ask: 'If our mothers have favoured their male offspring, our brothers, who is there to suckle us?' We can only turn to ourselves and to the spirit world'. This question of Vietnamese women psychologically nursing themselves from within is occasionally connected with their taking on lovers.

What I believe is misunderstood, especially by the man who happens to play the role of actual physical lover, is that (as far as the woman is concerned) the lover is not there as an outside entity brought in whole to be loved and understood for his own sake – he is merely a stand-in for the real lover, the dream lover, who is pure and can only exist within the woman.[21] Truly, as she nurses her secret yearnings for love, the physically real lover ultimately fails in comparison to the dream lover.

Can her husband be the lover? Generally, no. The reason is fairly simple: Vietnamese women marry quite young and learn to relate to their private psychological space very early on in their marriage. By the time that space is fully defined, the husband has already shown himself to be imperfect and his imperfections have materially contributed to the design of the young wife's private space. Barriers are set up in that space specifically against the kinds of faults he possesses, and he is automatically excluded. If he is timid and afraid of his mother he will never ever be her dream lover. If her husband is boastful, her dream lover will be a quiet man. Only if a Vietnamese woman has reached maturity without having suffered significant male subjugation can her dream space admit the presence of a real lover; but for her own sake, and in the Confucian system, this is almost never the case.

There are, however, other entities that can intrude into this private space – the spirits. This has nothing to do with formal or organised religious ideology as we usually think of it. With few exceptions, formal religious organizations in Viet Nam, in much the same manner as formal political organisations, are under the clear and quasi-total domination of men.[22] The spirits I refer to can be the spirits of the dead or they can be other powers related to the Taoist pantheon. They are accessed via professional female mediums, who go into trances to commune with spirits who can penetrate the depths of a woman's life (a ceremony known as *len dong*). (See also Ngaosyvathn in this volume on Laotian spirit-mediums.) These spirits are themselves almost always feminine.

Another closely related phenomenon is the consultation of the *thay boi* or fortune-teller. The *thay boi* is nearly always female herself, and though men do come to learn the future from her, the bulk of her clients are women, with whom she maintains a semi-psychiatric relationship. No matter when or why the woman goes to the *thay boi*, she always discovers something: 'Go to soothsayer, she'll surely find a ghost; Sweep your house and you'll surely find dust.' The trump card which the *thay boi* always has up her sleeve is her combined knowledge of and sensitivity to the predictable psychological concerns of her women clients (faithless husbands, vicious mother-in-laws, prying sisters-in-laws, and rebellious children) and her control over the commonly accepted cultural signs and symbols needed to interpret these phenomena in an manner acceptable to her clients. The soothsayer becomes the only credible yet disinterested female confidante available to the Vietnamese woman suffering psychological pain. The latter comes seeking reassurance, and usually receives it.

Control

What do Vietnamese women do to gain control of their lives? As I have noted, there is a distinct tendency for Vietnamese women to control, or try to control, the family finances. This is seen from the woman's viewpoint as a defensive strategy (from the man's viewpoint this is at best an 'aggresive defence'), and the female desire for complete control within the home is thought of as something natural in Vietnamese culture. While the polite term for a wife is *noi tro* or 'interior helper', the common, not so polite epithet is *noi tuong* or 'general of the interior'. Some regions of Viet Nam, such as Ha Dong, are reputed to produce particularly fierce 'generals of the interior' who are often called *Su tu Ha Dong* ['Ha Dong Lionesses']. These Lionesses supposedly exercise dominion over their husbands who, in turn, are said to belong to a very ancient club, the *Hoi So Vo* or 'Society of Men who Fear Their Wives'.[23] The *Hoi So Vo* is the subject of hundreds of Vietnamese jokes, some of which are very hoary. One of the oldest and best-known goes as follows:

> A peasant was being scolded loudly by his wife for not having the presence of mind to bring in the laundry, drying on the clothes-line, before it rained. His neighbour heard this, came out and said, 'Why do you let yourself be treated like this by a woman – I would never let this happen to me.' She came out and said, 'Oh, yes? And what would *you* do?' 'Why, my dear', replied the neighbour, 'I would surely remember to take in the laundry before it got wet.'

Lame humour aside, it is martyrdom on the part of women that is more often the unseemly counterpart to perceived male domination, and this, of course, is not limited to Vietnamese culture or even to Southeast Asia in general. This martyrdom reflects an effort to seek control by directing the attention of others to one's misery, to arouse shame. This is usually directed over those people to whom one cannot simply give explicit orders. In a Western context this would be closely related to the 'Jewish mother' or Swedish Protestant mother syndrome, except that these European cultures are heavily reliant on guilt rather than shame as a mechanism of control over children's behaviour.

In Vietnam and other societies in Southeast Asia, however, the mother plays on the sympathy of the child, making the child feel culpable for the sadness of the mother, eternally responsible for her suffering. For example, instead of telling the child directly that he must eat his bowl of beans (which the child detests) because they are good for his health (which the child might refuse), the mother says that she worked many hours to acquire the money to buy beans, that she sacrificed buying something for herself with the bean money instead, that she slaved over a hot stove to cook the beans, and if the child does not eat them, his ingratitude will (as usual) kill her. While this tactic is not unknown among the Vietnamese, it usually undergoes a subtle but important variation, as follows: 'Everybody, your father, your grandparents, your brothers and sisters, see how hard I work to feed you, and if you don't eat these beans, they will know that you mistreat your mother and are ungrateful to the person who gave you life.'

In the case of the Jewish child, he will eat his beans, even if his mother leaves the room, because he knows that God can still see him and it would be a terrible thing to hurt her so. In the case of the Vietnamese child, he will definitely eat all his beans if anyone is looking, but if everyone leaves the room, he will throw the beans out of the window, and feel none the worse. In a culture which operates on shame rather than guilt, one knows when one is being manipulated.

By extension, a Vietnamese woman's sense of martyrdom, when applied to daily life, can only be effective if it is played out on a commonly accepted playing-field where everybody understands the rules and signals. This field is the *system of moral debts and balances*, where public shame is the umpire for the game. The system of moral debts and balances would appear to be Buddhist in origin; but it fits in so neatly with traditional Confucian moralising that the two reinforce one other rather well. In Buddhist metaphysics, life is in constant flux, all is change, there is no permanence, only ebb and flow (see Karim, Introduction, on the 'village community'). The only way to get ahead in the game[24] is to build up merit, which is done by acquiring the moral debts of other people, in the same way a banker buys up mortgage notes or a loan shark buys up gamblers' IOUs: 'If you drink the water, you should remember the source.'

There is constant social gift-giving and doing of unsolicited favours in Vietnamese society.[25] The object of these gifts conforms to the classic Maussian theory of the 'gift' which is to bind somebody morally or to balance off some previous benefit received from the person to whom the gift is given. The giver of gifts or renderer of services gains *on* or a moral IOU from the receiver, and is therefore in a position to demand something from the receiver;[26] the receiver knows this, is uncomfortable, and quickly acts to pay back the gift or service, often symbolically. One must thank someone with the statement, *cam on*, the meaning of which is to feel the moral debt arising from the acceptance of a gift. However, the Vietnamese believe that talk is 'cheap', and only actions count. The worst position to be in is *co no on ai*, or to owe a moral debt to somebody. Of course the people to whom one owes a continuing sense of *on* are one's parents. Parents go to great lengths to impress that fact upon their children. They also expect gratitude to follow them into the next life, through the constant veneration of their spirits after their deaths.

Because this system of debts and reciprocities is clearly understood by everybody, and because actions should be understood not at surface level but for their deeper implications, many Vietnamese women are continuously engaged in a game of manipulation and control through the acquisition of moral obligations. If a woman is wealthier than her friends, and can afford to buy them gifts which they are unable to reciprocate in kind (though they may ruin themselves trying), she may be able to gain power. But she must be careful, because that power is felt very clearly and keenly, and easily turns to resentment. The artful woman is subtle about the favours and gifts she bestows, always giving just enough more than she receives to keep the balance of *on* ever so slightly in her favour.

Vietnamese women seldom have male friends *per se* because they have very few social mechanisms for dealing with men on an equal footing. Men are always patrons or clients, fathers, sons husbands, or lovers. The psychological control of men and the off-setting of their formal powers still follows the basic Vietnamese principles of debts and balances, but involves special rules: unless there is a pronounced age-difference, a husband is controlled with the same strategies that a mother uses to control her son, while, age notwithstanding, a lover is usually controlled as a daughter controls her father.

Here I should like to refer to what I said above about moral versus metaphysical chastity. As was shown earlier, moral questions in

Vietnamese society are enforced by constraints of shame rather than guilt. A Vietnamese woman can cheat (in the Western sense) on her husband without regret as long as it is not known.[27] The following saying illustrates the point: 'Flirtatious with desire, I wore a wedding ring for protection; I lost my wedding ring, but my desire remains.'

Contrary to Western notions (enforced by guilt) of freedom before marriage but faithfulness afterwards, in societies where shame and the notion of virgin marriage[28] is operative, extramarital affairs outnumber premarital ones. If a Vietnamese woman takes a lover and can keep the fact secret (avoiding shame), she can maintain an upper hand. The Vietnamese man, while much less bound by problems of public shame for having a girlfriend, is more likely to be worried about surrendering self-control. Loss of self-control, inability to control one's anger for example, for the Vietnamese male is a major loss of 'face'. Hence Vietnamese men in positions of power tend to be very quiet, and anger is effectively shown by a lowering of the voice, not by raising it. A surrender to the act of love, though desired by the man, is to experience the moment of supreme loss of self-control. Vietnamese men thus tend to think of love-making in almost medical terms, concerned about the maintenance of their potency, psychological as well as physical. In this context it is easy to see why tales of female sexual insatiability also attach themselves to the Ha Dong lioness myth. Because it is important for a Vietnamese man to maintain control of himself, the Vietnamese woman's immediate control over her lover is therefore not moral but existential.

Reintegration and Reflections on Gender in Southeast Asia

It is difficult to come up with more than a just few theoretical proposals about what is happening between men and women in Vietnamese society. Many of these notions may be so generally applicable to women everywhere as to be of no analytic value for the understanding of Southeast Asian women in particular, but I do have one idea that might be productive. Confucianism was a holistic system that tended to work to the benefit of male power. However, Vietnamese women, in the deep recesses of their nation's history, played an openly powerful role and countered this Confucian male power with strategies of their own which appear to be very old. One could go on to say that Vietnamese women are the main inheritors of indigenous traditions in Viet Nam, and that they employ this equally holistic tradition in gender struggles. My question is: Are we looking at a more generalised Southeast Asian pattern? In Malay society, for instance, Karim (1992) states that women are the guardians of an older indigenous tradition (*adat*), which expresses itself in the gender arena where they face Malay males armed with the patriarchy of Islam. And is not the *machismo* of Filipino males reinforced by the very Spanish traditions out of which the word *machismo* comes? In Thailand and Laos, where the *Sangha* is tightly controlled by men, does Indic Buddhism confer a power on males which is countered by women using strategies common to Shan and Chuang, Lowland Thai and Upland Lao, and other Tai peoples? What about the Burmese or the Khmer? In each case is the male tradition a classical, literate, imported tradition, buttressed by patriarchal terminology expressed in languages whose mysterious power partly derives from their exotic origins in India, China, Arabia or Iberia?

What we are talking about here is the layering of various cultural and ideological traditions upon one another to form a composite 'society' which operationalises these traditions in disparate ways, allowing women to find their own level of accommodation which is personally and socially satisfactory. The greatest threat to these gender accommodations is possibly the development of *atomistic* forces of Western science and technology in the region. The same can be said for the introduction of technological Western capitalism, as opposed to Marxist socialism which, owing to its very inefficiency (inefficiency due, in turn, to a misrepresentation of Marxism as 'holistic') has had little significant impact on traditional gender relations, other than to re-enforce them.

Southeast Asian women intellectuals, writers, artists, educators, and political activists who are working on the relationship between technological capitalism and gender relations cannot prepare themselves better against the onslaught of rapid social and economic change than by recognising the subtle complexities of male–female relationships in Southeast Asia. Obviously they cannot know where they will go unless they have some clearer idea where they have been.

Notes

1. Although I was trained as a linguist, most of the observations made in this chapter have been a result of my life experiences in Hanoi and my relationships with the Vietnamese for the last two decades.
2. To the extent that Marxist ideology has intervened in daily life in Viet Nam, it has largely left family relationships intact and has primarily been concerned with the 'macro' society, though it is interesting to see that what is considered

to be moral behaviour on the part of party cadres has many parallels with the proper behaviour of the Confucian gentleman.

3. While nuns are not uncommon in Viet Nam, and the tradition of elderly widows' shaving their heads and entering Buddhist orders is widespread, their influence on priesthood is difficult to detect. Somehow, perhaps by losing their legitimate sexual function, they have been effectively neutered and thus neutralised. Public ideology, frequently indistinguishable from religion in any case, includes political ideology, especially where there is a prescribed State system of thought, as in Viet Nam. Here again, men dominate. Female members of the National Assembly and of the Communist Central Committee do exist, but they represent an infinitesimal portion of the whole and exercise almost no real decision-making power. To my knowledge, the *Politburo* has never had a female member.

4. In one of the earliest extant Chinese paintings on silk, K'u K'ai-ohih's 'Admonitions to the Court Ladies' (British Museum, fourth century), the inscription on the scene in the bedchamber emphasises that this is the best place for the concubine to ask for what she wants.

5. There are even occasional reports of young women being married to already defunct husbands, probably for ceremonial purposes. Excesses of this order were most probably confined to the more sinicised upper reaches of society. In general we can say that Confucian principles tended to be honoured as a direct function of the social rank of the family in question.

6. The Vietnamese have gained the reputation among their Southeast Asian neighbours of being a very tough group of people. In addition to a half-century of war, one reason for this may be that, especially in central and northern Viet Nam, life itself has often been much tougher than elsewhere in Southeast Asia. In looking back over French colonial statistics for the recent history of the country, I was particularly struck by a medical survey done in 1912 of the population of Hue, the imperial capital, which showed that 69.63 per cent of the population over forty years of age had tuberculosis. In addition, a pre-Second World War economic survey of the Tonkinese peasantry showed that the average farmer had a wage equivalent to only one-quarter of the income of the average Moroccan farmer (and French statisticians thought of Morocco as a typical example of colonial poverty).

   In point of fact, a simple division of farm revenues by the known population yielded a figure below what was considered to be subsistence level, and the only conclusion one could draw was that the average peasant was literally dying of hunger.

7. As opposed to Chinese-run shops (many Chinese merchants have fled the country).

8. Though they are more often small merchants, it is interesting that supposedly the richest private capitalist in Viet Nam today is a woman, the owner of a food-processing combine in the south, *Mrs.* Nguyen thi Thi.

9. Whether this verse originated as a folksong or is from the pen of Tu Xuong (*circa* 1890) I am not clear, but it admirably illustrates the point. Songs and

sayings cited hereinafter are to be found in Vu Ngoc Phan, Hanoi, 1978.

10. To give a women a piece of fine jewellery in Vietnamese tradition is to help confirm her independence as a human being, and for a mother to hand over a piece of her jewellery to her daughter is a universally understood gesture, for which the sub-text is 'may this protect you from misery'.

11. Though Confucian tradition permits the husband to take lesser wives (theoretically to be chosen for him by the first wife), economic realities (and relatively innocuous modern laws) usually force him to content himself with one at a time.

12. In most areas of Viet Nam, women are also employed in heavy field labour. This tendency increased during the war, when men were at the front, and continued in view of the number of working-aged males who were killed or injured. According to a colleague, Christine Pelzer-White, up to 80 per cent of the field work in an area studied by her was carried out by women (personal communication).

13. Fishman shows that young Vietnamese mothers are often ignorant of proper feeding patterns when isolated from their own mothers, as often occurs during periods of forced migration.

14. Because the eldest daughter has usually been given the responsibility for much child-rearing, she is often one of the last to marry, particularly if her mother is unwell and there are still siblings to tend. Another reason for her to worry is that, while marrying the eldest son may lead to fortune for the young bride (this is not a foregone conclusion, since Vietnamese eldest sons also tend to be terribly spoiled), young Vietnamese men may be afraid to marry an eldest daughter. Throughout his life, the husband of an eldest daughter can expect to be pestered, directly or indirectly; but his younger in-laws consider his wife to be a substitute mother and therefore obliged to be helpful to them; in Southern Chinese families, where the same pattern occurs, this is known as the *jie-fu* syndrome.

15. In this connection, I find it interesting that, because the vocative system of the Vietnamese language is largely devoid of pronouns (instead, it uses static kinship terms) husband and wife enjoy a fictive incest: the husband speaking to his wife uses the same terms he has always used towards his real younger sisters, referring to himself as 'older brother' [*anh*] and calling his wife 'little sister' [*em*].

16. One is especially struck by the use of the phrase *nhà tôi* [my home] in this folk song, as if to say that her real home is where her mother is and not where her husband is.

17. Basically the Red River area of today's northern Viet Nam, sometimes called *Ton[g]kin[g]*, and the coastal littoral down to the region of modern Huê.

18. Not all aspects of traditional Chinese civilisation are male-centred, but those which emphasise the importance of female roles, outside the Confucian ethic, were probably not implanted in Viet Nam by the primarily male immigrant Chinese population. I should add that I believe the patriarchal aspects of Confucianism were not new to Confucius, but were incorporated into

Confucianism on the basis of the pre-existing traditions. Confucianism in many ways represents a codification of some of these pre-existing ideas, much as Islam contains the codification of certain pre-sixth century Arabic tribal traditions. The mass of Chinese immigrant males in Viet Nam were obviously not well-read Confucian scholars.

19. Young couples in Hanoi, even married couples, face great difficulty in finding a place for private encounters. The evening stroller through the city's lakeside public parks must step carefully to avoid interrupting lovers hard at work.

20. Its enemies risk becoming legion. The most common exaggeration of this state of mind is a tendency towards paranoia, a condition frequently attributed to the behaviour of a Vietnamese woman by Westerner interlocutors, who can only explain the woman's actions by supposing that she is mentally deranged. The problem is that what is normal in one culture is abnormal in another. The model constructed in the woman's inner world, her only solace, becomes the explanation of the real world she must deal with, and since Vietnamese culture has always filled the language of interpersonal relations with layers upon layers of innuendo, indirect criticism, and dissimulation, it is only prudent for her to think that any word or deed whose aim is not perfectly clear to her is probably a threat.

21. While I have not been able to look at the question closely in the case of Vietnamese women, because the mass media industry of manufacturing public idols is not yet developed in the country, I suspect that the dream lover has many feminine qualities, and 'he' may even be of indeterminate sex in previously heavily Confucianised cultures. I find it interesting to contemplate the androgynous images that are projected by Tokyo pop singers (or Michael Jackson, for that matter) and the fascination that many young Japanese girls have with Takarazuka male impersonators and female television wrestlers.

22. There is little overt female power in public ideological institutions in Viet Nam. The Catholic priest is male, celibate, and arbiter of the public life of his co-religionists. Catholic priests led the mass exodus from northern Viet Nam after the Geneva Accords of 1954 – whole villages, men, women, and children, pulled up stakes and left for the South on the word of their village priest. The Buddhist priest, far more numerous, is equally male and celibate, though his political influence has varied.

23. The Vietnamese claim this club now has branches in most countries of the world.

24. The very idea of being able to get ahead by striving is anathema to sophisticated Buddhist thinkers; but popular Buddhism, abetted by ignorant and (metaphysically) corrupt monks relies heavily on strategies for gaining merit in this world to be cashed in the next world (or sooner, if at all possible).

25. The common Asian notion that it is shameful to come empty-handed is one which is often misinterpreted in the West, especially in North European Protestant societies, where material gifts are usually reserved for special

occasions. In Western societies this emphasis on a multitude of small gifts is felt somehow to be materialistic and it is seldom reciprocated. The Asian ends up feeling scorned and unappreciated by the Westerner (who he suspects 'is all talk and no action'), while the Westerner feels that the Asian is trying to 'buy' his affections.

26. The greatest *on* is gained from self-sacrifice. Thus in military graveyards across the nation there are markers inscribed *To Quoc Ghi On* [the Fatherland Inscribes its Moral Debt]. The Japanese who have a similar concept of *on* 恩 acknowledge the origin of the word as Chinese. However Cong Huyen

    Ton Nu Nha Trong (personal communication, 1995) a specialist in Vietnamese folklore and literature states, '"Ồn" (pronounced like "un" in "undo", as distinct from the Japanese 'on' which is pronounced like 'ong' in 'pingpong') is an authentic colloquial Vietnamese word. It is not of Chinese origin and cannot be transcribed in Chinese script. Formerly it was transcribed in *chu nom* (a demotic script created around the 13th century wherein two Chinese characters are combined to represent a Vietnamese word as it was spoken); from the 19th century it has been represented as "ồn" in *quoc ngu* (or national script which makes use of the alphabet with added diacritics to mark the tones). The same notion was referred to by the Confucian scholar gentry as "ân", a Sino-Vietnamese word, or a Chinese word/character pronounced the Vietnamese way. Thus "ân" is of Chinese origin, but "ồn" is not.'

27. Vietnamese men, on the whole, though every bit as amorous as their Western counterparts, know the rule of the game and have less of a tendency to brag publicly about their conquests.

28. Premarital intercourse is quite common in Vietnamese villages; but there is an obligation on the man's part to marry the girl he has deflowered, and she reminds him of the fact in the strongest possible terms.

Bibliography

Fishman, C. (1985). Child Nutrition Patterns in Refugee Vietnamese Families in the US, Unpublished Doctoral dissertation, University of Pennsylvania.

Karim, W. (1992). *Women and Culture: Between Adat and Islam*. Boulder: Westview.

Mauss, M. (1954). *The Gift*. London: Cohen and West.

O'Harrow, S. (1979). 'From Co Loa to the Trung Sister Revolt: Viet Nam as the Chinese Found It'. *Asian Perspectives*, 22.2, 140–64.

O'Harrow, S. (1986). 'Men of Hu, Men of Han, Men of the Hundred Man: The Conceptualization of Early Vietnamese Society'. *Bulletin de l'Ecole Française d'Extrême-Orient*, 75: 249–66.

Poirier, M. (1913). 'La Conquête de la Femme Indigène en pays d'Annam', *La Grande Revue*, 10 Dec., 717–36.

Vu Ngac Phan (1978). *Tuc ngu ca dao dan ca Viet Nam*. Hanoi.

8

Performance and Gender in Javanese Palace Tradition

Felicia Hughes-Freeland

'When a person dances, their character appears – you can see the person.'[1]

'"Male" as hot as fire/ "female" cool as water/ "Transsexuals" – what do we call them?/That's what they say'[2]

The analysis of general ideas about human nature has become part of the agenda for restoring the Other to its own terms within the framework of anthropological discourse. This analytical orientation has proposed that the categories 'woman' and 'man' are social constructions rather than given biological universals,[3] and has produced studies which question how universal the notion of 'women' is cross-culturally, and what indigenous data can tell us about this. One example is the discussion of women in the Hagen Highlands of Papua New Guinea, whose cultural denigration has been analysed not as a derogation of the women themselves as persons but of what they stand for (Strathern 1981: 178). In Java this distinction between persons and what they stand for has been deemed unfeasible because of Javanese systems of prestige and power. Although Javanese people make distinctions between individuals on the basis of style and status as much or even more than gender, women are seen as inherently inferior to men, and incapable of obtaining authority in the eyes of the community: 'Women do not possess, exercise, or really understand potency to any appreciable degree. They are said, by Javanese men and women, to be flighty, incapable of concentration, and self-control' (Keeler 1987: 241).

Javanese genders are ranked in a hierarchy on the basis of a concept of potency which is the preserve of men. Men are superior to women, who are identified as 'containers' (*wadah*);[4] women may excel in lower orders of material transaction, but are denied access to exchanges which bring status and power.

Javanese women's reputation as economic agents is not in question here, but the assignation of women to a sphere of secondary and inferior control which is 'mundane and obvious' (Keeler 1987: 104) cannot be taken as general or representative of Javanese constructions of gendered identity. Approaches to gender ideologies and relations based on contrastive dualisms of this kind have already been challenged by indigenous categories which emphasise a relationship between male and female based on 'creative complementarity' (Waterson 1990: 65). Indeed, Keeler has recently modified his position on the gender hierarchy, which he claims is situated in the polarised essentialism of how Javanese speak about genders, although characteristics of both stereotypes can be found in persons of both genders (1990).[5] However, while conceding to Strathern's point that men and women may behave in a male or female way, he nonetheless insists that women are denigrated as a category and have an inherently inferior status, unlike the women in the Hagen Highlands.

Material from urban Java, however, does not support the view that women are inferior, and presents different interpretations of female capacities from village data, capacities which are culturally highly valued, as data from a study of performance in the Sultan's palace (*kraton*) at Yogyakarta and the place of gender[6] as it figures in characterisation and representation will show. Staged performance is never a simple reflection of the everyday, and Javanese interpretations and evaluation of performance bring out the interconnections between performance and life's daily dramas. This set of evaluations of court-associated performance consitutes a discourse which organises responses to persons and actions as well as roles and performances and therefore has implications for the conceptualisation of gender and person within court culture in Yogya. As this culture serves as a model in contemporary Indonesia, the data raise questions about the interpretative emphasis given to the concept of potency in Keeler's paper and the volume in which it appears, and while they do not substitute for Keeler's village-based analysis, they demonstrate that there are more Javanese ways of speaking about gender than his argument suggests. Also, given the recent emergence of the nation state of Indonesia and the transformation of court performance into the classical performance of this nation state, a related question is the importance of *gender* identity as opposed to ethnic and class identities in the determination of persons with regard to opportunity and development in the emerging Indonesia.

Court Patronage in Java

Written and visual references to all manner of performing arts in the courts of Java are found from the the tenth century onwards (Holt 1967). Court patronage of performance is a long-established practice, which has continued through the rise and fall of kingdoms and the Islamicisation of what became the central Javanese dynasty in the sixteenth century (Moedjanto 1986). Within this framework, there has been intense variation in the forms of court patronage and the relationship between court and performers over time, across regions, and also between different genres. For instance the control of a specific performance personnel for the *Wayang Wong* dance drama, today regarded as a high prestige form in Yogyakarta, was a mid-nineteenth-century development: until then troupes of performers from the village would be invited to perform in the *kraton* (Lindsay 1985: 88). However, court ceremonial provided a context through which performance genres for both men and women attached to the court by birth or occupation developed. During the establishment of the Mataram kingdom during the sixteenth century, women performed ceremonial dances in the court which paralleled performance by women at village fertility rituals after the harvest, and duels between male soldiers became the basis for choreographies. These performance contexts became instituted as a sign of the ruler's politico-spiritual prestige, and we can see ritual and militarism as determining the development of performance within the *kraton*, in contrast to performance brought in from outside as entertainment.

To a certain extent there is a correlation between performance genre and gender: militaristic representations are performed by men, ritual abstractions by women. These correlations altered following the division of the central Javanese kingdom in 1755 and the setting up of the Kingdom of Yogyakarta. The senior palace of Surakarta retained the culture of its agricultural origins, while the younger courts, the *Kasultanan* in Yogya and the *Mangkunagaran* in Surakarta, which arose from rebellion, are militaristic in ethos. The result has been a divergence in gender representation in performance staging.

For example, in the *Kasultanan* in Yogyakarta, women's genres such as *Bĕdhaya* and *Srimpi* are militaristic and rigorous compared to their romantic mood in the *Kasunanan* palace at Surakarta. In the *Mangkunagaran* palace in Surakarta women play all the roles in the dance opera *Langĕndriyan*. Both these courts have had female personnel serving military functions. In popular dance drama in Surakarta it has become conventional for the male character of Arjuna to be played by a woman.

But in Yogya court culture, cross-dressing was confined to men representing women in all forms except *Bĕdhaya* and *Srimpi*. For instance, *Bĕdhaya* and *Srimpi* are performed in all the *kraton* of Yogya and Surakarta.[7] *Bĕdhaya* is part of a powerful myth of unification between the male and the female. The dance is said to have been devised in memory of a mystical marriage of the founder of the sixteenth century kingdom of Central Java to the Queen of the South Sea, *Kangjĕng Ratu Kidul*. In the kingdom of Surakata the *Bĕdhaya Kĕtawang* is regarded as the first *Bĕdhaya*. The Yogyakartan version is called *Bĕdhaya Sĕmang*, a long and complex dance which was regarded as a sacred heirloom, ridden with taboos and mystical associations, and ceased to be performed in the palace after 1914 (Hostetler 1982), among other reasons because people became too afraid to play the melodies of *Kangjĕng Ratu Kidul*, the Queen of the South Sea. *Bĕdhaya* has special status as the oldest and most revered genre of court culture; some *Bĕdhaya* choreographies are regarded as sacred and are subject to strict taboos. *Srimpi* is a dance for four women, and is less grandiose than *Bĕdhaya*. In the Surakarta *kraton* they have always been performed by women but in Yogya they became available for men from around 1840 to 1914 (Hostetler 1982: 137).There was a difference in the social status of male and female *bĕdhaya*. The males were called '*abdhidalĕm bĕdhaya*' and were close to the Sultan. Until the 1920s female *bĕdhaya* and *srimpi* were of different ranks in the palace prestige system. The *srimpi* were children and grandchildren of the ruler; the *bĕdhaya* the daughters of court officials. During the reign of Hamĕngku Buwana VIII (1921–39) it became usual for the sultan's wives and daughters to participate in the training and performance of both dance forms. Sixty trainees from families of officials or villagers were recruited; they lived in the female quarters (*kĕputren*), and trained daily. This contrasts with the *Kasunanan* palace in Surakarta; here the *bĕdhaya* were a hereditary professional group, while the *srimpi* were related to the *Sunan*.

Such variation within one cultural region already shows the danger of making generalisations about the basis of gender and role identifications. The phenomenon of theatrical cross-dressing in general is yet to be fully examined, but the point here is that there appears to be a place both on and off stage for less rigid and dualistic ideas about a person's relationship to their gender than in the West. But the nature of this variation is not necesarily the same across regions. Gender-ascription to performers has varied over time as well as across place, and there has been increased formalisation with the intensification of court patronage, and a reification of the values which court performance expresses in contrast with other courts and also with performance outside the court. For instance, although professional female dancers (*ledhek*) from villages used to be hired to dance with noblemen of the court at parties to which the sultan would be invited, the dancing of these women is ideologically held by practitioners of the court traditions to represent the antithesis to what *Bĕdhaya* and *Srimpi* performance expresses, and their place in the culture of palace circles has been ideologically excised until recent re-evaluations, as we shall see.

In Yogyakarta the ethos of performance has been militaristic and more accessible to males, who were required to represent both male and female roles in the dance drama. With the exception of *Bĕdhaya* and *Srimpi*, females did not represent females in performances within the court. There had been more flexibility about female performance in the residences of royal princes and high-ranking officials; but it was the establishment of the *Kridha Bĕksa Wirama* dance school in 1918 by two princes with the support of the Crown Prince who shortly afterwards became Sultan Hamĕngku Buwana VIII which altered the status of female performers. The first dance school of its kind in Yogya, it made female participation in other genres outside the palace more respectable and removed slurs of immorality from female performers who participated. It was in a *Kridha Bĕksa Wirama* production in 1928 that females were first seen in *Wayang Wong* (dance drama) and in the fighting duets (*Bĕksan*) which were excerpts from dance dramas. In 1935, *Kridha Bĕksa Wirama* staged the first 'mixed' fight, using bows and arrows, which allowed a physical distance between male and female to be maintained on stage. In 1949 a production by a newly formed dance association, *Irama Citra*, presented a 'mixed' fight for the first time using daggers (*kĕris*) bringing the fighters much closer than previously. In 1952 a woman playing Srikandhi in a dance-drama rode on a *garudha* (eagle) played by a man for the first time; fights between women mounted on these birds have been a favourite in Yogyakarta ever since, and are now regarded as part of the palace repertoire. However even *Kridha Bĕksa Wirama* resisted the incorporation of the *Golek* dance into its repertoire until 1954; the dance was considered too like that of village professionals (Choy 1984: 57).

It was only after the declaration of independence in 1945 that the *kraton* followed suit. During the years of struggle leading to the recognition of the new state there was little court performance, and in 1952 the *kraton* delegated its arts activities to the *Bĕbadan Among Bĕksa* until 1973. Performances during this time were given in the residence of Prince Purwadiningrat, and for the first time females performed in palace-sponsored *Wayang Wong*. Other venues for training that introduced practices which brought men and women together on stage were also being established.

With the establishment of *Kridha Běksa Wirama*, palace performance was taught outside the palace for the first time. Just as performance was reaching its heyday inside the palace there was an attempt to democratise palace performance and make it more widely available. This perception of the need to democratise was one expression of a growing nationalist movement within the ruling élite and the merchant classes. By supporting the establishment of *Kridha Běksa Wirama* outside the palace, the eighth sultan was able to demonstrate a modernist approach to change while preserving the court's role as exemplary centre of Javanese society. This association still stands, and the reign of Haměngku Buwana VIII is regarded as the golden age of court performance, and provides standards for the what is considered to be classical Yogya dance today. It it could be argued that performance has become important in the cultural agenda of the nation state because of the place it was given in the nationalist struggles of the 1920s and 1930s by *Kridha Běksa Wirama*, which removed court performance from the court, ensured its development and broadened its appeal by altering the terms of respectability.

Performance and Socialisation

The gender implications of dance training in education and its role in sex role scripting have been analysed by Hanna (1988). Her approach is based on a number of assumptions about person, role and gender; I will here concentrate on whether the gendered dualism that Hanna speaks of is in fact instilled by the educative force of Javanese court performance.

Élite modernists of the 1920s realised that a Javanese nationalist identity could be enhanced through an educational system. What emerged was the principle of 'From behind bring influence to bear'. Educative strategies to develop Javanese character for the new age should have a traditional Javanese subtlety. The eighth sultan used performance to train and educate nobles and retainers in codes of speech, gesture, and general comportment. Self-control and orientation are two elements basic to all Javanese social interaction, and Javanese terms for physical action and moral actions are not easily separable. Knowing one's place (*ěmpan papan*) within choreography and within social interaction are analogous, and generate associations across action contexts. Knowing one's place involves a practical grasp of *tatakrama*, a word which describes politeness in action in a weightier sense than mere 'etiquette', and constitutes a philosophy of action.

Performed movement interlocks with music to produce an effect called 'flowing water' (*toya mili*), an aesthetic value which is of central importance in Yogya palace culture. The three measures of music, movements, and direction create this effect, which should be pleasing (*luwĕs*), fitting (*patut*), and clean (*rĕsik*). Unsuccessful and undesirable performance is coquettish, stiff, clumsy, dirty, flat, empty, and so forth (Suryobrongto 1981). While referring to the sensibility and spirit of the dancing, these evaluations are also applied to the person and their behaviour: 'That person doesn't understand measure' is a total criticism. Successful dance, like successful living, is evaluated in terms of time (measure) and space (orientation).

Performance and its movement dimension, therefore, is a moral activity, and performance aesthetics are related to the ethics of social relations, particularly in public situations. Non-Javanese in Indonesia and beyond notice the importance of 'performance' in Javanese behavioural style. To assess the place where one finds oneself and to adjust behaviour accordingly is crucial, particularly in public events, ceremonies associated with rites of passage (circumcision, marriages, funerals or professional advancement), which are held, if the host is wealthy and traditionalist, in the front of the house, the *pĕndhapa*, which is also where dancing takes place.

A prince who was formerly in charge of palace protocol explained *tatakrama* with reference to four elements: orderly gestures (*trapsila*), such as sitting for two hours without fidgeting in performance, men holding the front of a *bathik* skirt to prevent the flap from opening, and women carrying their arms so that the armpit does not show indecently; politeness or correct attitude (*subasita*); correct attention to codes of respect and deference in language (*unggah-ungguh*); and keeping one's word (*udha nĕgara*). 'These four', he said, 'all come into performance.'

A recurrent theme in conversations about performance is its improving and educative capacities. For some, dance has a moral significance, for others a spiritual one: in performance, 'one's inner self (*batin*) goes straight to God'. Anecdotes were told about individuals or groups who were so unruly as to be causing their parents and teachers problems, who learnt Javanese dance and changed in behaviour completely, becoming more self-controlled, less noisy, and so forth. One man spoke of a girl so changed by dance training that he did not recognise her. Stories from elderly palace performers also spoke of the valour and discipline of performers who went on stage with malaria, or endured bees crawling up their noses without flinching. In 1989, after a major *Bĕdhaya* performance, tales were told of performers fainting after the one-and-a-half hour dance. It is the performers' endurance while in the public eye that is valued.

This view of performance as education has been taken up by Indonesian government strategists. Such are practical, not symbolic: whatever ritual function performance once fulfilled, its educative role today means that it provides practical knowledge for Javanese life. Dance drama training is gender-linked in terms of the ways it figures in the life courses of male or female, although in terms of representation it is not simply a question of sex-role scripting. The interpretations of performance that follow arose in the context of radical social change and the emerging hopes placed on education. Although the palace is no longer a power centre politically, it has been a real university as well as a microcosm of the universe,[8] and remains a key reference for Javanese identity in contemporary Yogya.

Today small Javanese boys and girls are encouraged to move to music of all kinds and to appear in community celebrations of independence and so forth. They may learn from the age of seven in primary school, where performance is now being integrated into the main curriculum as part of national development, or they may also join the many dance clubs and associations in Yogya. There is a tendency for most organisations to attract more girls than boys, the ratio in one case being in the region of five to one. This suggests that while Javanese traditions continue to be supported by educational policies, there are competing activities for children's time, and that boy children are either better at resisting their parent's wishes, or that parents themselves are more inclined to encourage the male children to engage in 'modern' activities. Given the prioritisation of male education in a family which finds itself short of funds, the latter seems likely. Conversely, participation in traditional performance for girls appears to be a 'safe' activity, which nonetheless offers valuable opportunities for them to avoid being tied down to household chores after school and to engage in wider networks. One effect of such activities is that girls are able to establish contact with males outside their family and neighbourhood, with the teacher, who may be male – and many are not scrupulous about following palace protocol which restricts touching a trainee of the opposite sex with, at the most, a pencil or ruler, never the hand – and with other trainees who are male. In most organisations boys may watch girls, but the girls retire when it is the turn of the boys. While this might seem to be a sign of Islamic influence, informants always insisted that it was 'Javanese custom'. Javanese custom continues to influence male–female separation of teenagers who start to become interested in mixed activities; and in general young women tend to think of getting to know young men as a prelude to selecting a husband. Court dance is an excellent venue for improving one's chances of making a good match: in the palace performers often acquired promotion or wealthy spouses as a result of their skill. But this was conceived of as a side-effect. Performers of palace dance performed for honour, not money, and any material benefits were regarded as good fortune, rather than one's due.

After marriage, the ratio of men and women who dance changes. Mothers rarely appear in performance; but the skilled and enthusiastic will teach. There are some exceptions, such as the dancer who until recently could be seen performing on Sunday rehearsals in the palace with her two teenage sons and daughter, while her father trained the next generation of male performers. This kind of dance dynasty is becoming rarer, but it is not extinct, and family connections to the palace by blood or occupation continue to influence enthusiasm for the traditions. Older people say that dance in the male life-cycle is only for boyhood; shadow puppetry or music are the appropriate artistic interests for the mature. Others recalled the days of palace specialisation, when a male dancer would not reach his peak until his late thirties and forties; a young man would be too concerned with technical brilliance to attend to the inner spirit of performance. In palace productions today, the massed ranks of the gods are normally played by older men – directors of academies, heads of government arts offices, the most famous dance teachers – their chests bared, bellies strapped in by the costume, unrecognisable in their make-up. Once past the rigours of performance, men will satisfy their interest by teaching, playing music and singing. This is different from the female life-cycle, where in palace custom singing and dancing have come to be mutually exclusive, with the exceptions of the dance operas *Langĕndriyan* and *Langĕn Mandrawanara*. In all these cases, the performer does not seek profit; rather, the object is the preservation of tradition and the maintenance of the Javanese identity in the context of the Indonesian state.

By considering the impact of dance training on the *individual*, however, we are importing presuppositions about persons which are not necessarily relevant. Performance associated with the palace is a *collective* phenomenon. An important element of mastering *ĕmpan-papan* in the performance is to be in harmony with the other performers as well as within oneself: an underestimated element of performance skill is being able to avoid bumping into other dancers. During the making of a documentary film about *Bĕdhaya* I structured the narrative around one dancer whose daily life and interest in dance technique formed the first part of the film.[9] Some viewers were annoyed that she was subsequently lost in the *Bĕdhaya* dance. This is an important moment in the narrative, because it represents a switch from a Western perspective to a Javanese one. What is important about the dance is not the dancer Susindahati, but the collectivity of performers which is named *Bědhaya*.

The Hierarchy of Expression in Male and Female Dance

Javanese people do not speak of 'dance' as a category of activity; they refer to the specific form or genre associated with particular events, or to movement styles (*běksa*), which I shall call 'mode'. A dance mode is a prescribed system of movement which is named. In the Yogya court tradition there are twenty-two masculine modes which represent male characters, and a single feminine mode, *putri*. It is usual for all girls to start dance training by learning *putri*,[10] although dance academies now train girls in masculine modes and boys in *putri*, to maximise teaching, among other things. Boys normally begin with *impur*, the most gentle

Figure 8.1: *Langêndriyan*

masculine mode, and one used to represent esteemed heroes, which is most similar to the feminine mode. They then study the mode which best fits their physical development. It is in this context that a common explanation of the fact of there being so many masculine modes occurs: that the male physique and musculature is less able to adapt to a preferred standard than the female body. Javanese value adaptability and flexibility above brute strength; there is no 'macho' ideal, and the mastery of the *putri* by male as well as female dancers in the past and by male trainee teachers today is very much respected. So while *putri* denotes feminine qualities, these qualities are considered generally desirable, for male persons as well as female persons to emulate.

The modes are used most extensively in dance drama and are explained with reference to characterisation in the shadow play (*wayang kulit*), which in human performance is expressed in costume, make-up, voice style, dance mode, and physique (Suryobrongto 1981). For example the noble, modest, restrained but confident hero Arjuna, a small, low-voiced puppet, is represented in movement through *impur*, the mode closest in style to the feminine mode.

The classification characters in shadow play and dance drama comprise a range of types, from the controlled, modest heroes such as Arjuna to unrestrained ogre-types with untrammelled instincts. *Alus* types are found in palaces and other social enclaves, while the ogres come, typically, if not exclusively, from the forest. Ogre kings however, live in palaces, as befits kings. Characters are classed not only on a nature–culture axis, but also according to their social rank, which makes simple binary classifications inappropriately reductive. For example, a role such as Gathutkaca, the son of the Pandawa Bima, requires a heroism combined with beastly qualities inherited from his mother, who was an ogress; this is a difficult balance to achieve.

Despite the discrepancy between homogeneity of female representation and heterogeneity of male, Javanese intepretations of modes and genres do not support the notion of a fixed ranked gender hierarchy. The contrasting pair of Javanese concepts, *alus* and *kasar*, have been associated with a contrast between refinement and roughness and invoked to rank gender, correlating women as secondary and *kasar*. And Javanese interpretations relate them to what is approved of and disapproved of in the context of everyday social life, to the extent that they represent a culture–nature contrast (Hughes-Freeland 1986). But dancers explain that the contrast between *alus* and *kasar* cannot be applied to dance movement (*běksa*), because such movement is incorporated into a non-natural culturalised control, the physical control being enhanced by inner control.

Figure 8.2: Women training in the *putri* mode in the Sultan's place, Yogyakarta

Figure 8.3: Ledhek performed at a *tayuban* in the Gunungkidul district of Yogyakarta

It is in this sense, then, that *alus* and *kasar* take on the sense of unnatural and natural.

When a person performs in dance drama, s/he 'sits' in the *watak* and *wanda* of the puppet character being portrayed. *Watak* is the character and *wanda* the face which expresses it; in shadow theatre, one puppet may have several *wanda* to express different moods: warlike, enamoured, and so forth. *Watak* is the foundation (*dasar*) of a person, but spirit (*jiwa*) and sensibility (*rasa*) are also important parts of the person. As we have seen, performance conventions within the palaces have varied over time, and this includes the casting of roles and the statuses which performance made available to persons within the palace hierarchy. During the reign of the eighth sultan palace resources made it possible and desirable that a male performer should concentrate on one role for years. The male performer would be constrained by his physique and his presence: his scope as a performer was chiefly dictated by his shape, size, and facial expression: Arjuna would be played by a small-framed man. Access to roles in the plays was determined *to a certain extent* by the court hierarchy. Princes tended not to play lower characters, but talented soldiers might climb the ranks to play noble characters in the play.

People could be selected for roles because they have the right 'face' (*wanda*) or 'build' (*dĕdĕg*) because of the importance of control and spiritual sensitivity in people's discussions of dance. There has been more to casting than simple physical determinism. A well-known example was the performer who was too small for the heroic part he is remembered for: he compensated for his physical lack with the excellence of his sensibility and the bigness he brought to the role through his spirit. One informant said that even if a *bĕdhaya* dancer is not objectively very pretty she will look beautiful in the dance if her spirit is good; he reinterpreted the proverb 'an ugly face, an ugly heart' to 'a beautiful person is one with a fine spirit'. Casting therefore showed a flexibility with regard to rank in the palace, and men of noble and commoner status recalled their dancing days as coy heroines on the palace stage. Today there is more scope for male and female performers, and they are required to be more adaptable.

In palace performance ideology, excellence of expression is achieved by inner control. The effective performer is the one who no longer has to try. Movements move by themselves, s/he is absorbed by the spirit of the role, which infuses the face. This effect cannot be achieved by trying to look like Arjuna or Gathutkaca. Facial expression (*pasĕmon*) is not the result of muscular action (*polatan*), but the reflection of the dancer's spirit (*jiwa*). To try to put on *alus* behaviour is to be operating in the world of outer reality, to be motivated by self-interest (*pamrih*). Dancers should not be aiming for success; their object is to achieve a balance between sensibility and physique, the harmonisation or the fusion of the physique and the inner self. *Joged Mataram*, the palace 'philosophy' of performance, requires that a dancer should never feel as if s/he has succeeded. The dancer should never desist from the search for perfection. Self-interest damages one as a person as much as one's reputation as a performer.

These remarks make it clear that Western ideas of expression do not apply in Java, where a show of emotion, passion, or individuality is not approved of: such behaviour is classed as *kasar*. Emotion and desire should be channelled and restrained, not unleashed into the world of others. Javanese expression therefore is not about showing effort. Young dancers who spoke of being aware of trying to please their audience during performance are operating in the physical world, and are at risk from inflaming the passions (*hawa nafsu*) rather than generating the kind of expressive communication which is understood among older dancers to be proper. The dancer, according to performance philosophy, has a spirit which is in a state of contemplation (*sěmědhi*), s/he 'feels nothing', not a state of emptiness but of being 'empty but full'. One sees one's fellow-dancers and the pillars in the building, but neither these nor the audience interfere with the dancer's concentration. Informants conceded that there is an element of trance or forgetting in the dancer's loss of social inhibitions and constraint about rank. Therefore, although characters in dance drama represent the range of types, performance for both men and women inside the palace is classified as *alus*, as controlled and denatured: it appears natural only in so far as skill in performance makes it seem so. The different modes together represent a set of characteristics which *may* of themselves be violent, forceful and so forth, but are represented in action within an encompassing frame of control. Indeed, Javanese people do not like to refer to persons in terms of *kasar* at all; negative appraisal is in terms of smaller classifications.

The feminine mode *putri* is homogeneous, but allows the spirit to animate the particular role. In shadow theatre different female types are marked by the different angles of the head and pitches of the voice. Although there is only one feminine mode in human performance, there are a number of ways in which it is performed; distinctions operate at the level of inner expression, not different kinds of physical action. These distinctions are *luruh* (gentle, obedient), the most subdued and submissive feminine character type; *branyak* (bold), the most aggressive; and least usual, *tumandak* or *těmantu*, in-between. Javanese correlate these to the characterics of Arjuna's three wives: Sěmbadra is submissive and demure, Srikandhi is belligerent and lively, and Larasati, the first wife, is in-between.

It would be very wrong merely to see in female dance training the instilling of feminine grace, beauty, and passivity. The feminine mode looks graceful and fluid, but looks are deceptive: *putri* appears easy only through strenuous muscular control and the rigours of a strict training which stresses disciplined standards, particularly concerning elbows, wrists, and eyes, which should be kept lowered, looking at a point on the floor at a distance equivalent to twice one's height. *All* Yogyakartan palace modes and forms are strenuous, and conform to Javanese ideals about behaviour that effort should be dissimulated in order to create an impression of easy control. A dancer should look as if s/he has no bones, only muscles, concentrated but not stiff, and while dance movement is measured it is not slow, as beginners attempting to master fighting sequences have found to their cost. This training is more appropriately identified with the participation of females in the martial arts. It strengthens their muscles, improves their timing (both of which enhance their dance ability), and also gives them the capacity to defend themselves.

One cannot stress too much the tendency today to favour the Srikandhi spirit in characterisation and the representation of women in performance. Srikandhi is the brave and brazen female type, the warrior wife of Arjuna.[11] The Srikandhi factor has prompted historians to reconsider colonial stereotypes of Javanese women as gentle, self-effacing and sensual. Javanese palace chronicles and memoirs provide alternative images of women who play important dynastic, religious, and military roles (Carey and Houben 1987).[12] Women's influence declined in the mid-nineteenth century; but the heroic, active model of woman exemplified by Srikandhi is again being recognised by contemporary policies and propaganda to activate the women in the burgeoning republic. Women of today may see their models in the guise of dance heroines brandishing keris, bows and arrows, and most recently, lances. Although in the past males had access to the staged representations of male and female, with certain exceptions in regions apart from Yogya, female students of palace dance and drama in government academies are now learning masculine modes and taking on parts reserved for males, such as the four clowns in the dance drama. Nonetheless, within the palace ideology, the distinct between spirit and sensibility remains. When females enact soldiers in *Běksan* duets or dance drama, they portray the martial *spirit* of a soldier out of a refined (*alus*) sensibility. It is important to notice the distinction made here between spirit and sensibility; they are two different elements.

Militarism and the staged representation of fighting is not only understood as a literal reflection of Yogya's military origins – origins it shares with the Indonesian republic. Javanese men and women interpret performed fights in ways which reveal the capacity ascribed to the feminine in palace ideology. Apart from the literal militaristic invocations, militaristic metaphors are also used mystically to refer to an inner spiritual struggle in which military codes of chivalry (*satriya*) centred on self-control (*mawas diri*) (Onghokham 1983). Men and women partake equally in this struggle; but there is a difference in the evaluation of male and female performance and capability in the interpretation of fights which reveals a hierarchisation of expression with respect to gender representations.

The fights in dance drama (*Wayang Wong*), duels (*Běksan*) and the newest palace genre, *Běksan Golek Menak*, are valued for their dramatic quality; but those in *Bĕdhaya* and *Srimpi* by contrast are interpreted symbolically. The *Srimpi* fights between two pairs of women are symbolic, but less so than *Bĕdhaya*: *Srimpi* fighting sequences use a greater variety of dance patterns, and choreographers point out that *Srimpi* fights have been influenced by the drama of fights in the *Wayang Wong* and *Bĕksan*.

Let us consider *Bĕdhaya* in more detail here. *Bĕdhaya* is the most abstract palace form, and is denied simple referential mimetic or narrational capacities by performance practitioners (Hughes-Freeland 1991). Movement in *Bĕdhaya* exemplifies the aesthetic of 'flowing water', and is not divided up into units of signification, nor do costumes and make-up differentiate the dancers. In most *Bĕdhaya* dances, the performers are dressed identically, and a beautiful dancer is yellowed out with the traditional turmeric make-up. Yogya interpretations of *Bĕdhaya* emphasise unity, although there are named positions within the dance. The entrance and exit formations represent the human body: *Batak* (Head), *Endhel* (Follower), *Jangga* (Neck), *Pĕndhadha* (Chest), and *Bunthil* (Rear) form a central line and are flanked to each side by four dancers representing the arms and legs. In the formations that ensue, *Batak* and *Endhel* are in conflict. Regardless of what they represent in the particular choreography, the important general principle is that they are necessary opposites, between which conflict and reconciliation occur (Hughes-Freeland 1986). *Bĕdhaya* as performance event elicits ideas about process rather than structure. In *Bĕdhaya* philosophy two elements in shifting opposition and harmony show in abstract form how life is a process of complementary forces, not structural oppositions. Whereas conflict in other forms is valued for its dramatic excitement, the conflict in *Bĕdhaya* is valued for reasons which go beyond instant entertainment or gratification. The form has come to be associated with the capacity to evoke the large questions of existence beyond the humdrum daily divisions, but to bring the ideas of balance and process which concern the philosophers and metaphysicians into the frameworks by which daily interactions and perceptions are understood and evaluated (Brong-todiningrat 1981).

Interpretations such as this and the explanation of *alus/kasar* ideology in performance have important implications for how gender characteristics are understood and reveal something about perceptions of gender roles and capabilities which has been overlooked in ethnographic examples from the region so far. The asymmetry between the homogeneous feminine mode and heterogeneous masculine modes is not a sign of lower female status or the imposition of a repressive standardisation for females. The difference rests on an evaluation which emphasises responsiveness and subtlety of expression, which the female is better at achieving. To return to the problem of the Javanese gender hierarchy introduced at the start of this article, I would suggest that there is a conceptual problem in Keeler's representation of prestige systems in Java and women's exclusion from the sphere of 'potency', a word which has strong male associations. The word which Keeler translates as 'potency' is *sĕkti*, more often rendered as 'power', although 'energy' is another possible translation (Slamet 1982: 27) that removes associations of a masculine 'potency' and restores to the concept the Sanskritic sense of *shakti*, the female energy, from which *sĕkti* derives.[13] Whether *Bĕdhaya* is performed by male or female, it is ascribed female susceptibility and sensitivity, and remains the genre which has the power to express the most subtle and complex ideas: it exemplifies the grace of the feminine mode.

Female movement, performed by men or women, is classed as inherently more *alus* than masculine movement, and certain esteemed male roles are danced in masculine modes which are close to the feminine style. This evaluation confirms the limitation of a general model associating female and nature (Ortner 1974; MacCormack and Strathern 1980), and it indicates that the characterisation of the female as a class excluded from refinement and prestige is not a representative Javanese model of interpretation. Dance movement in the feminine mode, which is available to male and female, is ascribed a greated flexibility, a more innate capacity for learning and adaptability than the masculine modes, which are highly differentiated in order to accommodate the male performer, who is constrained and muscle-bound and, in many instances, literally type-cast. In palace performance today the male person tends to be tied to a role represented by a particular mode, while the female person may be different persons within the performance, using a single movement system by virtue of the animation of her spirit. There is no need for crude gestures or make-up to indicate who she is. In these terms, female is conceived as subtle and responsive: her nature is amenable to taking on cultural forms of grace and control. The same applies to male performers used to performing *putri*, and who now perform the 'gentle' masculine movement mode which is the closest to *putri*.

Today *Bĕdhaya* serves as more than the jewel in the Sultan's crown. It is performed by young Indonesians who hold neither allegiance to a king nor committment to a court. *Bĕdhaya* is not the stately show of servitude it might have been before independence; but there is a sense in which the capability of the female participants and the representation of the feminine has been created by the power system of the palace. I have suggested that the flexibility of the female in the lack of differentiation and the abstract capability of *Bĕdhaya* is a particular indication of female energy or power in Java, that the significant dimension of the energy of the female in palace performance is its control. It could be argued that performance within the palace ultimately redounded to the benefit of the ruler, expressed in restrictions which prevented women from appearing in palace forms other than *Bĕdhaya* and *Srimpi* until after independence. The control of the performer and the resulting style of expression can also be understood as an internalisation of political control by the State. Palace ideology controlled the form of female expression and energy shown in performance, especially the eroticism, the antithesis of the 'refinement' of female performance. The abstract *Bĕdhaya* does not express in any overtly erotic style the female capacities implicit in its mythic origins in the the legitimising love-making of the sultan and the Queen of the South Sea: the dissimulation of sexuality in the expression of the performance is evident to anyone who has watched *Bĕdhaya* and marvelled at its discipline and control.

The interpretations of concepts of power and their gender associations are not limited to anthropological arguments; such arguments are political, and indicate changing ideas and opportunities for women in society. Indonesian Javanese are currently debating the values by which they legitimise their cultural distinctiveness, and one of these arguments concerns the status of women who participate in a kind of performance which stands in opposition to everything that *Bĕdhaya* and female palace dance represents. These dancers (*ledhek*) once played a part in the rites preceding the annual harvest (*bersih desa*), a custom associated with fertility which continues to be associated with well-being in many parts of Java today (Hughes-Freeland 1993). The association with male partners has caused *ledhek* to be regarded as dancing prostitutes, bringing to their dance all the sexuality that palace performance has squeezed out. But palace polarisations tend to overlook the fact that not more than fifty years ago dancers such as these performed a similar role to palace dancers in the residences of regents and princely houses in the court centres, and in the past very good *ledhek* might be recruited to be trained as palace dancers. Recent research is attempting to correct the false dichotomy between *bĕdhaya* and *ledhek*, and to recognise the *ledhek* as the predecessor of palace dancers, as priestess rather than profanity (Suharto 1980).

Current interpretations pertaining to this sphere of Javanese practice are polarised between Indic and Islamic accounts. The Indic quality of female energy seen as curbed by Islam, a polarisation which has transformed the Hindu goddess Durga from her role in Hindu–Buddhist Java, where her statues provided cures for infertility (and still do, unofficially), to the malevolent demoness of today's shadow theatre. Indic and Islamic provide contrastive poles that structure divisive binaries and limitations rather than potentialities, complementarities, and the multiplicity of persons. As in India, to watch Javanese dance is to watch not the dancer but the dance. The aesthetic is ascetic, an asceticism which combines Islamic ideas with earlier Indic notions. The Javanese rationale of action as self-control may be understood in terms of Islamic or Hindu codes of spiritual discipline and progress: *Bĕdhaya* is the summation of the asceticism which Islam and Hinduism share. It is also a conjunction of two categories of asceticism (*tapas*) and desire (*kama*), chastity and sexuality, which it has been argued should be seen as complementaries, not opposites (O'Flaherty 1969). The chaste expression of the female dancers is not the exclusion of sexuality, and O'Flaherty's idea helps to account for resonances in Javanese material that are beyond crude polarisations of Indic and Islamic. Female energies contribute to a performace which is highly regarded in the Yogya *kraton* culture: the energies may be hidden or dissimulated, but they are still a weapon to be used.

It is often claimed that the Queen of the South Sea is Durga, the malevolent female force who has been overcome by the patrilines of Mataram. The myth of origin of female dance may be read as a legitimising strategy based on the agreement of the forces of the South Sea to marry Javanese sultans, since which time sultans have controlled women in the courts, expressed in dances celebrating the rule of men. But the myth can be read differently. The ruler has not *tamed* the female energies; the female energies concede to his rule, and *Bĕdhaya* is a sign of the female energies agreeing to visit the court. Divine visitation is a theme in other origin myths about dance in the region: *bĕdhaya* are sometimes said to be nymphs created in heaven by the divinity Brahma, who came down to earth. Javanese womanhood can take this myth of marriage between the sultan and the spirit queen as a way of representing the complementarity between the genders.

Performance: From Type-Casting to Options for Identity

Perceptions of women in anthropology and women anthropologists remain caught up in a lively and ongoing debate. Stereotypes are often invoked by both Western and non-Western feminists to structure new orders of gender action and ideology. Sometimes Western stereotypes are taken as fact by non-Western feminists: for instance, there has been a rejection of so-called 'Western values' in a statement often made by Indonesian women that they do not need Western-style 'women's lib'[14] because they have already been liberated by Kartini, the young noblewoman who struggled for education for women in the early twentieth century. Kartini was inspired by Dutch liberalism, at a time of struggle for opportunities and education for native Javanese (Jayawardena 1986: 140–6), and the educational projects in the sphere of dance training may also be seen as the result of Western values which gave the Javanese the wherewithal to define an anti-colonial position and develop politicised notions of national identity.

By the beginning of the twentieth century, the social stratification centring on court circles which themselves had been assimilated into the colonially sanctioned social order shifted its idiom and focus when the Indonesian power centre was established, first in Yogya, and finally in Jakarta. However, the revolution of independence is represented as having been built on continuities of hierarchy as much as on the breakdown of traditional Javanese social processes and possibilities. Formal performance on the part of the court was expanded beyond the court sphere in 1918, as court performance itself entered its 'golden age', which was supported by colonial subsidies to the ruler, and attested to by colonial administrators for whom performance was offered as a display and for entertainment. Non-courtly traditions meanwhile came and went as they always had, depending on the availability of surplus to sponsor such activities. It was only after national independence had been secured that the State set about defining, censoring and patronising village-type performances (Hughes-Freeland 1992).

Performance in Yogya demonstrates that persons and roles are gendered so as to cross-cut biological identities. Performance is gender-ascribed, but available to both sexes, according to specific conventions. Masculine dance modes are rigidly classified; the feminine mode is multiplex and sensitive: more flexible and fluid than masculine, more responsive and malleable; and such traits are culturally approved over and above the assertive, dominant, and fixed. Rather than the feminine role's being seen as that of constrained 'containers' that represent an impoverished counterpart, female energy is both *enabling of* and *complementary to* male potency. Also, males do not have to be constrained by notions of masculinity or male roles: the representation of males in drama acknowledges a range of types of masculinity, permitting men to represent 'gentle' heroes in a style that is masculine and yet feminine, without any stigma of sissiness or the comic–grotesque that Western representations of this kind often show. In contemporary Indonesia, transsexuals (*banci*) are an accepted 'third gender', with their own nationwide association and success stories in the world of showbusiness and beyond (see Hobart, this book).

The ritualised action of staged performance is part of a continuum of cultural action where male–female roles are complementary without necessarily being hierarchical. Dance training that enhances the capacity to dissimulate strong feeling in the approved manner provides individuals with the capacity to manipulate hierarchies and to be effective social actors. Control of one's physical person, like control of language codes, leads to control of a situation: the force of deference is to compel efficacious response from a patron. The cross-cutting effects of status allow women of higher status to compete with one another and with men in the arts as in other spheres of social and economic reproduction. But finally the achievement of control achieved in dance transcends the gendered individuals who contribute to its production and performance. Through performance men and women form a collectivity: the shared venture is ranked over and above individual interests.

It is important, though, to recognise that the struggle of women and men in Indonesia today is concerned with personal fulfilment and realisation in the broadest sense. Gendered identity is not a distinct agenda, but part and parcel of the construction of a national identity, which is the predominant political and cultural dynamic in contemporary Indonesia; and individuals switch from collective conformity to individual intepretations of appropriate action. A person may use the collective 'I' strategically some times, while at others s/he drops the Javanese 'I' in contexts of argument or bargaining.[15] The negotiated face of social interaction in process is not concerned with legitimisation, but efficacy. This is why there is a problem with the influential image of power attributed to the Javanese in Keeler *et al.*, an interpretation which is concerned with the legitimisation of a status quo and explanations for its possible disruption. The problem is that it does not explain how things are happening and where they will go. Many styles of action are also available in the culture, but dissimulated efficacy continues to be an important model for action and achievement in Javanese culture. As more overtly aggressive 'Westernised' models come into favour in urban circles female styles of behaviour for men and women alike will be challenged as appropriate for modern life, and thus models for genders will diverge. Alongside the Srikandhi factor are contesting images of women as wives and mothers in the domestic environment (Tomagola 1990). Whatever direction it takes, given the characteristic fluidity of performance interpretations over the years, the interpretations will be adapted to changing Javanese thinking about the roles of men and women in changing times.

Notes

1. Statement by senior female dance teacher.
2. From the pop song 'Semua itu katanya' by the singer Etrie Jayathie: 'Dia "lelaki" panas bagaikan api/Dia "wanita" sejuk bagaikan air/ Dia "waria" ih apa kita dipanggil/ Ada apa/ . . . Semua itu katanya.' I cannot think of any mainstream pop lyrics in the West with this kind of gender angle.
3. This reappraisal has offered a challenge to anthropology, As Moore puts it, 'feminist anthropology must not claim that women cannot be confined to and defined by their biology while simultaneously refining female psychology into a cross-cultural, social category' (1988: 7).
4. This binary image also determines an analysis of the gender classifications of the Javanese house following the Dutch structural anthropologist Rassers (Keeler 1983).
5. He also discusses cross-gender behaviour and people's responses to it.
6. I use the word 'gender' as used by Illich: 'Sex can be discussed in the unambiguous language of science. Gender bespeaks a complementarity that is enigmatic and assymetrical. Only metaphor can reach for it' (Illich 1983: 4).
7. Although there is numerical variation in numbers taking part in different *Bĕdhaya* choreographies,the dance for nine performers is the most dignified expression of the form and is generally the prerogative of the king.
8. Following the declaration of independence in 1945, the ninth sultan gave over part of the palace to house the first Indonesian university, Gadjah Mada university.
9. *The Dancer and the Dance*, 1988. Produced by the Royal Anthropological Institute and the National Film and Television School, United Kingdom.
10. During first fieldwork in the early 1980s participation in dance training was crucial to my research for methodological and theoretical reasons. It made my presence in Yogya less incomprehensible to locals than it might have been, and made possible a detailed semantic analysis of dance movement. I learnt the dance mode *putri* ('girl, daughter'). Although *putri* expresses movement styles and character attributes associated with femininity, it is not limited to female persons.

11. Indianists might note that Srikandhi is the Javanese version of the character Shikhandin in the Indian *Mahábhárata*, who after practising austere penance has been granted a boon by Shiva to be born as a male warrior in order to avenge her humiliation by Bhisma of the Kurawa clan in a previous life. In Java, Srikandhi fights valiantly for her man, her kin and her country. In Balinese shadow play, Srikandhi is viewed with disfavour, as a *banci*, a gender-bender.

12. In nineteenth-century Yogya there was a female cavalry corps, the *Langěnkusuma*.

13. The etymology of the word *shakti* relates to the Sanskrit root *shak-*, a verbal root meaning 'to be able to'. The *shakti* is the one who enables a man to act, to be a *kartta*, a doer: 'women and the domestic sphere seem to be in the Hindu life-world the potent core of an outward growing spiral' (Marglin 1985: 300–1). This observation comes from a study of temple priestesses and their relation to the king; but rather than implying a comparison between these *devadasi* and the *bědhaya* or the *ledhek*, it is the conceptualisation of the model of female capability which is significant for my argument about Java.

14. While anthropology struggles to overcome perceptions of ethnocentrism in the gender debates, other anthropologies, such as Islamic anthropology, have yet to make an impact: it is still difficult for feminist anthropology to accept at face value statements made by Indonesian women that to wear Islamic dress is to be liberated *from* the unwelcome attentions of men. This is one option among many culturally available rationales and ideologies for liberation *to be* a women; it is also a way of being liberated in a non-Western way. For a comparative discussion of self-presentational options available to females living in the Muslim world, see Nagata on the subject of Malaysian women in this volume and Abu Odeh on how feminists might think about the 'ideology of the veil' (1993).

15. In the filming of *The Dancer and the Dance* Susindahati twice rides pillion on a motorcycle: with her father, she sits sidesaddle; with her boyfriend, she sits astride. Before filming this second scene her father said that this style was unsuitable; but Sus argued forcefully, saying that she was wearing trousers to ride astride (*gagahan*, which refers to a set of 'strong' masculine modes). The two styles of pillion-riding reveal a fragmentation of the self: the Javanese collectivity, and a person who rebels against that identity. This variation of expression, however, can only occur because at that point in her life, when she was 21 years old, Sus relied on males to provide motor-cycle rides.

Bibliography

Abu Odeh, L. (1993). 'Post-colonial feminism and the veil: thinking the difference'. *Feminist Review*, 43: 26–37.

Brongtodiningrat, K. P. H. (1981). 'Filsafat Bedhaya'. In Yayasan Siswa and Among Bĕksa (eds), *Kawruh Joged-Mataram*. Yogyakarta: Arts Council, Yogyakarta, pp. 17–21.

Carey, P. and Houben, V. (1987). 'Spirited Srikandhis and Sly Sumbadras: The Social, Political and Economic Role of Women at the Central Javanese Courts in the Eighteenth and Early Nineteenth Centuries'. In E. Locher-Schoten and A. Niehof (eds), *Indonesian Women in Focus: Past and Present Notions*. Dordrecht: Foris, pp. 14–42.

Choy, P. (1984). 'Past texts of Golek dance'. In S. Morgan and L. J. Sears (eds), *Aesthetic Tradition and Cultural Transition in Java and Bali*, Monograph 2. Madison: Center for Southeast Asian Studies, University of Wisconsin, pp. 51–81.

Hanna, J. (1988). *Dance, Sex and Gender: Signs of Identity, Dominance, Defiance, and Desire*. London: Chicago University Press.

Holt, C. (1967). *Art in Indonesia: Continuity and Change*. Ithaca: Cornell University Press.

Hostetler, J. (1982). 'Bedhaya Semang: The Sacred Dance of Yogyakarta'. *Archipel* 24, 1127–42.

Hughes-Freeland, F. (1986). 'The Search for Sense: Dance in Yogyakarta', Ph.D. thesis (Social Anthropology), London University.

Hughes-Freeland, F. (1991). 'Classification and communication in Javanese palace performance'. *Visual Anthropology* 4:3–4, 345–66.

Hughes-Freeland, F. (1992). 'Packaging Dreams: Javanese Perceptions of Tourism and Performance'. In M. Hitchcock, V. T. King and M. J. G. Parnwell (eds), *Tourism in South-East Asia: Theory and Practice*. London: Routledge, pp. 242–56.

Hughes-Freeland, F. (1993). 'Golek Menak and Tayuban: Patronage and Professionalism in Two Spheres of Central Javanese Culture'. In B. Arps (ed.), *Performance in Java and Bali*. London: School of Oriental and African Studies, University of London.

Illich, I. (1983). *Gender*. London: Marion Boyars.

Jayawardena, K. (1986). *Feminism and Nationalism in the Third World*. London: Zed Press.

Keeler, W. (1983). 'Symbolic Dimensions of the Javanese House', Centre of Southeast Asian Studies Working Paper 29. Melbourne: Monash University.

Keeler, W. (1987). *Javanese Shadow Plays, Javanese Selves*. Princeton, NJ: Princeton University Press.

Keeler, W . (1990). 'Speaking of Gender in Java'. In J. M. Atkinson and S. Errington (eds), *Power and Difference: Gender in Island Southeast Asia*. Stanford: Stanford University Press, pp. 125–52.

Lindsay, J. C. (1985). 'Klasik Kitsch or contemporary: a study of the Javanese performing arts'. PhD Thesis, Sydney University.

MacCormack, C. and Strathern, M. (eds) (1980). *Nature, Culture and Gender*. Cambridge: Cambridge University Press.

Marglin, F. A. (1985). *Wives of the God-King: the Ritual of the Devadasis of Puri*. Delhi: Oxford University Press.

Moedjanto, G. (1986). *The Concept of Power in Javanese Culture*. Yogyakarta: Gadjah Mada University Press.

Moore, H. (1988). *Feminism and Anthropology*. Oxford: Polity Press.

O'Flaherty, W. (1969). 'Asceticism and Sexuality in the Mythology of Siva'. *History of Religions*, 9: 1–41.

Onghokham (1983). *Rakyat dan Negara*. Jakarta: Sinar Harapan LPES.

Ortner, S. (1974). 'Is Female to Male as Nature is to Culture?' In M. Rosaldo and L. Lamphere (eds), *Woman, Culture and Society*. Stanford: Stanford University Press, pp. 67–87.

Slamet, I. (1982). *Cultural Strategies for Survival: the Plight of the Javanese*, CASP 5. Rotterdam: Erasmus University.

Strathern, M. (1981). 'Self Interest and the Social Good: Some Implications of Hagen Gender Imagery'. In S. Ortner and H. Whitehead (eds), *Sexual Meanings*. Cambridge: Cambridge University Press, pp. 169–91.

Suharto, B. (1980). 'Tayub: pengamatan dari segi tari pergaulan serta kaitannya dengan upcara kesuburan', unpublished research report. Yogyakarta: ASTI.

Suryobrongto, G. B. P. H. (1981). 'Penjelasan tentang pathokan baku dan penyesuaian diri', etc. In F. Wibowo (ed.), *Mengenal Tari Klasik Gaya Yogyakarta*. Yogyakarta: Dewan Kesenian Propinsi Daerah Istimewa Yogyakarta, pp. 60–109.

Tomagola, T. A. (1990). 'The Indonesian Women's Magazine as an Ideal Medium', Ph.D. thesis (Sociology), University of Essex.

Waterson, R. (1990). *The Living House: An Anthropology of Architecture in South-East Asia*. Singapore: Oxford University Press.

PART III

Methodological Issues

9

Redefining the *Maybahay* or Housewife: Reflections on the Nature of Women's Work in the Philippines[1]

Jean Frances Illo[2]

The work females do is widely assumed to be central to the support of families. Much of this work, however, is consigned to the realm of domestic, household, or home work, and none of this is reflected in economic statistics as productive. Only wage work or a profit-earning activity is acknowledged as 'economic' or 'productive'. In economies and societies like the Philippines and the rest of Southeast Asia, rural women perform work activities, apart from home work, which do not earn a wage or directly yield a profit. They also undertake tasks which are part of a household enterprise, earnings from which are generally attributed to the household head or the principal producer. Throughout the region, reported female labour force participation rates range from less than 40 per cent in Malaysia to a little over 60 per cent in Thailand. The majority of the women who are not counted in the labour force are generally classified as 'housekeepers' or 'housewives'.

The economic conditions obtaining in the rural areas of Southeast Asia dictate a reassessment of concepts and methods better to understand the nature of women's work. To this end, this paper explores the concept of *maybahay* (literally, owner of the house), the Pilipino term often used to describe married women in parts of the Philippines, and elaborates on the life-cycle context of women's work. While it draws heavily on the life stories collected in a fishing village in the Philippines, it focuses on the salient points either articulated or alluded to by the women in the course of the interviews.[3] This chapter concludes with a note on the divergence between the women's construction of their work, on the one hand, and the assumptions of labour force surveys and the views of policies and programmes about women and their work, on the other.

Perspective and Method

Work is defined here as the production of goods and services for the market or for home consumption (Wallman 1979; Tilly and Scott 1987, first published in 1978; Beneria 1982). It is a means towards the support and maintenance of the family or the household.

Work in the family farm, trade or business, as well as wage work, including domestic service, are part and parcel of the family calculus for survival. Women's (as well as men's) work tends to be rooted in a sense of responsibility for the care of family. Such a family orientation captures the essence of the housewife or the *maybahay*. It also embodies the lessons girls are taught from childhood. It likewise shapes the work activities of women in different phases of their life-cycle.

Tilly and Scott, writing about women and work in France and England from 1750 until the last decade, observed: '. . . in all periods different kinds of work for women represented family economic strategies of adaptation to changed conditions' (1987: 6). A family's circumstances are reflected in its resource base, its anchor for survival. And as family fortunes shift, so does the work configuration of its members, female and male.

The changes in the nature of women's work over the women's lifetimes have been investigated through intensive, in-depth interviews of selected women geared towards reconstructing their life story.[4] The choice of life history as a research methodology was guided by a particular perspective and objective. This perspective confronts the complex realities of women's lives. Its objective is to give women a voice and their experience a name. The aim of naming women's realities, of 'addressing women's lives and their experience *in their own terms*' or as women articulated these, proceeds from a recognition of the power of naming.

> . . . Naming defines the quality and value of that which is named – and it also denies reality and value to that which is never named, never uttered. That which has no name, that for which we have no words or concepts, is rendered mute and invisible: powerless to inform or transform our consciousness of our experience, our understanding, our vision; powerless to claim its own existence (Du Bois 1983: 108).

In collecting life histories, one asks the women to retrieve their past. In so doing, a meaningful discussion of work and the crucial roles which women's work plays in the production and reproduction of life can take place. Likewise, it would be in assuming the women's delineations of significant events of their lives that concepts such as division of labour, accumulation of assets, and production and reproduction as distinct spheres of the world of work can take on their meaning.

The Site and The Women Studied

The data used in this paper are drawn from the life histories of women in the fishing village of Bantigue, a community located eight kilometres from Lucena City, the capital of Quezon, a southern province in the Luzon Islands. Bantigue typifies fishing communities, usually physically distant, economically and socially removed, from the larger regional and national society. It is basically a farming and fishing village, situated at the southernmost tip of the town. It is linked to the town centre in terms of political administration, social services and markets. It is also linked to markets, jobs, schools, and patrons in Lucena City.

While the fishery resources of Pagbilao Bay may strike fishers from other areas as abundant, Bantigue residents have witnessed the distressing depletion of the bay's marine resources and the decline of their fishery catch. Local fishers have gone to explore other nearby fishery areas. Some fishers have tried to join crews of trawlers based in Lucena City. Other fishers have also realised the profitability of marketing their fishery catch to, as well as buying fish from, the commissioned middlemen at the Dalahican fish market in Lucena City.

The Research Site
Bantigue occupies about 560 hectares in the western coast of Pagbilao Bay. More than half (304 hectares) of the village land area was planted to rice. In 1985, the population of Bantigue numbered 1000 (487 females and 546 males) and its households totalled 200. About 54 per cent of the households relied exclusively on farming, 16 per cent on fishing, and 30 per cent on a combination of fishing and farming. Farming households resided in the inner sections of the village such as Ilayang Bantigue. Meanwhile, fishing households tended to be concentrated in the southern end of Bantigue, called Ibabang Bantigue.

In 1986, about 59 families lived in Ibabang Bantigue (Table 9.1). Among these, 82 per cent partly or fully depended on fishing; 13 per cent relied mainly on farming or *panganganihan* (contracting the management and harvest of rice crops) and 3 per cent depended completely on earnings from *rigaton* (trading in fishery products). A number of fishing families, however, simultaneously engaged in rice farming and fishing. Most other fishers were rice harvesters (*nanganganihan*). This extension of one form of livelihood to another had partly enabled the Bantigue fishers to maintain their daily sustenance. A few families in Bantigue (five in Ibabang Bantigue and one in Ilayang Bantigue) had neither land to till nor gears for fishing. And finding a lot where a hut could be built was extremely difficult. Negotiations for land use were often conditionally resolved, and landless families were driven from one homelot to another. As one landless woman remarked: '. . . *Para kaming mga hayop na itinataboy-taboy . . .* ' (which roughly translates to, 'We were like animals being constantly driven away').

Individual fishers employed varying fishing strategies, preferring certain fishing grounds at different times of the year. In addition, while some specialised in fish, others caught crabs and squids as well as fish. A typical fisher in Bantigue used a *banca*, or a small dugout canoe weighing no more than 0.3 gross ton, and operated other fishing gears which might not require the use of boats. The relatively narrow *bancas* were made out of light marine plywood; these were sometimes equipped with outriggers for stability in rough waters. Apart from these boats, bamboo rafts were likewise utilised for fishing, particularly close to the shores.

In 1986, several village-level mechanisms and institutions for resource-sharing were apparent in Bantigue. Although a variety of options were available in the village, access to a number of these required prior access to land (rice cultivation) or to capital (as in the case of own-account fishing, trading, or operating transport facilities like pedicabs). Families that had no access to land or fishing capital could negotiate with resource owners for the use of the land or fishing equipment under share tenancy or *kasama* arrangements, while families that could not buy their own animals could raise pigs or cows under an offspring- or profit-sharing system called *pangingiwian*. (The managers could be male or female Bantigue residents, while the fisher-*kasama* were often male spearfishers who came to the village from Bohol. These men found having a manager advantageous, since the latter provided them with a hut and a boat.) Moreover, landless households could also contract the management and harvest of crops (or *panganganihan*) for a percentage share of the harvest.

Table 9.1 Percentage distribution of households in Ilayang Bantigue and Ibabang Bantigue, by principal means of subsistence, late 1986

Means of subsistence	Ilayang Bantigue	Ibabang Bantigue
Fishing only	—	34
Fishing and farming	3	8
Fishing and *panganganihan*	—	33
Fishing, farming, and *panganganihan*	—	7
Subtotal[a]	3	82
Farming only	27	5
Farming and *panganganihan*	67	—
Panganganihan only	3	8
Rigaton only	—	5
Total	100	100
(Number of cases surveyed	30	59)

[a] Includes *rigaton* by the female spouses in fishing households.

The rice-harvesting contract was often drawn between two landless households: the non-owner-tiller household (share tenant or *kasama*) and the harvesters (*nanganganihan*). The *kasama* family often granted the rice-harvesting rights to relatives. As in the case of the *kasama* system, *pangingiwian* and the rice-harvesting contract enabled assetless households to gain access to the fruits, if not the ownership, of income-generating resources. In Bantigue, where many families existed close to the subsistence line, the cash which the sale of an animal could bring has enabled some families to finance a child's education, pay hospital and medical bills, and/or buy fishing gear. Additionally, large amounts of cash for production and/or home consumption could be supplied by a collective savings scheme (known locally as *turnohan*, literally, 'taking turns') involving at least 20 people and/or families. These village-level support sources helped expand the survival options of Bantigue women and their families.

The Women Studied

The ten women interviewed in Bantigue lived in households composed of members of their conjugal families. The only exceptions were Mina, whose mother moved in with them after her father died in early 1985; and Berta, whose family had adopted a young boy in 1985. Of the households, nine were reportedly headed by the male spouse; only one (Caring and her husband, David) claimed that they jointly headed their household (Table 9.2).

All ten families had at least a boat and jiggers, pots, or nets. Two owned a motorised boat, while the rest had a paddled *banca*. Six owned a fishing net, while four relied mainly on fish or crab pots, jiggers and/or spears. Not all, however, were engaged in fishing in 1986. Mina and her spouse had shifted to non-fishing ventures in early 1986. Mina ran her *sari-sari* (variety) store, while her spouse operated a pedicab (a motorcyle with a side car for passengers and baggage). In the other nine cases, survival depended partly on fishing, and partly on what could be earned from crop farms and/or from wage jobs in the village or elsewhere. All the families also claimed to raise their own animals – pigs, cows, goats or carabaos – and/or animals owned by other families on an *iwian* arrangement.

Table 9.2   Distribution of cases in Bantigue, by reported household headship and resource base, late 1986

Reported Household headship	Resource base		
	Land and fishing	Wage labour and fishing	Trading capital
Male-headed	Atang Rosing Gloria Clara	Eva Ramona Lani Berta	Mina
Jointly-headed	Caring		

The women who were interviewed in Bantigue in 1986 included a 27-year-old woman, five women in their thirties, three in their forties, and one who was 53 years old. Their mean age was about 38 years (Table 9.3). They had been married for an average of 18.5 years. Age at marriage varied among the women, with the mean age computed at about 19 years. Five women had spouses of their own age, one was a year older than her spouse, while four were 1 to 5 years younger than their spouse. The couples also tended to be evenly matched by education; the average amount of education of the women and the men was less than the six-year elementary education.

The women had had an average of four pregnancies and live births. About half of the women's living children were females, the other half, males. Six of the women had all their children still living with them by

1986; three had a daughter who had left home; and one had three daughters and a son who were working elsewhere or had begun their own households. The out-migration of young family members indicated the paucity of job opportunities for young villagers as well as a desire of parents and children to wrest the latter away from the back-breaking, low-earning production work in the village. The fact remains, however, that many of the children continued to live with their parents, and thus continued to share with them the uncertainties of survival, which hinges on the elusive access to the sea and the land.

The Life-Cycle Context of Women's Work

Their reproductive roles loomed largely in the lives of the women interviewed. This was apparent in the recurring usage by the women of life-cycle markers in their stories, markers primarily associated with pregnancies and childbirths, sicknesses and deaths. The women were viewed and were trained to view themselves in terms of nurturing roles. As probably elsewhere, the social construction of gender revolved around

Table 9.3 Selected personal and familial characteristics of the women interviewed, late 1986

Item	Range	Mean
Years married	10–35	18.5
Age at marriage		
Woman	17–23	19.3
Man	16–24	20.7
Woman's age as of 1986	27–53	37.8
Education (years of formal school attendance)		
Woman	4–9	5.5
Man	2–10	5.6
Number of pregnancies	2–6	4.4
Number of live births	2–6	3.7
Number of living children	2–6	3.7
Female	1–5	2.3
Male	1–3	1.4
Number of resident children	1–6	2.9
Female	1–2	1.2
Male	0–5	1.7

the women's reproductive function. Even Gloria, a tomboy, confided that it was only when she was nursing her baby that she felt 'like a woman'.

The bodily changes that accompanied pregnancy tended to dictate a new work rhythm. The women were forced to move more carefully, and to refrain from strenuous activities. Care was taken especially by those who had miscarried earlier pregnancies (as in the case of Atang), an unfortunate event generally attributed to overexertion during pregnancy. Atang, for instance, blamed her sewing with a pedalled machine while she was pregnant for her miscarriage and stillborn baby. In the case of Gloria, her frequent trips to market, which involved walking long distances carrying a basket of fishery products, almost cost the lives of two of her babies.

A number of the women desisted from engaging in physically exhausting, non-domestic work during the last three months of pregnancy. The range of tasks they could accomplish became more and more limited as their bodies grew larger with child. Certain activities, such as weeding the field or staying out in the bay to fish, became awkward if not difficult. However, the state of poverty in which some of the women lived compelled them to continue their field work or their *rigaton* until the week of their expected delivery; premature withdrawal from these activities could adversely affect their households' survival. The pressure to work was particularly great among women whose spouses were ill or unable to secure the family's basic needs. Thus, a few women recalled having their first labour pains while working in the field or out in the sea. Moreover, whether engaged in non-domestic work or not, pregnant women also remained responsible for the many home chores necessary to sustain home life, stopping only when labour pains persisted. Thus, they cooked the meals, washed the laundry, mended clothes, looked after toddlers, cared for sick family members, and so on.

With the coming of the children, women whose spouses were earning enough or whose natal families could subsidise their needs refrained from work activities that would take them out of the house for extended periods. They rejoined the village's economic life only after the children were old enough to be left alone. This labour-force participation pattern suggested women's entry into the workforce at an early age, periodic withdrawal during the formative years of the family, and return on a full-time basis after several years.[5] The economic-participation curve, thus, was much flatter for the women in Bantigue than what the macro data depict, because complete withdrawal was never possible.

Moreover, work withdrawal was associated mainly with actual fishery capture. Many of the women resumed a regular work schedule after a short lying-in period of two to four weeks. As soon as the women were able, they undertook housework and home- or neighbourhood-based enterprises (such as running a store, raising animals, washing or making clothes for pay, cooking food items for sale) which provided their households part of their food or cash needs. After a few weeks more, those who previously traded in fishery products and/or worked as rice harvesters took them up once more. As was indicated by some of the women studied, the short lying-in period provided them with their only rest from work.

The women's almost unnoticed withdrawal from market-oriented work was made possible by specific features of village life: the early initiation of children into work, the livelihood-opportunities structure that allows women to venture into home-based economic work, and the presence of kinswomen who could watch over the children when the women had to resume their *rigaton*, field work, and fishing. To many of the women (and the men), therefore, life was an unending toil. While some help with the children could be taken advantage of, their care and that of the home generally fell on the women. Moreover, although every new-born was a delight to the women and their spouses, the child was also an added mouth to feed until he or she could begin to earn his/her keep.

Closely associated with the normal life-cycle of village households was accumulation of resources. Building-up of human and other resources was generally undertaken jointly by the women and their spouses. The jointness lay not only in the process of decision-making, but also in the work involved in the acquisition of the resources.

At the outset, the couples invested in a minimum of fishing gears that would serve as their livelihood base. They also arranged for secondary income sources by negotiating the rights to cultivate a farm as share tenant, contracting the management and harvest of standing crops, and/ or acquiring animals for fattening or breeding under the *iwian* system. These various ways of earning a living provided the Bantigue families with their basic requirements at different phases of their life-cycles.

Accumulation of resources by Bantigue couples, however, seldom followed a straight time trajectory. Rather, it was marked by twists and turns denoting the shifting fortunes of women and men, as some assets were acquired, and others, lost.

The effects of changes in household resource status affected the work burdens of male and female household members. Acquisition of animals for fattening or breeding often meant additional chores for the women and their children, while acquisition of cultivation or rice-harvesting rights required more work for the men as well as the women and children. Because these offered more livelihood options, households strove to create a multiple-activity security net, a hedge against failures in any one component of their survival package.

As economic options helped women and men generate more resources, they also tended to diversify their work activities further. Women like Atang and Gloria's mother ventured into management of fishers, thus acquiring their own fishery-catch supply independent of their spouses' catch. Others, like Eva's mother, ventured into moneylending with cash earnings from fishery trading. Acting as petty capitalists, the women expanded their households' resource base, and enabled them to finance the education of their children. More importantly, as is shown by the story of Mina, the women could build their own resource base. This seemed to give some women the confidence in their ability to support themselves and their children. Along with the feeling of self-confidence came the leverage to deal with recalcitrant spouses and a reshaping of the domestic balance of power.

Women's Work, Self-Image and Worth

Work and Identity

Wallman posits that 'the extent of individual or group identification with one kind or aspect of work rather than another ultimately depends on the structure and the values of the society of which that work is a part' (1979: 16–17). This identification is a dynamic process, with its roots traced to the work roles females and males are socialised into since childhood, and to the relative value imputed to different work activities.

In the Philippines, cultural ideals define female work as destined to be done for and in the home, while male work basically covers tasks performed outside the home (Gonzales and Hollnsteiner 1976). The norms are transmitted to children through chore assignments, instructions or encouragements concerning loci and types of games boys and girls can play.[6]

In Bantigue, the females' home focus was diluted, principally because women and girls usually travelled to town to sell fishery products. Nonetheless, females and males tended to define themselves according to the gender division of work spheres. The females associated themselves with the world of their mothers, consisting of services to other family members (cooking meals, doing the laundry, caring for children) as well as 'female' cash-earning ventures (running a store, selling cooked food). Meanwhile, the males viewed themselves in terms of the world of their fathers, a world revolving around fishing, farming, and/or wage work.

The formation of gender-based ties was never straightforward. Like children elsewhere in the country, boys and girls in Bantigue were trained to cook rice and simple dishes, wash up after meals, and keep the house clean. In addition, older children shared the tasks of tending the younger ones. Children were given more defined gender-based work assignments at puberty, when boys began helping their fathers fish and mend nets, while the girls assisted their mothers with housekeeping and other productive ventures.[7] But in some cases male adolescents continued to perform home chores, while the girls were drawn into fishing activities. Some girls, therefore, spent their childhood and youth not only in their mother's world but also in their father's, and actual fish capture was not the exclusive domain of men. This point was evident in the life stories of Gloria and Berta who occasionally fished by themselves, and of four other women who occasionally joined their fathers to help with the net or the oars. Because Gloria and Berta admittedly enjoyed doing 'male' tasks (such as handling motorboats, working with nets, and going out to sea alone) during their youth, they were branded tomboys by the villagers. In the case of Gloria, the label stuck even after her marriage to Mario.

Whatever contradictions existed between actual and ideal gender roles were mitigated in part by an admonition that couples should share burdens, and by the fact that women had learned to play multiple roles. In most cases, however, while the men stayed in the male world of definite livelihood pursuit, the women increasingly took on 'male' activities in addition to the various chores that characterise their own world. Providing one striking exception, Gloria and Mario equally shared the responsibilities of earning a living, accomplishing home chores, and raising children.

To minimise domestic conflicts, the women tried to stay home when their children were small. Failing this, they kept their activities close to home, limiting their ventures to collecting *turnohan* pledges, operating a small store, raising animals, and making dresses and other products. When they needed help with their children and home chores, they usually sought the help of other females: daughters, mothers, sisters, female in-laws, friends and relatives.[8]

All the women interviewed recalled both their parents endlessly toiling to feed their children. More than the men interviewed, however, the women had vivid memories of their mothers forever bent over *something*: an infant or a toddler, an open stove while cooking their meals, a load of washing, a basket of fishery products. Soon enough, the women were acting like their mothers, and taking on home chores and a host of other activities: making dresses, trading in fishery products, joining rice-harvesting teams, managing fishers and/or a collective-savings group, raising animals.

The 'femaleness' of domestic work weighed heavily on the women. Despite their diverse livelihood package, they associated themselves with their home work, their being a *maybahay*.[9] Those who went fishing alone or with their spouses described themselves as the latter's helpers (*katulong*). They tended to downplay their incursions into the men's world, and reaffirmed their status as secondary producer *vis-à-vis* the male. Even Ramona, who singlehandedly supported her family for a few years, explained her livelihood activities as performance of a wife's duty to help the spouse support the family.

Like Ramona, the women tended to view their livelihood activities as secondary to their being a wife and mother. Three women, however, took pride in their own enterprise: Mina, who ran her own store; Atang, who managed and financed a group of spearfishers; and Gloria, who showed great aptitude and guts (*lakas ng loob*) in pursuing livelihood opportunities. Unlike Mina and Atang, however, Gloria had very little interest in housekeeping. To her amusement, the Bantigue residents found her to be 'more manly than womanly'.

The data from Bantigue suggest that their multi-activity work portfolio outside of housekeeping had made it hard for the women to associate themselves with just one work type. The exact activity mix might change according to their personal preferences, market opportunities, life-cycle, and available resources; but the women were at once traders, fishers, rice harvesters, farmers, and fund managers, as well as housekeepers. Because they considered all these activities as related to being a *maybahay*, a status imbued with a social value, the Bantigue women were identifying with a generalised status or lifestyle (Wallman 1979: 19). In its broad context, therefore, the status of a *maybahay* was also attributed an economic value. The valuation of women's work, however, remains a problem.

Work and Worth

The sense of self and self-worth among the women interviewed could have arisen, as Chodorow (1974) suggests, from strong ties between the women and their mothers. Because the Bantigue females were inured to both housekeeping and economic roles, their self-worth emanated not only from their performance of domestic duties but also from their ability to contribute to the support of the family. The integration of the non-domestic with domestic work, however, tended to cloud the issue concerning the nature and the associated incentives of the array of work women do.

Among the families studied in Bantigue, women's work at home seemed to be valued for the comfort and convenience it affords to their members, the stability it lends to the group, and the care it gives to the succeeding generation of citizens and workers. Because even market-related production activities of women were geared towards the support of family, the high social value accorded to being a wife, a mother and a worker tended to rest on the premiss that the self is sacrificed for the group, in this case the family.

The story of Eva highlighted the steadfastness of family support as an incentive for women to take on work, whether purely household, or a double burden, consisting of housework and market activities. Although Eva grew up watching and helping in her mother's fish-trading business, the first decade of her own married life was spent at home, being a 'good wife and mother'. She narrates:

> I used to stay home when the children were still small. My husband wanted to keep me at home. This was my place, he said; his was working to support us . . . We had a hard life. We often relied on my parents for food, cash, and even the education of my eldest daughter . . . In Infanta, we depended on my older sister . . . I engaged in *rigaton* only after my youngest child turned six over the initial objections of my spouse. It was then I realised what a big help a woman's income could be [to the family].

While the support of the group might have provided the stimulus for men and women to work, the value of a person's work tended also to be associated with the control which one could exert over the product of her or his work.[10] Ramona, whose life was marked by long work periods and little rest, felt helpless and worthless when she could not use the fruits of her labour to realise a personal dream. Yet some of the women interviewed considered themselves in control, with incentives to work emanating as much from the monetary returns as from the control over their own fate. Gloria and Mina were such cases. Gloria learned to do things on her own and for herself from an early age. Meanwhile, Mina's wilfulness, enterprise and personally built-up resources enabled her to do what she wanted when she wished to. These two women strove hard to keep their autonomy throughout their youth and married life. Of the remaining women, seven had, at most, moments when they felt 'in control', a feeling engendered by a certain degree of financial independence at certain periods of their life-cycle. In contrast to all these women was Ramona, whose hard work had benefited first, her natal family, and later, her conjugal family. Not even Ramona, however, thought of herself beyond being a *maybahay*, a housewife.

Concluding Notes

A review of the Bantigue data as well as other studies in the Philippines indicate that, from an early age, girls are trained at home and in school to be home managers, housekeepers, housewives, or *maybahay*. It is as a *maybahay* that a girl undergoes training from her mother. As a *maybahay*, she would have her own house, her own household, her own family life.

The concept of *maybahay*, which is used to define married women 'who do not work for wages', is imbued with different shades of meaning, but largely associated with household work. As such, it is considered non-economic by labour force surveys, which tend to view work as either of two mutually exclusive categories: economic or non-economic.[11] As the Bantigue data suggest, however, the *maybahay* is more than the 'housekeeper' as defined by labour force surveys. To these women, economic and non-economic work are not separable, and their being a *maybahay* means being a total worker, producing both goods and labour. The Bantigue data challenge existing concepts and definitions. By extension, they also challenge the development of policies and assistance programmes to women who have been classified so far as non-workers, as 'merely' *maybahay*.

Notes

1. This essay draws heavily on a monograph (Illo and Polo 1990) which is based on a research study on women's work and family strategies funded by the International Development Research Centre. Publication funds were provided by the United Nations University (UNU). The study formed part of a regional research network on women's work and family strategies sponsored by the UNU, and co-ordinated by Vina Mazumdar, Director of the Centre for Women and Development Studies based in New Delhi, and Hanna Papanek, Research Associate of the Center for Asian Studies at Boston University.
2. The author is a research associate of the Institute of Philippine Culture of the Ateneo de Manila University. She co-ordinates the institute's women's studies programme.
3. Details of the life histories are presented and discussed in Illo and Polo (1990).
4. At least two other approaches can be used for achieving a longitudinal view of women's work. One approach involves the projection of women's work from a cross-sectional study of strategies of women and families at different

life-stages. Another would entail observing or monitoring a sample of women and their families over time. For a recent discussion of the life-history methodology, see Jones (1983).
5. This u-shaped pattern of women's economic participation imitates, to a certain extent, the macro pattern based on cross-section, age-specific labour force data from surveys and population censuses in the Philippines (see, for instance, Mangahas and Jayme-Ho 1976 and Angeles 1982).
6. Studies undertaken in the late 1950s and early 1960s suggest that gender-based differentiation in chore assignments was rarely noted before children turned ten (Nurge 1965). However, girls from an early age were enjoined to play close to home (Guthrie and Jacobs 1966) and to do home chores (Mendez and Jocano 1974). In contrast, boys could play far from home, and are often assigned to do errands. As Guthrie and Jacobs noted, girls who would rather play boys' games with boys are called *tomboy* (1966: 139). Separation of the sexes became more marked in the fifth and sixth grades, which stressed agricultural science and industrial arts for the boys and home economics for girls (Nydegger and Nydegger 1966: 160).
7. Nydegger and Nydegger (1966: 167) describe adolescence in an Ilocos village of the late 1950s as a 'period of growing intimacy between a father and a son'; the boy works closely with the father and joins him in his cockfighting. During this period, too, a girl takes on increasing responsibilities, and is enjoined to be a good worker and to be womanly. Control over female, but not male, sexuality becomes marked at this stage. Guthrie and Jacobs describe this control thus: 'The physical changes at puberty also necessitate certain behavior changes in the girl. Her behavior becomes more inhibited and controlled. She is expected to be more careful about her person . . . [She] may continue to play . . . but she does this less frequently because of her increased household duties and the awareness of her developing body' (1966: 140).
8. Viewed from the mother's end, Nurge (1965) suggests that daughters in her Leyte (Philippines) village are seldom free of their obligations to their mother. The only times they could be excused from answering their mother's call for help are their own child-bearing and illness, or, sometimes, pressure of their own work. The tie between daughter and mother is one nurtured from childhood, when obedience to elders is a value in the village, and when it is a natural thing to do because 'love makes one obedient' (1965: 104). Using data from groups with 'strong matrifocal tendencies' (East London, Java, and Atjeh), Chodorow (1974) further notes that mother–daughter ties (and ties among female relations), which arise from companionship and mutual cooperation, appear to enable the women to develop 'a strong sense of self and self-worth, which continues to grow as they grow older and take on their maternal role' (1974: 61–2).
9. Apropos housework and the ideology of the *maybahay*, Marilyn French writes of the housewife: '. . . She was an unpaid servant, expected to do a superlative job. In return, she was permitted to call this house hers. But so did [the others]' (1978: 107).

10. Papanek argues that unequal power and authority within a group are reflected, first, in persistent inequalities in the allocation of work and resources: 'Those who make the decisions that affect others and who make these decisions stick are also in a position to benefit most when work is divided and resources distributed – if they are not prevented by feelings of responsibility or norms dictating self-sacrifice' (1987: 21).
11. The economic–non-economic opposition seems to have also influenced the concept of household head as used in labour force surveys as well as in development programming. With household headship attributed to an assumed male producer, rural economic ventures that involve the female spouses and children are generally attributed to the 'male household head' (Illo 1989).

Bibliography

Angeles, E. (1982). An Economic Analysis of Migration and Work Behavior of Married Women in the Philippines, unpublished Ph.D. dissertation, School of Economics, University of the Philippines, Quezon City.

Beneria, L. (1982). 'Accounting for women's work'. In Lourdes Beneria (ed.), *Women and Development: The Sexual Division of Labor in Rural Societies*. New York: Praeger Publishers, pp. 119–47.

Chodorow, Nancy (1974). 'Family structure and feminine personality'. In Michelle Zimbalist Rosaldo and Louise Lamphere (eds), *Women, Culture, and Society*. Stanford: Stanford University Press, pp. 43–66.

Du Bois, B. (1983). 'Passionate Scholarship: Notes on Values, Knowing and Method in Feminist Social Science'. In Gloria Bowles and Renate Duelli Klein (eds), *Theories of Women's Studies*. London: Routledge & Kegan Paul, pp. 105–18.

French, Marilyn (1978). *The Women's Room*. New York: Jove/Harcourt Brace Jovanovich.

Gonzales, A. M. and Hollnsteiner, Mary R. (1976). *Filipino Women as Partners of Men in Progress and Development: A Survey of Empirical Data and Statement of Goals Fostering Male and Female Membership*. Quezon City: Institute of Philippine Culture, Ateneo de Manila University.

Guthrie, George M., and Jacobs, P. J. (1966). *Child Rearing and Personality Development in the Philippines*. University Park: Pennsylvania University Press.

Illo, J. F. I. (1989). 'Who heads the household? Women in Households in the Philippines'. In Amaryllis T. Torres (ed.), *The Filipino Women in Focus: A Book of Readings*. Bangkok: UNESCO, pp. 245–66.

Illo, J. F. I., and Polo, Jaime B. (1990). *Fishers, Traders, Farmers, Wives: The Life Stories of Ten Women in a Fishing Village*. Quezon City: Institute of Philippine Culture, Ateneo de Manila University.

Jones, G. R. (1983). 'Life History Methodology'. In Gareth Morgan (ed.), *Beyond Method: Strategies for Social Research*. Newbury Park, California: Sage Publications, pp. 147–59.

Mangahas, M. and Jayme-Ho, T. (1976). 'Income and Labor Force Participation Rates in the Philippines', Discussion Paper, No. 76-03. Quezon City: Institute of Economic Development and Research, School of Economics, University of the Philippines.

Mendez, Pepita P., and Jocano, F. L. (1974). *The Filipino Family in Its Rural and Urban Orientation*. Manila: Centro Escolar University Research and Development Center.

Nurge, Ethel (1965). *Life in a Leyte Village*. Seattle: University of Washington Press.

Nydegger, William F., and Nydegger, Corinne (1966). *Tarong: An Ilocos Barrio in the Philippines*, Six Cultures Series, Vol. VI. New York: John Wiley.

Papanek, H. (1990). 'To each less than she needs, from each more than she can do'. In Irene Tinker (ed.), *Persistent Inequalities*, Women and World development, New York: Oxford University Press, pp. 162–181.

Tilly, L. A., and Scott, Joan W. (1987). *Women, Work and Family*. New York: Methuen, Inc. (First published in 1978 by Holt, Rinehart and Winston).

Wallman, S. (1979). *Introduction: Social Anthropology of Work*, ASA Monograph 19. London: Academic Press.

10

The Significance of 'Eating': Cooperation, Support, and Reputation in Kelantan Malay Households

Ingrid Rudie

In this chapter I attempt to address some general problems in household studies, at the same time as I seek to explore essential features of Malay household organisation. In the following discussion I shall draw on my own field experience for exemplification, trying to show how an understanding of Malay households developed in a dialogue between pre-established analytical concepts on the one hand, and vernacular concepts and local practice on the other. The dialogue took place on two occasions – one, fieldwork as far back as 1965, and the other a new study which was undertaken through three consecutive visits in 1986, 1987 and 1988. This particular history will necessarily add a reflexive mood to the analysis. Reflexive anthropology is a risky game, because it may easily lapse into self-centred stories. It has a job to do, however, if it can be carried forward as a serious attempt to unveil the influences that shape our theoretical understanding.

This analysis will, then, be a small paragraph in the general story about how anthropological concepts develop and sometimes fossilise; but it will also suggest some measures to escape fossilisation. In anthropology, perhaps more than in any other social science discipline, concepts and definitions are constantly challenged when the analyst faces material from very different societies.

Household Concepts

Households are apparently simple and straightforward social units, but pose some intricate problems to the analysis because as organisations they are also remarkably 'multi-purpose'. This offers many possibilities for pursuing a variety of different topical interests: households are small units in which primary familial loyalties have to come to terms with some requirements for efficient resource management, and they are fields of interaction in which deep-seated features of a gender system are reproduced through social practices that seem particularly resistant to analytical penetration.

Starting from a preliminary definition of the household as *a co-residential unit, usually family-based in some way, which takes care of resource management and primary needs of its members*, I argue that this has primarily invited two foci, each of which seems to carry its own particular traps, or invite its own particular exaggerations. One of these stresses the fact that households are family-based, the other stresses the fact that they are concerned with resource management.

The *family focus* may have led to the development of one kind of stereotype, which Olivia Harris criticises as a tendency to look at households as a universal entity, being and doing the same thing in all societies – 'natural' units, because households are seen as places where women give primary care, at the same time as women are associated with nature – something that Harris – building on de Beauvoir – sees as deeply embedded in European thought (Harris 1981: 136). The unfortunate consequences of this strain of thought she sums up like this:

> Some have argued that domestic labour is a hidden form of exploitation; others that women's responsibility for the personal, emotional lives of household members structures their lives in such a way as to exclude their participation in social and political life; others have pointed to marriage as the key social relation by which women's subordination is secured; yet others have argued that women's status in the public domain can be positive only when there is little separation or differentiation between domestic and public spheres (ibid. 137).

Harris further argues that discussions tend to fall into this groove even when analysts are aware of the wide variation that is found in division of tasks between the sexes as well as in kinship systems and residential arrangements. She even notices such lapses in her own work, and argues that this happens because deep-seated presuppositions in European thought 'meet' the occurrence in different societies of co-residential units which are family-based and take care of primary needs.

I suspect that the flaws noticed by Harris have tended to intensify during a phase in which anthropologists have concentrated more on women and on societies advanced into modernity. Rosaldo´s influential hypothesis about universal male dominance resting in the division between domestic and public spheres (Rosaldo 1974) pulls in the same direction.

The other approach to household studies – the one that takes its departure from resource management – largely escapes Harris's criticism. That approach can be traced back to Chayanov, and – of a more recent date – Goody's and Stenning's contributions in the Cambridge Symposium on the development cycle of domestic groups. All these contributions take their departure from an insight that there must be a certain balance between consumers and producers for the group to survive. The Cambridge symposium appeared before the issue on gender had become obligatory; but still women are remarkably present, both as domestic producers in Stenning's essay on the pastoral Fulani, and in Freedman's description of how the women of the Iban longhouse inherit and determine residence on an equal footing with men.

The approach that builds on notions of resource management, however, has tended to produce a different exaggeration from the one that is criticised by Harris, an exaggeration and omission arising out of the way in which households are primarily analysed as units organising production and consumption. Production and consumption are general economic concepts, and basically there is nothing wrong with them; production and consumption must necessarily take place in all societies of the world. But their localization in social space varies. In pre-capitalist societies – particularly those of a 'peasant' type – the household organises both activities. That calls for quite complex organisational solutions, and it activates both men and women – not necessarily in similar tasks, but in tasks that are undoubtedly related to both production and consumption. When anthropologists try to apply such models in the study of capitalist societies, where production is no longer organised within the domestic group, the models become cumbersome. There does not seem to be much left in the household except consumption; many tasks fall into a dubious category, as non-work and non-productive; and the need arises for a revision of concepts like *viability, production,* and *work.* One research area in which such problems have been visible is Norwegian 'anthropology at home', where a number of empirical as well as critical works have tried to do undertake such a revision by re-conceptualising some of the activities that get lost between the narrowed economic concepts (see for example Larsen 1981; Rudie 1982; Gullestad 1984; Melhuus and Borchgrevink 1984, 1987).

The resource argument has been developed in a somewhat different direction by Marxist anthropologists, who have been mainly interested in the historical process through which the household has passed from being a productive and reproductive unit, to becoming reproductive only. The Marxist perspective represents a shift in focus, and introduces the concept of reproduction. For my present analytical purpose I still classify it as another materially oriented approach that does not quite come to terms with emic understanding and the symbolism of practice.

Facing the risk of gross simplification, then, I have offered a brief characterisation of two influential trends in the study of household – one that carries the notion of the 'natural' family along in its luggage and is in danger of reproducing stereotyped images of gender, and one that carries the concept of economic viability along, and tends to lose gender altogether, along with the finer qualitative aspects of human relations.

Meeting the Informants' Practice and Concepts

Fieldwork was carried out in a cluster of villages in the central and most densely populated part of Kelantan. In 1965 these villages were communities of small cultivators, where cultivation was often supplemented with other activities, mostly part-time, but where access to land was the basis for security, and hence an ultimate goal for economic strategies. In this system women had a firm grip on the means of production and the exchange processes. They were landowners in their own right, they contributed heavily to agricultural production, and they were responsible for the marketing. Responsibility for marketing the products of the household provided the women with a basic skill for trading, which some of them cultivated further into a specialised full-time occupation. A female dominance in market trade was, and still is, a strong feature of Kelantan society. Women's identity as productive persons was very striking; the notion of women as essentially self-supporting was a central one.

Important vernacular concepts relating to the house as a physical structure and to features of household organisation are: house, ladder, fireplace, eating together, and eating separately. The notion of *house* carries a load of meaning. It is connected with belonging, hospitality, and ceremonial duties. Children, youths and adults generously extend the invitation 'Come to my house!' or sometimes 'Come to my mother's house!' To accept food in someone's house is a matter of politeness and trust. Sleeping in someone's house lies one step further towards a deeper and more intimate friendship. Invitations to sleep in the house are sometimes issued even if there is no practical reason for doing so. It is as if a line is crossed from a formal to a more intimate kind of hospitality.

Houses are reference points in village ceremonial, which mainly takes the shape of rather formal, communal meals. Their purpose is mostly to mark life-crisis events, or else to mark important points in the Islamic religious calendar. Invitations to such occasions are issued to *houses* rather than to *individuals* or *families*, and it is important that each house is represented by at least one adult person – sometimes of specified gender, sometimes not.

Those who inhabit the house do not necessarily make up a resource-managing unit for all purposes. This is indicated by the expressions 'eating together' and 'eating separately'. 'Eating together' is shorthand for at least sharing food expenses. 'Eating separately' then implies having separate food budgets. *Dapor*, carrying a wide meaning of 'kitchen' and a more restricted meaning of 'fireplace' is also sometimes used as an idiom to describe how the human content of the house is organised. A house, in other words, may contain social subunits who either 'eat together' or 'eat separately', and if they 'eat separately' they may use one or two fireplaces. Rosemary Firth started to unveil these features in her pioneering book, to which later students, including myself, have been greatly indebted (Firth 1966). Three features of her analysis are particularly important – she utilised the native distinction between 'eating together' and 'eating separately', drew attention to the pooling principle at work between household members, and showed clearly the power and responsibility of women in handling the household's monetary resources. Her focus was, however, firmly on the aspect of resource management, which leaves many organisational and symbolic problems unexplored.

In an effort to bring out the symbolic and practical links between gender, food and money, and to sort out the different forms that pooling and exchange can take, I will henceforward consistently apply the following terms:

House unit, which is the group sharing a dwelling at any point of time.
Food unit, which is the group *eating together* at any time.
Family, which denotes relations of close kinship. An intact nuclear family will always eat together. An extended family contains personnel that are eligible to eat together, but may choose to eat separately if they share a house.

The choice of the analytical terms *house unit* and *food unit* instead of the more familiar terms *dwelling unit* and *consumption unit* is not just a mannerism, but is made in the hope of conveying more precise meaning. *House unit* will convey not only the technical aspect of sharing a location, but also the more ample connotations of house – the sharing of symbolic capital. The food unit is not necessarily a consumption unit in a more total sense. There are many shades of sharing and separation before all expenses are shared; practice varies. *Food unit* also plays on a wider symbolic and role aspect: it brings into focus the close connection between women and food.

Exploring the Household as a Resource-Pooling Organisation

When I went to Malaysia for the first time the household model in my luggage was one stressing 'economic viability' rather than 'natural family'. It was with this point of departure that I met the local reality and the vernacular concepts and went into the first dialogue with them. This dialogue was conducive to working out an abstract and quite gender-neutral analytical model of the organisational dynamics of households, but was not sufficient to capture the more subtle aspects of gender symbolism.

According to this model the food unit is not the smallest module; there is another building-block inside it, which can be called a unit of support. The evidence and reasoning are as follows: In 1965 about 60 per cent of households in some villages differed from the nuclear family. They were often complex structures, in which ties between closely related women were the integrating link and, as we shall see below, the concept of eating together was of crucial significance. The striking organisational feature of such house units was their flexibility: they could change their composition and structure more often and less regularly than they would have done if governed by life-crisis events only. Individuals could leave, or attach themselves to a house unit; eating together could change into eating separately, or vice versa.

The concepts of eating together and eating separately can themselves be taken as implicit emic analytical statements about different organisational solutions. In 1965 this distinction was carefully applied by informants to describe all house units that differed from nuclear families or other simple constellations of adults and minors. When people found it necessary to make such an explicit statement, I took it to indicate that a voluntary decision had been made about creating, or not creating, a composite food unit. In other words, there seems to be an implicit notion of some 'natural' units from which the composite ones can be built up. A married couple, a nuclear family, or an adult with minors attached will be a food unit as a matter of course – no decision has to be taken to establish commensality. As soon as any combination is made between such entities, it *is* necessary to make a decision and give the decision a label. In contrast to the composite food units, the 'natural' ones are irreducible – they are the smallest building-blocks, implicitly recognised as potentially independent. It is this building-block that I prefer to call a unit of support.

How, then, is the unit of support identified? That takes a closer look at persons as consumers and producers, and the mode of relationships that connect them.

On the most abstract level we can strip people of their qualitative differences and specificities of gender, age, and structural position in a family, and sort them out in purely material terms in two categories – productive and unproductive. The productive are those who are able to support themselves. In the village society of 1965 that meant having either land or labour or both. The unproductive are those who do not possess any productive assets, be they land or capability for work, and have to be supported.

Some individuals control many resources; others few, or none. Some can get access to resources only through others, by exerting rights *vis-à-vis* those who are productive. This is what happens when productive family members maintain those who are unproductive: here we have the unnegotiable relation of support that rests on a moral principle, and can only be ended through life-cycle events, as when a child grows up and becomes a producer. On the other hand, when two persons pool their land resources, their different skills, or land with skill, we get a kind of cooperation: the two both control productive assets. Then we have the negotiable relation of cooperation that contains a contractual element and can be ended by agreement.

We are now ready to sum up the characteristics of the *units of support*. A unit of support consists of at least one productive person, possibly with dependants. It is a resource-controlling and right-administering entity that contains elements of all that is needed to be viable in material terms. That means being productive – controlling resources, or being able to survive by exerting one's own working capacity.

The degree of abstraction in the above paragraph has revealed what we may call a gender-neutral deep structure. On this deep-structure level the resource person can be either male or female. Women as well as men are landowners in their own right, men and women share productive responsibility, men or women may form the crucial reference points through which right of sharing can be established.

The relationship between resource person and dependant (productive and unproductive) inside the unit of support is a non-negotiable, moral tie, qualitatively different from the negotiable relation of cooperation that links the units of support together.

Put differently, the food unit, which may consist of more than one unit of support, is seen as balanced around conditional practical relationships of cooperation, and unconditional moral relationships of support. Such ties can be obtained within the extended family whether it cohabits or not. In cases of cohabitation, however, the ties are amplified and fill a larger space in the individuals' lives.

Many food units in 1965 were large, multicentric and multifunctional units, and demonstrated a flexible mode of organisation. By calling them multicentric I mean to say that strings of units of support were added together into composite structures through relations of cooperation. Their multifunctionality consisted in the principle of pooling a large number of often very small resources in such a manner that material viability is secured, and better secured than it would have been for each individual unit of support. Flexibility consisted in the relative ease by which the ties of cooperation were established and dissolved. Establishment and dissolution happened more frequently than they would have done if governed only by life-cycle factors – in other words, important parts of the process were governed by social rather than biological events.

This was ultimately possible because of a considerable degree of economic individualisation, and a considerable degree of economic equality and even substitutability between men and women. When presented in its most generalised form, this model appears *gender-neutral*, because both men and women can be centres of units of support.

On another level, however, kinship and gender act selectively to bring about specific patterns of composition or surface structures. We must reckon with a more-or-less clear division of work between men and women, as well as with symbolic links between gender and reputation and gender and food, and finally with the blurred zones between the positions of cooperation and support. The distinction between producers and consumers is by itself a gross simplification, and needs to be constantly judged against circumstantial factors. There is a fact that should not be undercommunicated: namely that the borderline between productive and unproductive states is by no means clear-cut. The borderline may be situationally defined, and depend on the demand for particular services in a household. For instance, in 1965 additional female labour tended to be more useful in an adaptation centred on market gardening than in one depending on ricegrowing. Hence an additional woman might be defined as a productive person in the first situation, but as little more than an additional consumer in the second situation. Or an adult son or son-in-law who has a paid job will sometimes contribute more to the common good than one who can just offer his help on the limited area of land at a house unit's disposal.

In another case we might find two food units that correspond to two house units. Here a polygynous man and his first wife may belong to different food and house units, but maintain limited cooperation in rice production. But when he eats in the house of his second wife and her sister, it is as a guest rather than a member of the household. All the adults, having their own land and being all active in production, are analytically seen as centres in so many units of support. The two sisters have a clear role division between them: together they command a wide variety of skills and assets both of a gender-neutral and gender-specific kind. The older one was of a refined manner, did the indoor 'female' work, and was a skilled dressmaker. As a *Haji*, she also, so to speak, took care of the religious image of the household. The younger one did the rough, outdoor work, and was served prepared meals when she came in to rest. Both had grown children, and had so far secured continuity, the older one had a small grandchild living in. The role differentiation between the two sisters is not an uncommon one; the 'roughness' as well as the 'refinement' lie well within the symbolic possibilities of the Malay gender system. In this respect their age – past childbearing, but still strong and active – gives them an ample range of images from which to build up their complete symbolic and practical viability. When reproductive functions no longer interfere with ritual purity, women can attain high religious merit. But they are also freer to cultivate a certain roughness which is associated with outside activities, mixed company, and a certain negation of female nicety in dress and behaviour. If the male world is characterised by the highest measures of ritual purity as well as of worldly roughness, women can come closer to this pattern in later years of life.

The two sisters explained their mutual closeness and the formal relations with the husband in these words: 'We are sisters, we share everything. He is a stranger (*orang lain*, i.e. non-relative).' Theirs may seem a special case, and 'exotic' from a European point of view, but therefore illuminating, and in tune with a cultural logic shared by less striking arrangements: according to this logic males and females are largely substitutable as economic resource persons, and sibling ties can take precedence over marriage ties for a number of economic and cooperative purposes. But gender enters and acts selectively, so that sisters, and mothers with their daughters, stand out as the most successful cooperators. It is not feasible in this brief paper to go into the complexities of kinship and economic processes that led up to this situation. Still, three important circumstances can be mentioned in brief. First, bilateral inheritance of land, together with an intricate patchwork layout of cultivated lots, tends to bind siblings in continued joint interests and almost forced practical cooperation. Second, owing to the possibility of interpreting Islamic law and customary law in different directions regarding the proportion of male and female shares, a certain tension easily crops up between the interests of brothers and sisters. Finally, the complex task system of housekeeping and primary production seems to tune mothers and daughters and sisters in to smooth and efficient cooperation. But this understanding still does not fully exploit the inner logic of the exchange between adult resource persons. To get further in this discussion we have to enter into the second dialogue, and pose the local practice and concepts against some more recent contributions to the analysis of exchange and gender symbolism.

Gender and the Domestic Mode of Exchange

To my knowledge, no one has coined an expression 'domestic mode of exchange' in analogy with the more established 'domestic mode of production', but such a concept seems to lie implicit in many approaches which see households as residues of gift-exchange constituting a breach with the commodity logic of 'wider society'. This is the essential reasoning in an analysis by Engelstad and Houg (1981), in which they argue that, in modern society, pieces of work that can be exchanged according to market principles are presented according to the gift logic within the household. Janet Carsten has brought the discussion of gift and commodity to bear on a Malaysian situation. In a recent article she suggests that there is a division of functions between men and women in the Langkawi islands: men bring in money as an impersonal commodity, and women socialise it – bring it into the sphere of personal loyalties in a household context (Carsten 1989).

Contrasting this with a Kelantan empirical situation, and trying specifically to penetrate the resource and symbolic relationships inside the household itself, I argue that this categorical division between the genders and between commodity and gift need not always be as clear-cut as Carsten's analysis suggests. To put it succinctly and slightly provocatively, my analysis suggests that instead of *socialising money*, women may sometimes come quite close to *commoditising the domestic sphere*, but also that these two tendencies compete, depending on contextual conditions. By contrasting two situations spaced in time, I will try to demonstrate that this open situation creates a space within which the symbolism of person- and resource-management may move in different directions – one of which comes to resemble the situation described by Carsten, while another alternative is to be found exhibited in some households that I have observed in Kelantan in the 1960s, and again, in a modernised form, in the 1980s.

The clear-cut distinction between a gift logic and a commodity logic, with its obvious bearing on Mauss's classical analysis, is perhaps another example of a thought scheme which emerges in a market economy and becomes 'naturalised' as part of the intellectual orientation in modern capitalist societies. To follow Marilyn Strathern's phrasing, 'Taking apart the image of the commodity (things produced for exchange) uncovers the gift (things produced by exchange); but the formula rests on a Western dichotomy in the first place. The result is that the knowledge I produce about the Melanesian societies is not commensurate with the form that knowledge takes there' (Strathern 1988: 343).

An argument which seems to agree with this has been offered by Parry (1986) in a critical examination of various anthropological interpretations of Mauss, together with aspects of Mauss's own conception of the 'pure gift'. According to Parry, the notion of a 'pure gift' is likely to develop in state societies with an advanced market economy, and is not a prototypical idea in pre-state and pre-market economic systems. In the latter case, gifts are part of social exchange, which in its turn is subject to evolutionary change.

In his much older examination of how forms of reciprocity are coupled with social closeness and distance, Sahlins (1965) evades the sharp distinction between gift and commodity but concentrates on a continuum of social closeness and distance, in which the household is seen as the innermost core that is governed by generalised reciprocity: 'the altruistic extreme'. The categories of exchange are opened up, and the household is placed on a continuum instead of on one side of a dichotomy.

In an analysis of Melanesian societies in transition Gregory, has demonstrated how economic institutions oscillate between gift logic and commodity logic (Gregory 1982). Drawing on Gregory, Marilyn Strathern has gone beyond this distinction and formulated a more fundamental one between mediated and unmediated relationships. Part of her argument is that in a gift economy (the Melanesian) exertion of labour is just a part of bodily activity in general, and therefore not a 'thing' that is exchanged. She suggests a contrast (valid for Melanesia) between (unmediated) domestic activities and (mediated) extra-domestic activities, where mediation takes the shape of gifts (Strathern 1988: 178–9, 318).

The other extreme could be found in Western societies, where political feminists of the 1970s advised women on how to make their domestic work visible by calculating its cost in market prices. It is as if their activities had to be re-cast in commodity terms in order to be recognised as work worthy of appreciation.

Between these two extremes there is a space in which the negotiation of domestic exchanges can take many forms. Crossing borders between different definitions of relationships and their content creates tension. This observation brings together into one perspective 'economic spheres' and 'role conflicts', which are conventionally conceived of as if they belonged in separate problem areas. In such fields of tension, relationships can be transformed. If we accept the idea that domestic relationships can be unmediated, they are also easily contaminated by mediated relationships in which their members engage, just as the gift definition of domestic work in modern society is contaminated by the commodity definition.

'The Significance of Eating' Reconsidered

The significance of eating crops up in different guises. One of them has already been dealt with: the way in which Malays have conceived of household organisation in terms of *eating together*, or *eating separately*. As was pointed out earlier in this paper, the pooling indicated by the arrangement of 'eating together' comprises food budgeting, but only to a varying degree – sometimes not at all – other expenses. The other guise in which the significance of eating appears is more directly concerned with what seems like a close connection between women and food. This is recognised by some analysts as a deep-lying and possibly universal connection. It is implicit in the analysis by Carsten cited above, and in another article she also suggests that women are associated with 'domestic' food, men with 'public' food (Carsten 1987). Building on Norwegian empirical material, Solheim and Borchgrevink (1993) unveil a deep symbolic representation of women as givers of food, a theme that is also treated by Melhuus and Borchgrevink (1987).

In the Kelantan Malay situation women's responsibility for food is clearly expressed when women describe their strivings for obtaining a money income as 'searching for food'. This idiomatic expression may be the same whether the woman sells goods in the market-place, or draws a salary in full-time employment. There is a fascinating track to follow from a peasant adaptation characterised by low expenditure into a present situation where the nominal sum of money needed to maintain a culturally sufficient standard of living has multiplied four or five times. In the first situation, to be accurate, the woman who went to market described her trade as 'searching for side-dishes' (*cari lauk*). The rationale behind this was clear: rice was the staple, which the household was able to grow itself through the joint effort of men and women. Other foodstuffs necessary to create varied and palatable meals could not always be produced in balanced quantities, and had to be obtained in the market. In 1965 a woman from a poor household might take a couple of gallons of rice to market and buy a few days´ supply of dried fish with the money it fetched. Such a transaction is indirect barter, only with money as a medium for convenience. In a slightly more affluent position were households that grew larger quantities of garden products aimed directly at sale. In a still more advanced position were, and are, women who turn the skill obtained through selling their own products into a more full-time occupation as market traders, making a profit from buying and selling. Most women who ventured into market trade were somewhere along a continuum between selling their own rice in indirect barter, towards becoming full-time traders. Modern women in employment still maintain that they 'search for food'. As an interesting feature it can also be observed that in many modern two-income families the wives report that their own income goes to cover food expenses and the electricity bill, while the husband's income covers durables like instalments on the house, and the car if there is one.

All this circumscribes the peculiar responsibility that women have for food. This is a responsibility for seeing to it that there is proper food, rather than necessarily for preparing it. For meals need not be prepared at home. Even in the more precarious economy of the 1960s it was quite common to buy a packet of *nasi kerabu* (cooked rice with fish and herbs) or some other dish from a stall, rather than actually preparing it at home. The more busy the woman was with directly procuring money, the more legitimate it was to buy cooked food – a rationale that still prevails. In the household women have the right of decision whether to buy food, and between women in the village cooked food was and is transacted partly as a commodity, and partly jointly produced as sacral meals (see Carsten 1987, 1989 and Rudie, forthcoming). We may well say that women run a food project, but also that they run a food-and-money project.

Beyond Gifts and Commodities

In this line of argument I suggest that in the Kelantan Malay peasant society, women's activities of searching for food in the market brought mediation into the core of domestic relations, and determined the nature of an exchange that did not fit the ideal categories of either gift or commodity. When I was fresh in the Malay field in 1965, it struck me that household relationships, among them marriage, were often represented in a quite explicitly contractual spirit. All relations of cooperation, including that between the married couple, were dissoluble, and continuation was contingent on worthwhile mutuality. When 'eating together' prevailed, there was a decision to relinquish the impending contractual definition of the situation. Peasant women who searched for side-dishes in the market took control of a long chain from production to commodity and back to a food gift that was made available for sharing in the household. In this way they had a power of defining domestic relationships through their 'food–money' projects. This has implications both for family structure and for women's and men's gain and loss of economic power.

A mother and her daughters have compatible food-money projects, which can include husbands, sons, fathers, and brothers. When a brother and son becomes a husband, however, he will also be included in his wife's food–money project, which is not compatible with that of his mother and sisters. If he brings most of the money in, and women are entitled to share men's money, there may be an area of tension between a mother-in-law's and daughter-in-law's domains. If the wife herself brings money in, she would rather submit her nuclear family of husband and children to her own than to her husband's extended family. The option of a married son and his wife living permanently with his parents was always a 'difficult' one in the Kelantan Malay village.

The female responsibility for food seems to govern a complex of push-and-pull forces in family relationships. On the economic level the links between female family members can dominate the surface structure of households as long as women have approximately equal rights with men in the means of production, and an important role to play in the household's market connections. There are two critical points in this adaptation. First, there is a built-in ambiguity in the marriage relation, because marriage turns sons and brothers into husbands and subsumes them under another woman's food project, and because marriage is also the start to a new nuclear family by which daughters' and sisters' food projects are drawn towards husbands and children.

Second, the whole system will be affected by changes in the macro economy.

Shifting Positions of Cooperation and Support

Modern development in Kelantan is uneven compared to that in the West Coast states of Malaysia. It is most advanced in education and the creation of infrastructure, while industrial development is still comparatively weak. The local labour market offers a number of job opportunities for women with specific educational qualifications – in teaching, health service, and clerical jobs; but very few opportunities in unskilled industrial work – which would be the outlet for those who lack more specific educational qualifications, or have failed to acquire the traditional skills of trade. In contrast, there has been a steady increase in male opportunities in such occupations as transport services and construction work, following public enterprise and the general growth of urban agglomerations. Male job opportunities are thus more evenly distributed to meet different levels of skill and education. It is this development in particular that has tipped the gender balance, in the sense that women's importance as providers has become less prominent, relatively, than it used to be. This situation has placed its stamp on the local villages in different ways. A large number of the adult men commute to jobs in nearby towns. In this process gardening declines, and with it an important impetus for reproducing female trading skills. Many women are turned into 'housewives' – in fact, a new word for housewife had become part of people's active vocabulary when I came back to the field in the 1980s.

This was followed by visible changes in household composition. In 1965, as mentioned above, the picture was dominated by flexibility and a noticeable overweight of female links in extended family households, which often changed their composition frequently, as a sister, a parent, or a child could easily circulate between alternative attachments. When young families set up their own dwellings in the village, they most frequently chose to do so in the compound of the wife's natal family if there was space available – this was described as a preference for 'following the wife' (*ikut bini*).

In 1987 nuclear families and virilocality had gained importance. Many unmarried and employed young men stayed with their parents; their sisters, who mostly failed to find jobs, tended to be married off as early as possible, and frequently 'followed their husbands' (*ikut laki*) out of the village, and the new households of married sons now seemed to be filling up the space in the family compounds.

When women 'searched for food' in the market, this became a special area of responsibility that also implied wider authority over money. This now spills over from a low-spending economy into a growing money economy. When economic growth creates more needs, and there is more money to meet these needs, the person who brings money into the household transfers her power to other areas beside food. Women who succeed in continuing as equal money-providers, keep this position. Those who do not, tend to lose it to their husbands.

If we take our departure from the position of productive person and provider, three different patterns emerge. The first pattern is of the husband as provider, and the wife as 'dependant' or supported person. The couple is asymmetrical, or unicentric in resource terms. The second pattern is of the husband as the main provider, with the wife as an auxiliary provider. This is an intermediate situation. Third, there may be a cooperation between two approximately equal providers. In that case there is a more symmetrical relation between the spouses; the couple is bi-centric in resource terms. These structural variations are mirrored in different versions of native descriptions of reality.

Women strongly express a wish to have their own incomes. This is not just a sign that they are trying to conquer a new position as income-earners. Rather, they seem to be trying against some odds to continue an established pattern of economic productivity and relative autonomy. In this process they are forced to conceptualise their productive status more explicitly (Rudie 1993 and forthcoming). However, they do so against the background of two different conceptions of what constitutes, so to speak, the universe of their responsibilities. These two conceptions are mirrored in two different rationales for wishing for an income – rationales given as explicitly voiced reasons by the women.

The first reason stresses the desirability of a measure of independence of the husband. It is characteristically voiced like this: 'When you earn your own money, you do not have to ask your husband for money, and you are free to spend it as it suits you. You can buy kitchen stuff or clothes, or give it to your mother.'

The second reason stresses cooperation with the husband. Its typical phrasing goes like this: 'We ought to be able to eke out our husbands' incomes. We must help them cover expenses.' Some will phrase it more strongly: 'It is a duty to help your husband cover expenses.'

I think the two rationales have different implications: they correspond to different, more or less explicit, perspectives on what constitutes a household. The first rationale represents the truly bi-centric structure, with the notion of a high degree of autonomy in a productive individual (male or female) as a potential centre in a unit of support; it stresses the maintenance of economic equality between the sexes, and an idea of cooperation rather than support.

The second rationale represents the notion of a male-centred family in which the woman's role becomes auxiliary. It subsumes the two first perspectives suggested above: that of the male provider and dependent wife, and of the male as the main provider and the wife as secondary provider. This brings us finally back to our more general issues of the household as a field in which the distinction between gift and commodity as well as the issue of gender complementarity can be negotiated.

Modern young women tend to be differentiated, falling into two different adaptations. Those who are educationally and occupationally successful, and in that way move farthest away from their peasant background, are the ones who reproduce a household structure built on cooperation and economic gender parallelism. Those who do not move as far have problems keeping up this equal position. When women lose recognition as providers, the *women–food link* changes its character. Instead of being responsible for the whole chain of production as well as preparation of food, the women become responsible for preparing it only. Instead of feeding other family members in a total sense, many now do so only in a partial sense. In such cases the women have lost control of the total process of acquiring the commodity and transforming it to a gift, and the area of ambiguous gift–commodity relations is relegated from the household, which emerges more unambiguously as a residue of gift relations within a commodity economy.

Conclusions

This paper has been exploratory rather than conclusive. It took its departure from an observation that our analytical concepts need to to be constantly checked against various practices in order to avoid distortions. I have tried to take this idea seriously and specifically, by confronting different analytical tools with my informants' practices and concepts. The household analysis has developed from a 'resource view' rather than a 'family view', and has come up with a few conceptual suggestions.

First, it has suggested a concept 'unit of support', which seems to have both drawbacks and advantages. To start with an advantage, this concept is able to merge a 'family view' and a 'resource view' and avoid the particular cost that each of them seems to imply. On the other hand, this high level of generality may also be a drawback, as qualitative criteria have to be reintroduced for the concept to be operative in empirical analyses. To take an example, a unit of support can be an individual in societies with a sufficient degree of economic substitutability between men and women, but may have to be a male–female pair in societies with a more rigid gender differentiation of economic roles.

Drawing on recent literature on exchange and gender, I have also tried to re-examine the conceptual distinction between gifts and commodities, and argued that an opposition which seems self-evident in a Western scheme of thought, should not be applied uncritically to every empirical situation. I am not saying that we should do away with the concepts. Gifts and commodities do exist in near-ideal form in most societies. But everywhere there are probably also social spaces in which they can be negotiated, and deep insights into cultural processes can be gained from seeking out these very spaces. Furthermore, in many societies the domestic field is a likely candidate to be such a space. This opens the possibility for some exciting renewal of household analyses.

Bibliography

Borchgrevink, Tordis and Solheim, Jorun (1988). 'A Rotten Text? On Gender, Food, and Interpretation'. In Tone Bleie, Vigdis Broch-Due and Ingrid Rudie (eds), *Carved Flesh, Cast Selves. Gendered Symbols and Social Practices*. Oxford: Berg Publishers.

Broch, Harald Beyer (1983). 'The matrifocal warp of Bonerate culture'. In Bo Utas (ed.), *Women in Islamic Societies*, pp. 144–59. London/Malmö: Curzon Press, Scandinavian Institute of Asian Studies.

Burling, Robbins (1965). *Hill farms and padi fields*. Englewood Cliffs, NJ: Prentice Hall.

Carsten, Janet (1987). 'Analogues or Opposites: Household and Community in Pulau Langkawi, Malaysia'. In Macdonald, Charles *et al.* (eds), *De la hutte au palais. Sociétés "à maison" en Asie du Sud-Est insulaire*, pp. 153–68. Paris: Centre National de la Recherche Scientifique.

Carsten, Janet (1989). 'Cooking Money: Gender and the Symbolic Transformation of Means of Exchange in a Malay Fishing Community'. In J. Parry and M. Bloch (eds), *Money and the Morality of Exchange*. Cambridge: Cambridge University Press.

Engelstad, Fredrik and Houg, Thora (1980). 'Arbeid og marked. Begrepsdiskusjon og problemstillinger'. *Arbeidsnotat til seminar i økonomisk sosiologi*. (Mimeograph.) Oslo: Institutt for samfunnsforskning.

Firth, Rosemary (1966). *Housekeeping among Malay Peasants*. New York: Humanities Press.

Gregory, C. A. (1982). *Gifts and Commoditie*. London: Academic Press.

Gullestad, M. (1984). 'Sosialantropologiske perspektiver på familie og hushold'. In Ingrid Rudie (ed.), *Myk start – hard landing*. Oslo: Universitetsforlaget.

Harris, O. (1981). 'Households as natural units'. In K. Young, C. Wolkowitz and R. McCullagh (eds): *Of Marriage and the Market*. London: CSE Books.

Larsen, S. S. (1980). 'Omsorgsbonden – et tidsnyttingsperspektiv på yrkeskombinasjon, arbeidsdeling og sosial endring'. *Tidsskrift for samfunnsforskning*, 21: 283–96.

Mauss, M. (1954). *The Gift. Forms and Functions of Exchange in Archaic Societies*. London: Cohen & West.

Melhuus, M. and Borchgrevink, T. (1984). 'Husarbeid: Tidsbinding av kvinner'. In Ingrid Rudie (ed.), *Myk start – hard landing*. Oslo: Universitetsforlaget.

Melhuus, M. and Borchgrevink, T. (1987). 'Familie og arbeid: Fokus på sjømannsfamilier'. *Arbeidsforknongsinstituttet, rapport nr. 27/85*.

Parry, J. (1986). '*The Gift*, the Indian Gift, and the "Indian Gift"', *Man* (NS), 21, 453–73.

Peletz, M. G. (1988). *A Share of the Harvest. Kinship, Property, and Social History Among the Malays of Rembau*. Berkeley: University of California Press.

Rosaldo, M. Z. (1974). 'Woman, Culture and Society: A Theoretical Overview'. In Michelle Z. Rosaldo and Louise Lamphere (eds): *Woman, Culture and Society*. Stanford, California: Stanford University Press.

Rudie, I. (1971). 'Between Market and Neighbourhood'. Manuscript, 330 pages.

Rudie, I. (ed.) (1984). *Myk start, hard landing. Om forvaltning av kjønnsidentitet i en endringsprosess*. Oslo: Universitetsforlaget.

Rudie, I. (1993). 'A Hall of Mirrors: Autonomy Translated over Time in Malaysia'. In Diane Bell, Pat Caplan, and Wazir Jahan Karim (eds), *Gendered Fields*. London and New York: Routledge.

Rudie, I. (forthcoming). *Visible Women in East Coast Malay Society. On the Reproduction of Gender in Ceremonial, School, and Market*. Oslo: Universitetsforlaget.

Sahlins, M. (1965). 'On the Sociology of Primitive Exchange'. In Michael Banton (ed.), *The Relevance of Models for Social Anthropology*, ASA Monograph No.1. London: Tavistock Publications.

Strathern, M. (1988). *The Gender of the Gift. Problems with Women and Problems with Society in Melanesia*. Berkeley: University of California Press.

Swift, M. G. (1965). *Malay Peasant Society in Jelebu*. London: Athlone Press.

11

Rewriting Gender and Development Anthropology in Southeast Asia

Penny Van Esterik

When anthropologists take up the opportunities available in international development work, they may experience subtle and not-so-subtle contradictions in the practice of development anthropology. For me, the contradictions come in the form of two little voices speaking at the same time. In one ear, a little voice reminds me that anthropology is very relevant and crucial for understanding processes of change and development. Development work provides new vocational opportunities for ourselves and our students. This voice urges me to become more involved in applied (for example, development-consulting) work, and climb down from my ivory tower (I have yet to find one, and if I did, I would not be comfortable in it). After all, anthropologists are underutilised and undervalued in development work. Why should economists and cross-cultural communicators walk off with all the consultancies? We can learn to speak development discourse.

But in my other ear (conveniently closed when I accept consultancies or projects) there is a quiet but persistent voice that says that what I do on development projects is not anthropology and not what anthropology is about: that without a critical perspective, and a constant struggle over definitions and priorities, anthropologists in development work will quickly come to be speaking development, not speaking anthropology. When we speak the language of development, we lose the opportunity to make a substantial contribution to development work.

Both little voices fought for ascendancy over the last few years, during the course of a project on the Women in Development Consortium in Thailand (WIDCIT) funded through the Institutional Linkage Program of the Canadian International Development Agency (CIDA). I direct the project in Canada, and work with the Thai project administrator, Malee Pruekpongsawalee, and a consortium of Thai universities working on women's issues in Thailand. Through this experience, I have come to question many assumptions about Women in Development (WID) or Gender and Development (GAD) in Southeast Asia, and the role of anthropologists in this work. In this essay, I will briefly review some background on women in Southeast Asia, and how development has influenced their work opportunities over the last decade. Then, I will allow the anthropologist a louder voice in considering some definitional dilemmas underlying women's work.

But I must let the other voice have the final word, by raising with you some of the contradictions I see emerging from gender and development work – contradictions that cause me to question what anthropologists are doing in international development.

Restating the Obvious and Not-So-Obvious

Southeast Asia is an area that defies generalisations and calls for historical and cultural specificity, particularly in questions related to gender and development. I am most familiar with mainland Southeast Asia, including work on refugee women from Laos. Southeast Asia has long been identified as an area where women enjoy 'high status', particularly in contrast to the male dominance characteristic of traditional Indian and Chinese societies. It has been characterised as an area of complementarity of male and female roles, with a lack of exaggerated opposition between male and female ideologies (Atkinson and Errington 1990). History and myth glorify powerful female political and legal figures – a fifteenth-century Burmese queen, the ruling Sultana of pre-colonial Acheh, or the Thai and Philippine reports of women respected for their legal prowess. Colonial experiences affected women's lives differently in the different countries of Southeast Asia (cf. Stoler 1991) – and I will not discuss this here, except to say that the aura of strength and competence of Southeast Asian women survived colonialism. The British were clearly shocked at the respect accorded Burmese women, 'When greater races bound the feet or veiled the face of their woman, or doubted if she had a soul, the Burmese held her free and enthroned her as chieftainess and chief' (Nyun-Han 1972: 100).

In the British colonial office in Burma in the 1880s a colonial officer struggled with this anomaly of the independence of Burmese women and the peace-loving nature of the Burmese, which must be destroyed for Burma to 'develop', to be 'on the road to progress'. To overcome their backwardness, Burmese men should learn to kill and to oppress their women (Mies 1986: 93). By the end of the period of direct colonial rule by British, French, Dutch and American, Southeast Asians had absorbed these lessons.

This image of Southeast Asian women as powerful figures in control of their lives and significant politically is to a certain extent a European discovery of the Oriental 'other'. This image would have appeared particularly striking in contrast to the position and condition of women in Europe and Victorian England. These idealised views of the past written by foreigners and locals are widespread in Southeast Asia.

The structural importance of women in Southeast Asia has been related to prevailing economic and social conditions such as:

1. availability of new frontier land and women as pioneers in land development;
2. low population density in the mainland, rendering women's work in agriculture a household essential;
3. wet rice production, with a farming management system dominated by women;
4. late development of centralised states, encouraging a distance between the patriarchal state and local culture;
5. predominance of bilateral kinship, with substantial matrilocal residence;
6. inheritance of land by daughters; and
7. women's control over money and management of family finances (cf. Van Esterik 1982).

In the post-colonial period, countries like Singapore, Malaysia, and currently, Thailand have undergone rapid economic development. For ASEAN countries, development and modernisation have not always benefited women, either as urban entrepreneurs or as village farmers. As early as the 1970s, it became apparent that development planning usually reinforced existing values, emphasising women's household and child-rearing tasks, and superimposed Western values regarding appropriate work for women (Tinker and Bramsen 1976; Boserup 1970; Stoler 1977). The next section identifies a few examples of work contexts that have changed owing to development and modernisation.

The Development of Work

These rapid changes have affected women's work patterns in many areas, including rice production, cash cropping, factory work, and the sex trade. The most dominant transnational forces influencing women's work in Southeast Asia include industrialisation and international tourism. Transnational corporations benefit from changes in wet rice production, shifts to cash cropping, factory production (particularly of textiles and electronics) and sex tourism, this last prefigured in the American military experiences in Thailand and the Philippines.

Rice Production

New rice technology includes high-yielding variety (HYV) seeds and the inputs associated with mechanisation. In some parts of Southeast Asia, these packages increased agricultural productivity, but also increased stratification in peasant communities. Few studies document whether HYV benefits resulted in women having increased access to money, food, or health services (Srisambhand and Gordon 1987; White 1985; Sajogyo 1985). Across the region, there are differences in the effects mechanisation has had on women's labour, depending on whether women are landless, own land, or employ other women. HYV of rice generally require more labour for weeding, harvesting, and post-harvest processing. In some countries, this is an opportunity for more wage employment for women. In parts of Indonesia, in contrast, mechanical threshing accompanying high-yielding varieties of rice reduces seasonal demand for labour or offers it only when it would interfere with the growing of subsistence crops. Throughout the region, development encourages the adoption of labour-saving technology, without finding alternative regular or seasonal employment for landless women.

Cash Cropping

Crops such as maize and cassava (for animal fodder), and plantation crops such as rubber and pineapple, provide employment opportunities for Southeast Asian women and men. The rapid expansion of plantations has immediate effects on Southeast Asian women by reducing their access to fuel wood and wild forest products for food and medicines as a result of deforestation. In the past, European administrators encouraged the transfer of rights in land from women to men. When communally-owned property was converted to individual ownership, property rights were more often vested in males than females. When market prices drop for cash crops, women have often been unable to find new sources of income to replace agricultural wage labour, and migrate to factory work in urban centres.

Factory Work

Young women migrants to Southeast Asian cities outnumber men, and they are all virtually assured of work opportunities in the new industrial areas. But factory working conditions are often intolerable, with problems of dust, noise, and heat for minimal wages. However, women are not accepting these intolerable conditions quietly, as many multinational companies expected Asian women to do. On 1 May 1988, thirty women workers from Winner Textile Company in Bangkok threatened to slash their wrists if they were not reinstated. They were among the 350 workers fired for protesting against working conditions following the breakdown of the air-conditioning in the factory in Nonthaburi, which brought temperatures in the work rooms to 38° Celsius. Management shut down the plant and re-opened it under a new name, rather than rehiring workers who had gone on strike or fixing the air-conditioning.

Many authors have discussed the semi-conductor industry in Malaysia and Singapore (Lim 1978; Grossman 1979; Henderson 1986; Ong 1987). These multinational companies exploit the female labour force with low wages, poor working conditions, and constant pressure to increase production. Recreational activities such as beauty contests encourage competitive individualism and promote the image of women as sex objects. Managers argue that electronics assembly work is suitable for women, who like routine manual work, and have been socialised to work obediently for others.

The Sex Trade

Women's groups, both national and international, have taken up the cause of sex tourism and child prostitution as it exists in cities like Manila and Bangkok. Again, research and reports on this topic are available, although the advocacy work does not always address the contradictions that academics in women's studies must explore – for example, contradictions regarding women's socialisation and the expression of sexuality that underlie the political economy of prostitution (cf. Truong 1990).

In Bangkok, prostitution was transformed through the military presence in Southeast Asia in the 1960s and international tourism in the 1970s and 1980s. Most tourists to Thailand are single males, and although tourism cannot be said to have 'caused' prostitution, it has affected the number

252 | **Penny Van Esterik**

of prostitutes, their public presence and display, and their availability. Work as go-go dancers, masseuse, waitresses and tour escorts is readily available, and more lucrative than other work for young, untrained, rural women.

As Thai research on this topic has emphasised (Pongpaichit 1982; Huntrakul 1988), it is poverty and landlessness in the rural areas that has encouraged young women to take up this work and parents to sell their daughters into lives of prostitution. Analysis is complicated by the wide range of conditions for women who work as prostitutes – from the brutal treatment of children chained to beds, to the glamorous lifestyle of escorts living in condominiums. What is constant is the importance of the income made available through prostitution. Money is sent home to support families, to pay debts, taxes, and school tuition for younger siblings, and to build houses for parents. These remittances help explain the ease with which women who have earned money from prostitution for a few months or years can return to village society, buy land, marry, and settle down to a rural lifestyle. This is only possible if the daughter has earned the respect of the community through supporting parents and younger siblings. The Thai perspective on prostitution as work which is 'family-supporting' should be compared to the external media view of sexual oppression and exploitation (Van Esterik 1992). From the perspective of Thailand's policy-makers, it is no longer possible to address gender and development issues without attempting to come to grips with this new work context.

Women and Work

Development has changed work experience for Southeast Asian women, but theoretical concepts about women's work have also changed, and these concepts have influenced the analysis of gender in Southeast Asia. In North America, early consciousness-raising about women's work protested that women's work was invisible and undervalued, and proposed wages for housework as a liberal feminist strategy. This logic continued into WID planning, as women's work was 'integrated' into the modern sector. This in no way challenged the double burden of women who were also responsible for household maintenance. As WID programmes increased, Third World women were saddled with yet a third burden – they became beneficiaries of women's projects or training programmes, and added attendance at seminars on sewing, crafts, or nutrition and child care to their already filled days. The objectives of WID, to spread the benefits of modernisation to women, were met through the establishment of women's bureaus and women's development plans. These growing bureaucracies may not have noticed, but in Southeast Asia, some women were already at the cutting edge of economic gains in the new modern sector as bank presidents, real estate developers, and owners of shopping malls. Many other women were harmed by these changes in working conditions brought about by development, and it is important to compare the gains and losses of different groups of women in the development saga.

In Southeast Asia, women's work is neither invisible nor undervalued, and since women have traditionally grown up with this idea of work, they are particularly alert to the many forms of exploitation of labour which occur in the new urban sectors. Significantly, in Malaysia, where a differential pay system is accorded to male and female production workers in most factories, rural girls no longer rush out in excitement when the loudspeaker of recruitment agents booms to announce work opportunities in the Free Trade Zones. They prefer to wait for other opportunities, causing a massive shortage of female operators in the Free Trade Zones in Penang and Seberang Prai (Wazir Jahan Karim: personal communication).

A second conceptual shift in Western analysis places more emphasis on the social reproduction of labour, the care and socialisation of children and the maintenance of adults. Some argue that women's reproductive activities determine their productive work patterns, the sexual division of labour, and gender subordination. Others stress the interaction between production and reproduction within changing economic contexts. In Southeast Asia, however, the distinctions between productive and reproductive labour, and public and private are blurred. For example, women prepare food for home consumption; but that act of preparation and presentation is often a public and political act. It is often an expression of 'power', of an ability to control food sources and resources. The same foods may also be sold in food-vending stalls in front of the home. Western analytical concepts such as women's invisible work and the opposition between productive and reproductive work, and public and private domains of women's work are inappropriate for the analysis of gender in Southeast Asia. Yet it is difficult to recognise how ethnocentric and value-laden some of our most common analytical distinctions can be. In my work in Thailand, I have tried to build on indigenous concepts of work. In so doing, I have begun to deconstruct the entire concept of work from a woman-centred perspective. Before we can attempt to analyse these new work contexts for women in Southeast Asia, we might benefit from re-examining the concept of work.

Rethinking Work

The Thai verb, *liang*, means to feed, nourish, nurture, care for, support, and bring up to maturity. The capacity to nurture others is the basis of women's social production, and is basic to their well-being, self-esteem, and self-reliance. By stressing that women's bodies were the first means of production of children and food, Mies argues that women consciously appropriated their own bodily nature to give birth and produce milk, forming not only units of consumption but of production as well. When women's productive and reproductive work are devalued, the activities of both become alienated from each other and harder to integrate. Thus, Mies argues that we need to develop a feminist definition of labour. The feminist concept of labour rejects distinctions between socially necessary labour and leisure, and uses a mother as a model of a worker. For mothers, work is always a burden and a major source of enjoyment, self-fulfilment, and happiness. She argues that this is because the goal of their labour is the direct production of life, not the production of things or wealth (Mies 1986: 216–17).

The Thai Concept of Work

Work (*ngan* in Thai) refers to task, job, unit of agricultural work, ceremony, or festival. The stress is on accomplishing or bringing about something. The Thai concept of work approaches Mies's feminist concept of labour. However, as both mode of production and relations of production are changing rapidly in Thai society today, particularly in urban society, the clashes between the indigenous concept of work and the realities of changing work situations are becoming more frequent.

In spite of exploitative work situations, Thai women workers have been very successful in modern work settings partly because of their capacity to detach themselves – their ultimate moral worth – from the task at hand, and their capacity to merge socially necessary tasks with pleasure.

Work or occupation does not necessarily equate with personal worth in Thai. That is, people's personal worth does not derive from the labour they perform; work and moral status, for example, are easily detached. If all tasks are equally valued, then there is no need to link personal worth to productive tasks. The Thai concept of work developed in rural contexts where social organisation and division of labour was more flexible and egalitarian, at a time when people could opt out of relations with their local princes, lose themselves in the forest, clear new land, and form new social units. The sexual division of labour contributed to complementarity in gender relations, as the work of both men and women was equally valued. In the official administrative system, officials were classified by four methods: (1) *Sakdi na* or dignity marks; (2) *Yosa* or honorific titles; (3) *Rajadinama*, elaborate names of the incumbents of official posts; and (4) *Tamnem*, terms indicating the rank or grade of a particular office (Dhiravegin 1978: 31). In the royal centres, then, officials were identified by an elaborate system of ranks and conferred names. These functioned as personal names, but changed as the person was promoted through the bureaucracy. They usually indicated the duties or function the person performed. This system of titles de-emphasised the individual, since he or she was known by different names throughout his or her career (Vella 1978: 129). Thus, in the state administration, when people have as personal names the position they occupy, these titles serve to further dissociate the persons from the tasks themselves. That is, the position or office is there, but the person filling the office constantly changes. This is also true in the realm of the supernatural. *Phra In* (Indra) is an example of a deity whose position is constant and unchanging, although the 'occupant' changes. Unlike caste systems, where strict occupational division of labour was necessary, the Thai concept of work allowed personal value to be separated from productive tasks.

On the other hand, work is not necessarily alienating drudgery either. Work is productive and accomplishes something to the extent that it is *sanuk* or fun. Women in office work and sales may speak of going to work as *'paj thiaw thamngan'* – to go and have a good time at work. When work ceases to be fun – usually for interpersonal reasons – then jobs are left. The back-breaking labour of rice production, without the related ceremonies and festivities, is no longer viewed by young women as appealing work; while detached, impersonal factory work in the city is sought to rediscover the fun of work, often with disappointing results. Ironically, both rural and urban work settings are being stripped of all pleasurable connotations. However, in Thai, work and celebration are in fact the identical word – both accomplish something in social settings.

Development Discourse

What happens to these indigenous concepts in the analysis of women's work? Is there no room for them within development projects? There is no room for these indigenous concepts because of the dominance of development discourse. And what is this language? It is the language of management embedded within bureaucratic discourse. Cultural complexity is reconceptualised through planning and management procedures into technical problems for action.

The dominant development discourse in Bangkok, Kuala Lumpur, and Manila – the loudest voice – is this bureaucratic discourse. The language and metaphors are provided by CIDA, AID, the United Nations and other bilateral and multilateral aid agencies. This results in, first, the over-bureaucratisation of the process of development assistance, often furthering the aims of the donor country, not the recipient. The development industry creates both efficiency and accountability by providing the primary categories for analysing projects – target groups, pre-project planning, implementation, monitoring, evaluation and follow-up. These terms are rarely translated, but used in English forms within Thai and Indonesian sentences.

If women's NGOs want to be funded, they are forced to learn this language. CIDA and AID development grants train Thai and Malaysian women to respond to externally defined issues and problems – and to respond to them within the project-planning framework. Throughout Southeast Asia, women's groups have internalised concepts such as needs assessment, income-generating projects (not work), curriculum development, and participatory workshops, as if these concepts had meaning for understanding gender subordination or inequalities in their communities. Development is now thought about in these terms, rather than through observing how conditions in real communities have developed, what sustains gender inequality, why institutions work as they do and what needs to be known about existing indigenous alternatives. Often data collected for gender and development projects are more useful to bilateral agencies in the monitoring and evaluation of projects, and for the researchers who collect the data, than to the women in the development projects.

Another consequence of this development by management is that advocacy discourse is often submerged or distorted. Protests about sex tourism in Thailand or factory conditions in Malaysia become funding risks for international development assistance. The most active and radical women's group in Thailand, Friends of Women, nearly disbanded for lack of money to cover modest rent and small staff salaries. At the same time, special management training courses for women entrepreneurs and for beauty schools are supported. Development assistance favours larger NGOs because they know how to handle proposals, evaluations, and accounting procedures, and can write reports in English, the language of donor money.

This is the era of the instant development expert – the expert without knowledge of the cultural context of the 'place' to be developed, but with knowledge of management skills, who acquires not the local language, but the language of development.

Is there a place for anthropologists here? We reject (and often resent) the 'acultural' instant development experts, and may respond critically to their development work in Southeast Asia, as superficial at best and often downright damaging. I remain confident that there is an important role for anthropologists in development work – particularly in gender and development work; but only if we resist development discourse. We are most useful when we speak and translate between the 'emics' of anthropology, 'the tools of the trade' of our discipline, and the conversations of our informants. In development discourse, the script is provided by the development industry; no constructs are disarticulated and no terms are questioned. Terms such as development, work, gender, and equity must all be deconstructed and interpreted through indigenous logic and not through management logic. This is an important task for anthropologists involved in development work.

Anthropologists have the skills for interpreting the historicity and specificity of situations, and they respect the enormity of the task of cultural translation and change. Therefore our most important contribution to gender and development could be in critiquing the givens of development discourse and conducting ethnographies of development encounters – and that includes the agencies that fund and manage gender and development projects in Southeast Asia.[1]

Note

1. The ideas for this paper were first developed for a plenary address to the Canadian Ethnological Society annual meeting in Ottawa, June 1989. The bibliography on current work on women in Southeast Asia was developed to update the bibliography for a second edition of my edited book, *Women of Southeast Asia* (1982), to be re-published by Northern Illinois University Press in 1993.

Bibliography

Atkinson, J. and Errington, S. (1990). *Power and Difference: Gender in Island Southeast Asia.* Stanford: Stanford University Press.

Boserup, E. (1970). *Women's Role in Economic Development.* New York: St Martin's Press.

Dhiravegin, Likhit (1978). *The Bureaucratic Elite of Thailand.* Bangkok: Thai Khadi Research Institute.

Grossman, R. (1979). 'Women's Place in the Integrated Circuit'. *Southeast Asian Chronicle*, No. 66.

Henderson, J. (1986). 'The New International Division of Labour and the American Semiconductor Production in Southeast Asia'. In C. Dixon *et al.* (eds), *Multinational Corporations and the Third World.* Boulder: Westview Press.

Huntrakul, S. (1988). 'Prostitution in Thailand'. In D. Chandler (ed.), *Development and Displacement: Women in Southeast Asia.* Centre of Southeast Asian Studies, Monash University, Clayton, Victoria.

Lim, L. (1978). *Women Workers in Multinational Corporations: The Case of the Electronics Industry in Malaysia and Singapore*, Michigan Occasional Papers in Women's Studies, No.9. Ann Arbor: University of Michigan.

Mies, M. (1986). *Patriarchy and Accumulation on a World Scale.* London: Zed Books.

Nyun-Han, E. (1972). 'The Socio-political Roles of Women in Japan and Burma'. Ph.D. Dissertation, University of Colorado.

Ong, A. (1987). *Spirits of Resistance and Capitalist Discipline: Factory Women in Malaysia.* Albany: SUNY Press.

Phongpaichit, P. (1982). *From Peasant Girls to Bangkok Masseuses.* Geneva: International Labor Office.

Sajogyo, P. (1985). 'The Impact of New Farming Technology on Women's Employment'. In IRRI, *Women in Rice Farming.* Aldershot, Hants, England: Gower Publications.

Srisambhand, N. and Srisambhand, A. Gordon (1987). *Thai Rural Women and Agricultural Change: Approaches and a Case Study.* Bangkok: Chulalongkorn University Social Research Institute.

Stoler, A. (1977). 'Class Struggle and Female Autonomy in Rural Java'. *Signs*, 3: 74–89.

—— (1991). 'Carnal Knowledge and Imperial Power: Gender, Race and Morality in Colonial Asia'. In M. di Leonardo (ed.), *Gender at Crossroads.* Berkeley: University of California Press.

Tinker, I. and Bramsen, B. (1976). *Women and World Development.* Washington: Overseas Development Council.

Truong, Thanh-dam (1990). *Sex, Money, and Morality: Prostitution and Tourism in South-east Asia.* London: Zed Books.

—— (1992). 'Thai Prostitution and the Medical Gaze'. In P. and J. Van Esterik (eds), *Gender and Development in Southeast Asia*. Montreal: Canadian Asian Studies Association.

Van Esterik, P. (ed.) (1982). *Women of Southeast Asia*, Center for Southeast Asian Studies, Monograph. DeKalb, Illinois: Northern Illinois University.

Vella, Walter (1978). *Chaiyo! King Vajiravudh and the Development of Thai Nationalism*. Honolulu: University of Hawaii Press.

White, B. (1985). 'Women and the Modernization of Rice Agriculture: Some General Issues and a Javanese Case Study'. In IRRI, *Women in Rice Farming*. Aldershot, Hants, England: Gower Publications.

Index

abuse of women, 51, 165
adat, 18, 19, 41, 44, 105, 110, 115, 176
adoption, 60, 107, 132, 250
affines/affinity, 25, 35, 38, 121–2,
    131–2, 134
after-life, 145, 148, 162
    see also rebirth, future-life,
        reincarnated
Akha, 52, 56–7, 78, 82
agnation, 128–35 *passim.*
agriculture/agricultural, 3, 29, 30, 39,
    43, 51, 73, 77, 79, 84–7, 132, 183,
    230, 249–51, 254
alcoholism, 17, 89
alimony, 105
Allah, 107–8
American, 8, 41, 51, 249
    see also military
ancestors/ancestral, 20, 56, 57, 78, 82,
    87, 129, 148, 150
Angakatan Belia Islam Malaysia, 106
animism, 39, 145, 150, 156, 161
apostasy, 108
ASEAN, 249
autonomy, 12, 15, 18, 27, 39–50 *passim.*,
    59, 76, 87–91 *passim.*, 221, 242–3

banca, 212, 214
bancih, 126, 133, 142, 202
baju kurung, 41, 107, 113
Bantigue, 207–23
barter, 92, 239
Batak, 37, 39, 46, 77, 197
batik, 105, 113, 187
Batara, 128, 131
Bedhaya, 179–204
behaviour, 3, 5, 6, 12, 17, 18, 35–8, 53,
    60, 103, 106–7, 113–6, 123–6, 138,
    140, 154, 163, 167, 173, 187, 194–5,
    202
beksa/Beksan, 185, 190, 191, 196, 197
bilateral/ism, 11, 16, 35–74, 79, 80, 86,
    87, 91, 105, 133, 135, 236, 249, 256
biology, xiv, 5, 15, 26, 29, 30, 35, 47,
    60, 121–31 *passim.*, 142, 181, 201,
    234
blood, 79, 167–8, 189
Buddhism, xiii, 14, 19, 21, 24, 26–7,
    39–40, 42, 53, 55–8, 116–7,
    145–56, 161–2, 173, 176, 200
    see also Theravada
budgets, 28, 29, 231, 238
bureaus, women's, 253
bureaucracies, 17–8, 42–3, 49, 53, 60,
    76, 82, 84, 164, 253, 255–6
business, 36, 39–41, 86, 164, 202, 210,
    221
Brahma/Brahmanic tradition, 38, 200
brothel, 92
bride wealth, 85

Canadian International Development
    Agency (CIDA), xii, 247, 256,
capital, 6, 28, 49, 50, 60, 135, 150,
    211–2, 214, 232
capitalism/capitalist, 11, 13, 16, 22, 43,
    49, 82, 90, 176, 218, 229, 237
career, 103–4, 109, 115, 255
cash, 49, 84–6, 89, 91, 135, 213, 217–8,
    221, 250
crop, 77, 79, 84–7, 250
caste, 121, 130–5, 255
causal/causation, 125–7, 130, 139
ceremonial, 36, 183, 230–1
ceremonies/ceremony 4, 19, 45, 81, 91,
    150, 153, 171, 187, 254–5
    see also rice, ritual
cigarettes, 140, 164–5
chastity, 163, 174, 200
childbirth, 3, 45, 53, 60, 125–6, 129,
    133, 167, 183, 214, 215, 235, 254
    see also pregnancies
child care, 109, 167, 252
childless, 139, 166
child-rearing, 148, 249
China/Chinese, 38–45, 79, 87, 110,
    116–7, 163, 167–9, 176, 248
Christian/Christianity, xiii, 40, 57, 80,

88, 103, 116, 117
circumcision, 45, 187
class, x, 12, 16, 18, 20, 26–7, 36–60
    passim., 89, 92–3, 103–4, 108,
    111–6, 128, 132–3, 140, 168, 182,
    186, 198
    see also hierarchy
classification, 25, 35, 37, 122, 124–5,
    140, 191, 195
colonial/ism, xiii, 7, 22, 38, 40, 44,
    46–8, 104, 106, 137, 166, 196, 201,
    248–9
colonisation, 13, 43, 77, 89, 113
commodities/commodity, 77, 79, 86–7,
    165, 236–44 *passim.*
communication, 37, 45, 59, 101–2, 113,
    195, 253
Communist/communist, 84, 161, 170
condominiums, 252
cohabitation, 234
conflict, 6, 8, 18, 23, 83, 85, 89, 105,
    109, 156, 161, 169, 197, 219, 238
conflicting roles, 149, 154, 238
Confucian, 26, 27, 30, 161, 162, 166,
    171, 173, 175
    see also ideology, patriarchal
consanguinal relations, 25, 35, 37, 39
Correspondence Theory, 123
cosmetics/make-up, 114, 189, 191, 197,
    198
cosmogonic forces and boundaries, 25,
    53
cosmology, 23, 42, 56, 78–82 *passim.,*
    88, 128, 145
courts, 22, 110, 111, 181–206
    syari'ah/sharia, 44, 110
crafts, 83, 90, 109, 252
crocodiles, 81

dadiya, 128–30, 134–5
dakwah, 101–20
dance, 22, 24, 36, 183–202 *passim.,* 252
    see also palace
Darul Arqam, 106, 109, 110
death, 24, 149, 150, 164, 174, 215
debts, 46, 149, 174, 252
    see also moral
decision-making, 12, 17–8, 27, 29–30,
    37–49 *passim.,* 55, 78–82 *passim.,* 86,
    116, 163–4, 217
deculturation/detribalisation, 51, 90, 91
deity, 25, 81, 128–33 *passim.,* 141, 150,
    255
    see also God, shrine

democracy, 39, 44, 153, 186
demographic displacement, 54, 57
demon/demoness 81, 200
descent, 35–6, 38, 40, 42, 49, 60, 79,
    128–30
determinism, 127, 142, 194
development, ix–xiv *passim.,* 5, 29–30,
    38–9, 43, 48, 51, 60, 76, 82–92,
    104, 111, 116, 176, 182–3, 186,
    188, 191, 222, 228–9, 241, 247–59
    see also projects, Women in
    Development
dialogue, 36, 41, 101–2, 124, 141–2,
    227–36 *passim.*
discrimination, 6, 7, 43, 102, 145
Divinity/divinity, 126, 142, 200
divorce, 51, 105, 129, 131, 147
donor, 256–7
dream, 26, 59, 170–1, 221
dress, 26, 41, 103–17 *passim.,* 184, 219
    see also, behaviour, *purdah*
drugs, illegal, 92
Dutch, 37, 40, 47, 201, 249

eating, 18, 112, 230–32, 238, 240
    see also food
ecology, 42, 53, 57, 77, 83
education, xiv, 40, 43, 45, 85, 104, 106,
    110–6, 186, 188, 201, 213–15, 218,
    221, 241
    see also projects
Egypt, 104, 111, 114
elopement, 135
employment, 43, 77, 84, 87, 110, 238,
    239, 250
    see also jobs, wage
endogamy, 136
England/English, 24, 25, 38, 40, 128,
    210, 249, 256–7
enterprise, 20, 28, 39, 41, 48, 82, 85, 88,
    102, 209, 217, 220, 221, 241
epistemological, 123, 139
ethnicity, x, 40, 43, 45, 76, 83, 84, 90,
    93, 103–6, 113–5, 150, 151, 168, 182
entrepreneurial/entrepreneurs, xiv,
    35–74, 109, 146, 249, 256
ethnocentrism, 15, 253
Eurocentric, 14–7, 26, 54, 121
Europe/European, 12, 15, 22, 23, 37, 38,
    41, 110, 123, 138, 145, 173, 228, 235,
    249, 250
environment, 28, 76, 77, 83, 91, 107,
    112
    see also ecology

exorcism, rituals of, 151,
exploitation, 16, 43, 51, 78, 89, 93, 102, 111, 228, 252–4
extended family, 28, 231, 234, 240, 241

factory, 43, 114, 166, 250–1, 255–6
faith, 11, 20, 115–6, 142
farms, 22, 39, 40, 49, 51, 52, 89, 164, 210, 214, 217
farmers, ix, 41, 59, 75, 76, 77, 83, 84, 87, 164, 220, 249
farming, 39, 51, 52, 75, 76, 82, 83, 164, 168, 211–8 *passim.*, 249
Federation
    of Lao Trades Unions, 154
    of Lao Women's Unions, 154
feminists, xiii, 5, 7, 8, 19, 20, 27, 37, 39, 49, 51, 53, 54, 59, 102, 201, 238, 252, 254
    see also Marxist, Western
feminism, 26, 47, 101, 103
    see also Western
fertility, 53, 57, 153, 199
    see also childbirth, rituals
festival, 6, 150, 254
fire wood, 250
firstborn, 40, 166–7
fishing, 5, 24, 86, 170, 209–25, 239
fighting, 23, 185, 196–7
finances, 6, 39, 42, 48, 111, 165–6, 172, 249
food, 19, 22, 28, 36, 50–6 *passim,* 79, 109, 129, 138, 217–8 221, 230–43, 250–4
    see also budgets, eating
folklore, 164, 168
forestation, logging, timber, 56, 82, 83, 87, 88, 250
Free Trade Zones, 253
    see also trade/rs
France/French, 12, 210, 249
fundamentalism/zealot, 44, 45, 103, 108, 110
funerals, 187
future-life, 144, 146, 148
    see also afterlife, rebirth, reincarnation

gambling, 165, 174
genderlessness, 25, 131
gift/s, 40, 174, 236–44 *passim.*
God, ix, 23, 24, 93, 107, 108, 173, 187
    see also deity
goddess/es, 88, 153, 154, 200
guilt, 109, 149, 173–5

hair, 108, 112, 114, 179
haj, 105, 113, 115
Haji, 235
harvest, 24, 149, 154, 183, 199, 212, 213, 217, 219, 250
health, ix, 107, 173, 241, 250
    see also nutrition
heir, 122, 131, 132, 133, 139, 169
hermaphrodite, 126, 133
hermeneutic, 59, 123, 139
heroes, 106, 134, 169, 191, 202
heroines, 46, 169, 194, 196
heteroglossia, 140, 141
heterosexual, 90
hunting, 57, 76–91 *passim.*
hierarchies/hierarchy, 12–8, 27, 35, 37, 40, 44, 47, 50, 54, 56, 58, 81, 82, 181, 182, 190–202 *passim.*
    see also class
Hinduism, xiii, 39, 40, 103, 128, 200
Holy Land, 113

Iban, 79, 80, 87, 88, 229
ideology, xiii, 19, 21, 26, 27, 40, 50, 51, 55, 58, 59, 76, 79–81, 86, 102, 106, 137, 161, 162, 176, 182, 194–201 *passim.*, 248
    see also feminist, religious, Theravada Buddhism
incest, 35
income, 28, 42, 51, 88, 111, 213, 217, 221, 238, 239, 242, 250, 252
    see also projects
independence, 44, 105, 185, 188, 198–9, 201, 221, 242, 248
Indian, 42, 101–2, 114, 116, 126, 133, 176, 200, 248
indigenous, xiv, 7–8, 14, 16, 38, 50, 76–7, 132, 137–8, 168–9, 175–6, 181–2, 253–7
infertility, 200
in flagrante, philandering, 91, 135
informality, culture of, 17, 22, 37, 38, 60
inheritance, 35, 36, 39, 44, 47, 75, 79, 80, 125, 139, 169, 191, 236
in-laws, 149, 166–8, 170, 172, 219, 235, 240
intersexual relations, 15, 36, 91, 162
Iranian women, 113
Islam/Muslim, x, 8, 14, 18, 24, 26, 27, 39–45 *passim.*, 101–17, *passim.* 170, 176, 183, 188, 199, 200, 231, 236
    see also Angakatan Belia Islam

Malaysia, dress, fundamentalism, laws, *Party Islamic Se Malaysia, Pertubuhan Kebajikan Perempuan Islam*

jewellery, 112, 165, 166
jobs, 19, 43, 49, 57, 77, 88, 92, 110, 122, 165, 211, 214–5, 227, 235, 241, 254–5
see also employment
jokes, 110, 172
Judaism, Orthodox, 103

Karma/karma, 55, 125, 138, 153
Kelantan, xi, 227–45
kindergartens, 116
kinship, ix, 3, 14, 20–1, 25, 35, 37, 39, 42, 47–8, 53, 60, 75, 78, 105, 121–7, 129–42 *passim.*, 167, 219, 228, 231–6
see also bilateral, classifactory, language, lineages, matrilineal, moral
Khomeini revolution, 113
kraton, 182–5, 200

labour, 19, 22, 28, 29, 36, 39, 49–52, 76, 78, 79, 85, 92, 109, 132, 149, 209, 210, 216, 221, 222, 228, 233, 234, 237, 241, 250, 251, 253,
division of, 5, 11–2, 77, 79, 87, 134, 211, 250–5
see also employment, wages
land, 11, 22, 39, 42, 47–9, 76, 82–92 *passim.*, 135, 169, 211–2, 215, 230, 233, 235, 249–54
inheritance, 39, 169, 236, 249
shortage, 56, 89, 133
landlessness, 49, 212–3, 250, 252
landowners, 230, 233
language, xi, 5, 23, 38, 59, 80–1, 90, 92, 101–3, 106, 122–4, 131–2, 140, 187, 202, 247, 256–7
Lao Front for National Construction, 152
Lao People's Revolutionary Youth Union, 152
law/laws, 40, 44, 48, 51, 58, 110, 111, 125, 169
see also courts, in-laws, Islam
legal, 40, 48, 51, 83, 109, 110, 111, 248
life histories/stories, ix, 102, 209, 210, 211, 219
lineage, 48, 78, 79, 81
see also kinship

Lisu, 16, 17, 76–80, 83–7, 89–91
longhouse, 79, 80, 87, 88, 229
lover, 170–5
lust, 138

machismo, 165, 176
mandarin, 162
management, 39, 42, 48–9, 51, 89, 114, 212, 217–8, 228–9, 231, 237, 249, 251, 256–7
markets, 49, 53–4, 59, 76, 85–9, 92, 142, 164–5, 210, 211, 216–7, 220–1, 230, 234–42 *passim.*
see also labour
marriages, 7, 35, 57, 85, 104, 107, 131–6, 149, 151, 163, 171, 175, 184, 187, 189, 200, 214, 215, 219, 228, 235, 240
martyrdom, 172, 173
Marxism, 15, 43, 48, 161–2, 176, 229–30
feminists, 43, 102–3
matriarchy, 11, 13, 47–8, 59
matrilaterality, 20, 35, 135
matriliny, 13, 35, 44, 47, 48
media, 51, 252
see also Western
medical/medicine, 19, 43, 81, 86, 109, 146, 163, 166, 175, 213, 250
see also health
mediums, 81, 151, 171
see also spirit
merit-making, 21, 56, 58, 143, 146, 147, 151, 156
metaphor, 16, 26, 41, 52, 80, 101–2, 114, 128–9, 137, 162, 256
metaphorical, 37, 59, 60, 130
metaphysical/metaphysics, 122–3, 127, 161, 163, 173–4, 197
metonymy, 130
Middle East, 106
migrant/migration, 43, 51, 54, 76, 84, 88, 89, 168, 215, 251
military, 82, 85, 183, 185, 194, 196, 250–1
see also soldiers, warriors
minorities, 16, 23, 42, 54, 79–86, 90, 110, 132, 151
see also ethnicity, faiths
mobility, 40, 44, 89, 93
modernisation, xiii, xiv, 28, 38, 43, 47–8, 85, 90, 249, 252
money, 18–9, 28, 79, 83–4, 89–90, 165, 173, 189, 221, 231, 236–42,

249–52, 256–7
see also cash, income, markets, wages
moneylending, 218
monks, 21, 55, 58, 146–9
see also nuns
morality, 17, 90–1, 108, 111–2, 116, 122, 125, 130, 161, 163, 173–5, 186–7, 197, 233–4, 254
see also kinship
movies, 59, 106
multilateral aid agencies, 256
multinational companies, 82, 89, 251
myth, 5, 81, 88, 175, 184, 150, 199, 200, 248
mystical, 126, 133, 134, 184

natal families, 216, 221, 241
see also shrines
native, 77, 87, 123, 124, 140, 231, 242
Negrito, 76, 77, 79, 83, 89
NGOs (non-governmental organisations), 256
nirvana, 148, 153
Nordic countries, 154
nuclear family, 28, 40, 48, 231–2, 240–1
nuns, 7, 54, 58, 107
see also monks
nutrition, ix, xi, 5, 252
see also food, health

occupations, 54, 103, 106, 109–15 passim., 182, 189, 230, 239, 241, 254–5
see also employment
offerings, 56, 91, 128, 131, 139, 147, 148
see also ancestral, sacrifices
Office of Tribal Affairs, 86
see also British
ordination, 145–6, 148–9
Oriental, 23, 102, 113, 249
Orientalism, 101
Orientalist, 59, 102, 113
opium, 77, 79, 82, 84, 85, 92
oppression, 15, 16, 41, 252

pain, 131, 151, 167, 216
see also psychological
pagoda, 144–50, passim.
palace, 189, 193, 196, 199
pastoral, 117, 229
Party Islamic Se Malaysia, 116
paternity, 131
patriarchy, xiii, xiv, 11, 12, 13, 17, 38,
39, 44, 46, 56, 59, 161, 162, 168, 176, 249
patrilateral marriage, 134, 136
patriliny, 35, 38, 39, 40, 48, 79, 133, 200
patrimony, 165
patronage, 13, 183, 184
pawning, 85, 90
Peasant Union, 59
peasants, ix, 21, 22, 75, 78, 89, 103, 105, 125, 134, 164, 168, 172, 229, 239–40, 243, 250
pedicab, 212, 214
Pertubuhan Kebajikan Perempuan Islam, 105
pilgrimage, 105, 113
Pisangkaja, 131–5
plantations, 85, 87, 88, 250
polygamy, 46, 57
polygyny, 40, 41, 109, 235
populations, ix, 38, 40, 75, 79, 82, 84, 92, 102, 114, 164, 168, 211, 249
see also farming
potency, 17, 106, 133, 175, 181–2, 198, 201
powerlessness, 14, 20, 27, 43, 46, 59, 210
predestination/predeterminism 151, 153
pregnancies, 125, 214–6, 237, 242
see also childbirth
prestige, 17–9, 26, 37, 44, 56, 76–81, 84, 91–2, 181, 183–4, 198
priests/priestesses, 134, 153, 154, 162, 169, 199
privacy, 59, 169, 170
private, xiii, 6, 11, 14, 17, 28, 52, 78, 110, 111, 170, 171, 253
see also property
productive and unproductive categories, 233–43
profit, 88, 189, 209, 212, 239
projects, x, 51, 85, 239, 240, 247, 248, 252, 256
see also development, education, income
property, 11, 40, 44, 47, 76, 80, 86, 139, 166, 250
see also private
prostitution, xiv, 17, 54, 87, 88, 92, 199, 251–2
psychology, 30, 44, 59, 136, 168, 170–5
puberty, 219
purdah, 107, 110, 112
full, 41, 109, 110
see also dress

purusa, 128–36
putri, 190, 191, 195, 198

Queen of the South Sea, 184, 199, 200
Qur'an, 110
Qur'anic, 109

rape, 92
rattan, 77, 79, 92, 94
rebirth, 138, 149
    see also afterlife, future-life,
        reincarnated
reincarnated, 138
    see also afterlife, future-life, rebirth
refuge, 115, 170
refugee, 165, 248
religions, 5, 14, 19, 21, 26–7, 38–9,
    41–2, 47, 49, 51, 56, 81, 106, 110–1,
    114, 116, 145–6, 148, 150–1
remittances, 252
residences, 20, 35, 39, 40, 76, 80, 85,
    103, 108, 115, 131, 133, 185, 199,
    229, 249
resettlement, 77, 88
Residual Unresolved Positivism (RUP),
    122
rice, 22, 24, 39, 51, 56, 77–93 *passim.*,
    126, 130–3, 140, 146, 148, 154, 170,
    211–3, 217, 219, 220, 234, 235, 239,
    249, 250, 255
rigation, 212, 213, 216, 221
rights, 8, 12, 40, 41, 45, 47, 49, 80, 86,
    110, 111, 217, 233, 250
    see also birth, customary, harvest,
        land, property, residence, rice
rite, 4, 134, 149, 153, 154, 199
    see also ceremonies
rites of passage, 44, 187,
rituals, x, 3, 21, 25, 27, 36, 39, 40, 45,
    49, 52–3, 55–8, 78–80, 128, 144–54
    passim., 161–2, 183, 188, 235
    see also ceremonies, rice
robe, 148, 149
rotating credit pools (ROSCAS), 25

sacred, 58, 113, 115, 136, 137, 146, 147,
    184
sacrifices, 45, 148, 148, 149, 150, 239
sakti, 133, 141,
salaries, 111, 135, 238, 256
    see also employment, wages
Sanskrit/Sanskritic, 128, 129, 198
school, 85, 105, 107, 185, 188, 211, 215,
    222, 252, 256

    see also education
security, 84, 86, 110, 218, 230
self-control, 175, 181, 186, 187, 196,
    200
sex objects, 249
sex trade, 250, 251
sexism, 20, 25
shamans, 36, 39, 81, 151
shame, 81, 173–5
share tenancy, 212–3, 217
shifting cultivation, 77, 78, 87
shrine, 25, 46, 128, 130, 131, 132
    see also deities
smallholders, 87
socialisation, 53, 186, 252, 253
socialism, 57, 58, 59
    see also Marxist
soldiers, 92, 165, 183, 194, 196
    see also military, warriors
soul, 14, 79, 81, 84, 88, 124, 149, 151,
    248
    see also rite
spirits, 20, 39, 43, 44, 54, 81, 82, 102–5,
    112, 113, 124–6, 130, 143, 146,
    148–54, 161, 171, 174, 187, 189,
    193–6, 198, 200, 240
spiritualism, 14, 17, 21, 24, 26, 52, 78,
    79, 81, 107, 156, 183, 187, 194, 196,
    200
Srimpi, 183–5, 197, 199
stereotypes, 7, 101–3, 137–8, 182, 196,
    200, 228, 230
stigma, 40, 109, 202
stratification, 50, 75, 201, 250
subordination, 14, 52, 81, 102, 228, 253,
    256
subjugation, 13, 171
submissiveness, 163–4, 195,
subsistence, 16, 77, 83, 84, 85, 87, 89,
    92, 213, 250
Sultan/sultan, 38, 182–200 *passim.*
supernatural, 56, 81–2, 149, 151, 154–5
superstition, 153, 15
swidden, 75–80, 84–5, 88, 91–2
symbols/symbolism, xi, 5, 13, 22, 26,
    92, 93, 107, 113, 149, 172, 230, 232,
    236

taboos, 184
Tai, 153
taxonomy, 124, 128
technology, 16, 82, 176, 250
temples, 25, 49, 128, 130, 131, 169
temptation, 87, 112, 146

theatre, 141–2, 193, 195, 200
Theravada Buddhism, 21, 55, 116, 117, 153
  see also Buddhism, ideology
titles, 36, 48, 255
tomboy, 216, 219
tourism, xiv, 250, 251, 256
traders, ix, 40, 77, 83–5, 89, 90, 210, 220, 230, 239, 241, 257
  see also sex, Free Trade Zones
trading patterns, 77, 89
trance, 171, 195
transnational, 106, 250
transsexuals, 133, 137, 181, 202
transvestite, 133
tribal, 76, 82, 84, 85, 90–2

ummah, 41, 106
United Nations, 256
university, 41, 105, 107, 109, 110, 113–5, 188, 248
usrah, 45, 108
uxirilocal, 88, 105

veil, 26, 41, 103–17 *passim.*, 248
venereal diseases, 17, 90
victim, 89, 91, 92, 103
virilocal marriage, 88, 241

virgin, 149, 175

wages, 43, 77, 86, 88, 92, 165, 209–10, 214, 218, 222, 250–2
  see also employment, labour, salaries
warriors, 80, 168, 196
  see also military, soldiers
weeding, 77, 216, 250
weaving, 80
wedding, 36, 82, 175
Western, xiii, 6, 8, 11–9, 24, 26, 29, 37, 41, 44, 47–53 *passim.*, 59, 83, 101–6, 112–7, 121–2, 129, 137–42, 173, 175–6, 190, 194, 201–2, 238, 244, 249, 253
  see also capitalism, dress, feminists, feminism, language, media
widow/widower, 139, 163
witches, 88, 133
Women in Development (WID), xiii, 247–8, 252
Women in Development Consortium in Thailand (WIDCIT), 247
worship, 25–6, 76, 121, 128–31, 145, 169

Yogya, 182–189, 193, 195, 196, 197, 200, 201